Contents

Objective Domain 3: Implementing, Managing, and Troubleshooting 71
Hardware Devices and Drivers

Objective Domain 6: Implementing, Managing, and Troubleshooting 219
Network Protocols and Services

Objective Domain 7: Implementing, Monitoring, ... 249
and Troubleshooting Security

Welcome to Installing, Configuring, and Administering Microsoft Windows 2000 Professional

Welcome to MCSE Readiness Review—Exam 70-210: Installing, Configuring, and Administering Microsoft Windows 2000 Professional. The Readiness Review series gives you a focused, timesaving way to identify the information you need to know to pass the Microsoft Certified Professional (MCP) exams. The series combines a realistic electronic assessment with a review book to help you become familiar with the types of questions that you will encounter on the MCP exam. By reviewing the objectives and sample questions, you can focus on the specific skills that you need to improve before taking the exam.

This book helps you evaluate your readiness for the MCP Exam 70-210: Installing, Configuring, and Administering Microsoft Windows 2000 Professional. When you pass this exam, you earn core credit toward Microsoft Certified Systems Engineer (MCSE) certification. In addition, when you pass this exam, you achieve Microsoft Certified Professional status.

Note You can find a complete list of MCP exams and their related objectives on the Microsoft Certified Professional Web site at *http://www.microsoft.com/mcp*.

The Readiness Review series lets you identify any areas in which you might need additional training. To help you get the training you need to successfully pass the certification exams, Microsoft Press publishes a complete line of self-paced training kits and other study materials. For comprehensive information about the topics covered in the Installing, Configuring, and Administering Microsoft Windows 2000 Professional exam, you might want to see the corresponding training kit: *MCSE Training Kit— Microsoft Windows 2000 Professional*.

Before You Begin

This MCSE Readiness Review consists of two main parts: the Readiness Review electronic assessment program on the accompanying compact disc and this Readiness Review book.

The Readiness Review Components

The electronic assessment is a practice certification test that helps you evaluate your skills. It provides instant scoring feedback so that you can determine areas in which additional study might be helpful before you take the certification exam. Although your score on the electronic assessment does not necessarily indicate what your score will be on the certification exam, it does give you the opportunity to answer questions that are similar to those on the actual certification exam.

The Readiness Review book is organized by the exam's objectives. Each chapter of the book covers one of the seven primary groups of objectives on the actual exam, called the *Objective Domains*. Each Objective Domain lists the tested skills you need to master in order to answer the exam questions. Because the certification exams focus on real-world skills, the "Tested Skills and Suggested Practices" sections emphasize the practical application of the exam objectives. Each Objective Domain includes a list of further readings to help you understand the objectives and increase your ability to perform the tasks or skills specified by the objectives.

Within each Objective Domain, you will find the related objectives that are covered on the exam. Each objective provides you with the following:

- Key terms you must know to understand the objective. Knowing these terms can help you answer the objective's questions correctly.

- Several sample exam questions with the correct answers. The answers are accompanied by explanations of each correct and incorrect answer. (These questions match the questions on the electronic assessment.)

Take the electronic assessment first to determine which exam objectives you need to study; then use the Readiness Review book to learn more about those particular objectives. You can also use the Readiness Review book to research the answers to specific sample test questions. Keep in mind that to pass the exam, you should understand not only the answer to the question, but also the concepts on which the correct answer is based.

MCP Exam Prerequisites

No exams or classes are required before you take the Installing, Configuring, and Administering Microsoft Windows 2000 Professional exam. However, in addition to the skills tested by the exam, you should have a working knowledge of the operation and support of hardware and software in standalone computers. This knowledge should include the following:

- Be able to use an operating system with a graphical user interface, such as Microsoft Windows 95, Microsoft Windows 98, Microsoft Windows NT 4, or Microsoft Windows 2000.

- Understand current networking technology.

- Successfully complete the *MCSE Training Kit—Microsoft Windows 2000 Professional*.

Note After you have used the Readiness Review and determined that you are prepared for the exam, use the Get More MCP Information link provided on the home page of the electronic assessment tool for information on scheduling the exam. You can schedule exams up to six weeks in advance, or as late as one working day before the exam date.

Know the Products

Microsoft's certification program relies on exams that measure your ability to perform a specific job function or set of tasks. Microsoft develops the exams by analyzing the tasks performed by people who are currently working in the field. Therefore, the specific knowledge, skills, and abilities relating to the job are reflected in the certification exam.

Because the certification exams are based on real-world tasks, you need to gain hands-on experience with the applicable technology to master the exam. You should consider hands-on experience a prerequisite for passing an MCP exam. Many of the questions relate directly to Microsoft products or technology, so use opportunities at your organization or home to practice using the relevant tools.

Using the MCSE Readiness Review

Although you can use the Readiness Review in a number of ways, you might start your studies by taking the electronic assessment as a pretest. After completing the exam, review your results for each Objective Domain and focus your study first on the Objective Domains on which you received the lowest scores. The electronic assessment allows you to print your results, and a printed report of how you fared can be useful when reviewing the exam material in this book.

After you have taken the Readiness Review electronic assessment, use the Readiness Review book to learn more about the Objective Domains that you find difficult and to find listings of appropriate study materials that might supplement your knowledge. By reviewing why the answers are correct or incorrect, you can determine whether you need to study the objective topics more.

You can also use the Readiness Review book to focus on the exact objectives that you need to master. Each objective in the book contains several questions that help you determine whether you understand the information related to that particular skill. The book is also designed to allow you to answer each question before turning the page to review the correct answer.

The best method to prepare for the MCP exam is to use the Readiness Review book in conjunction with the electronic assessment and other study material. A thorough study of the material combined with substantial real-world experience is the best preparation for the MCP exam.

Understanding the Readiness Review Conventions

Before you start using the Readiness Review, you need to understand the terms and conventions used in the electronic assessment and book.

Question Numbering System

The Readiness Review electronic assessment tool and book contain reference numbers for each question. Understanding the numbering format will help you use the Readiness Review more effectively. When Microsoft creates the exams, the questions are grouped by job skills called *objectives*. These objectives are then organized by sections known as *Objective Domains*. Each question can be identified by the Objective Domain and the objective it covers. The question numbers follow this format:

Test Number.Objective Domain.Objective.Question Number

For example, question number 70-210.02.01.003 means this is question three (003) for the first objective (01) in the second Objective Domain (02) of the Installing, Configuring, and Administering Microsoft Windows 2000 Professional exam (70-210). Refer to the "Exam Objectives Summary" section later in this introduction to locate the numbers associated with particular objectives. Each question is numbered based on its presentation in the printed book. You can use this numbering system to reference questions on the electronic assessment or in the Readiness Review book. Even though the questions in the book are organized by objective, questions in the electronic assessment and the actual certification exam are presented in random order.

Notational Conventions

The following Textual conventions are used throughout this book to differentiate various technical elements:

- Characters or commands that you type appear in **bold lowercase** type. Bold type is also used to identify key terms in the text that are defined in the glossary of the electronic assessment program.

- Variable information, URLs, and emphasized words are *italicized*. *Italic* is also used for book titles.

- Acronyms, filenames with extensions, and NetBIOS short names for domains appear in FULL CAPITALS.

- Folder names and interface elements, such as radio buttons and check box labels, are displayed in Initial Capitals.

Notes

Notes appear throughout the book.

- Notes marked **Caution** contain information you will want to know before continuing with the book's material.

- Notes marked **Note** contain supplemental information.

- Notes marked **Tip** contain helpful process hints.

Using the Readiness Review Electronic Assessment

The Readiness Review electronic assessment is designed to provide you with an experience that simulates that of the actual MCP exam. The electronic assessment questions are similar to those you will see on the certification exam. Furthermore, the electronic assessment format approximates the certification exam format and includes additional features to help you prepare for the real exam.

Each iteration of the electronic assessment consists of 50 questions covering all the objectives for the Installing, Configuring, and Administering Microsoft Windows 2000

Professional exam. (The actual certification exams generally consist of 50 to 70 questions.) Just as on a real certification exam, you see questions from the objectives in random order during the practice test. Similar to the certification exam, the electronic assessment allows you to mark questions and review them after you finish the test.

To increase its value as a study aid, you can take the electronic assessment multiple times. Each time, you are presented with a different set of questions in a revised order; however, some questions might be repeated.

If you have used one of the certification exam preparation tests available from Microsoft, the Readiness Review electronic assessment should look familiar. The difference is that the electronic assessment provides you with the opportunity to learn as you take the exam.

Installing and Running the Electronic Assessment Software

Before you begin using the electronic assessment, you need to install the software. You need a computer running Microsoft Windows 95 or Windows NT 4 with Service pack 3 or higher and Internet Explorer 5.01 or higher with the following minimum configuration:

- A multimedia PC with a 75 Mhz Pentium or higher processor

- Microsoft Internet Explorer 5.0 or later

- 16 MB RAM for Windows 95 or Windows 98, or

- 32 MB RAM for Windows NT, or

- 64 MB RAM for Windows 2000

- 17 MB of available hard disk space

- A double-speed CD-ROM drive or better

- A super VGA display with at least 256 colors

- A Microsoft Mouse or compatible pointing device (recommended)

▶ **To install the electronic assessment, perform these steps.**

1. Insert the Readiness Review compact disc into your CD-ROM drive.

   An autorun program will initiate, and a dialog box appears indicating that you are installing the MCSE Readiness Review Setup program. If the autorun program does not launch on your system, select Run from the Start menu and type *d*:**\setup.exe** (where *d* is the name of your CD-ROM drive).

2. Click Next.

   The License Agreement dialog box appears.

3. To continue with the installation of the electronic assessment engine, you must accept the license agreement by clicking Yes.

4. The Choose Destination Location dialog box appears showing a default installation directory.

   Either accept the default or change the installation directory if needed. Click Next to copy the files to your hard drive.

5. A Question dialog box appears asking whether you would like Setup to create a desktop shortcut for this program. If you click Yes, an icon will be placed on your desktop.

6. The Setup Complete dialog box appears. Select whether you want to view the README.TXT file after closing the Setup program, and then click Finish.

   The electronic assessment software is completely installed. If you chose to view the README.TXT file, it will launch in a new window. For optimal viewing, enable word wrap.

▶ **To start the electronic assessment, follow these steps.**

1. From the Start menu, point to Programs, point to MCSE Readiness Review, and then click MCSE RR Exam 70-210.

   The electronic assessment program starts.

2. Click Start Test.

   Information about the electronic assessment program appears.

3. Click OK.

Note The electronic assessment programs are designed to run one at a time and will not run simultaneously with other Readiness Review electronic assessment programs.

Taking the Electronic Assessment

The Readiness Review electronic assessment consists of 50 multiple-choice questions, and as in the certification exam, you can skip questions or mark them for later review. Each exam question contains a question number that you can use to refer back to the Readiness Review book.

Before you end the electronic assessment, you should make sure to answer all of the questions. When the exam is graded, unanswered questions are counted as incorrect and will lower your score. Similarly, on the actual certification exam, you should complete all questions or they will be counted as incorrect. No trick questions appear on the exam. The correct answer will always be among the list of choices. Some questions might have more than one correct answer, and this will be indicated in the question. A good strategy is to eliminate the most obvious incorrect answers first to make it easier for you to select the correct answers.

You have 75 minutes to complete the electronic assessment. During the exam, you will see a timer indicating the amount of time you have remaining. This will help you to gauge the amount of time you should use to answer each question and to complete the exam. The amount of time you are given on the actual certification exam varies with each exam. Generally, certification exams take approximately 90 minutes to complete.

Ending and Grading the Electronic Assessment

When you click the Score Test button, you have the opportunity to review the questions you marked or left incomplete. The electronic assessment is graded when you click the Score Test button, and the software presents your section scores and your total score.

Note You can always end a test without grading your electronic assessment by clicking the Home button.

After your electronic assessment is graded, you can view the correct and incorrect answers by clicking the Review Questions button.

Interpreting the Electronic Assessment Results

The Score screen shows you the number of questions in each Objective Domain section, the number of questions you answered correctly, and a percentage grade for each section. You can use the Score screen to determine where to spend additional time studying. On the actual certification exam, the number of questions and passing score will depend on the exam you are taking. The electronic assessment records your score each time you grade an exam so that you can track your progress over time.

▶ **To view your progress and exam records, follow these steps.**

1. From the electronic assessment main menu, click View History.

    All of your attempt scores appear.

2. Click on a test attempt date/time to view your score for each objective domain.

> The section score for each attempt appears. You can review the section score information to determine which Objective Domains you should study further. You can also use the scores to determine your progress as you continue to study and prepare for the real exam.

Ordering More Questions

Self Test Software offers practice tests to help you prepare for a variety of MCP certification exams. These practice tests contain hundreds of additional questions and are similar to the Readiness Review electronic assessment. For a fee, you can order exam practice tests for this exam and other Microsoft certification exams. Click the Order More Questions link on the electronic assessment home page for more information.

Using the Readiness Review Book

You can use the Readiness Review book as a supplement to the Readiness Review electronic assessment or as a standalone study aid. If you decide to use the book as a standalone study aid, review the Table of Contents or the list of objectives to find topics of interest or an appropriate starting point for you. To get the greatest benefit from the book, use the electronic assessment as a pretest to determine which Objective Domains to study. Or, if you would like to research specific questions while taking the electronic assessment, you can use the question number located on the question screen to reference the question number in the Readiness Review book.

One way to determine areas where additional study might be helpful is to carefully review your individual section scores from the electronic assessment and note objective areas where your score could be improved. The section scores correlate to the Objective Domains listed in the Readiness Review book.

Reviewing the Objectives

Each Objective Domain in the book contains an introduction and a list of practice skills. Each list of practice skills describes suggested tasks you can perform to help you understand the objectives. Some of the tasks suggest reading additional material, while others are hands-on practices using software or hardware. Pay particular attention to the hands-on suggestions, as the certification exam reflects real-world knowledge you can gain only by working with the technology. Increasing your real-world experience will improve your performance on the exam.

After you have determined the objectives you would like to study, you can use the Table of Contents to locate the objectives in the Readiness Review book. When reviewing a specific objective, you should make sure you understand the purpose of the objective and the skill or knowledge it is measuring on the certification exam. You can study each objective separately, but you might need to understand the concepts explained in other objectives.

Make sure you understand the key terms in each objective. You will need a thorough understanding of these terms to answer the objective's questions correctly. Key term definitions are located in the glossary of the electronic assessment on this book's compact disc.

Reviewing the Questions

Each objective contains three or more questions followed by the possible answers. After you review the question and select a probable answer, you can turn to the corresponding answer section to determine whether you answered the question correctly. (For information about the question numbering format, see "Question Numbering System," earlier in this introduction.)

The Readiness Review briefly discusses each possible answer and provides a specific reason why each answer is correct or incorrect. You should review the answer explanations to help you understand why the correct answer is the best answer among the choices given. You should understand not only the answer to the question, but the concepts that the correct answer is based on. If you feel you need more information about a topic or you do not understand the answer, use the "Further Readings" section to learn where you can find more information.

The answers to the questions in the Readiness Review are based on current industry specifications and standards. However, the information provided by the answers is subject to change as technology improves and changes.

Exam Objectives Summary

The Installing, Configuring, and Administering Microsoft Windows 2000 Professional certification (70-210) exam measures your ability to install, configure, and troubleshoot hardware resources, Windows 2000 Professional, and network protocols and services; implement and administer computer resources; monitor and optimize operating system performance; and implement, monitor, and troubleshoot Windows 2000 security. In addition, this test measures the skills required to manage, monitor, and optimize the desktop environment by using Group Policy. Before taking the exam, you should be proficient in the job skills listed in the following sections. The sections provide the exam objectives and the corresponding objective numbers (which you can use to reference the questions in the Readiness Review electronic assessment and book) grouped by Objective Domains.

Objective Domain 1: Installing Windows 2000 Professional

The objectives in Objective Domain 1 are as follows:

- Objective 1.1 (70-210.01.01)—Perform an attended installation of Windows 2000 Professional.

- Objective 1.2 (70-210.01.02)—Perform an unattended installation of Windows 2000 Professional.

- Objective 1.3 (70-210.01.03)—Upgrade from a previous version of Windows to Windows 2000 Professional.

- Objective 1.4 (70-210.01.04)—Deploy service packs.

- Objective 1.5 (70-210.01.05)—Troubleshoot failed installations.

Objective Domain 2: Implementing and Conducting Administration of Resources

The objectives in Objective Domain 2 are as follows:

- Objective 2.1 (70-210.02.01)—Monitor, manage, and troubleshoot access to files and folders.

- Objective 2.2 (70-210.02.02)—Manage and troubleshoot access to shared folders.

- Objective 2.3 (70-210.02.03)—Connect to local and network print devices.

- Objective 2.4 (70-210.02.04)—Configure and manage file systems.

Objective Domain 3: Implementing, Managing, and Troubleshooting Hardware Devices and Drivers

The objectives in Objective Domain 3 are as follows:

- Objective 3.1 (70-210.03.01)—Implement, manage, and troubleshoot disk devices.

- Objective 3.2 (70-210.03.02)—Implement, manage, and troubleshoot display devices.

- Objective 3.3 (70-210.03.03)—Implement, manage, and troubleshoot mobile computer hardware.

- Objective 3.4 (70-210.03.04)—Implement, manage, and troubleshoot input and output (I/O) devices.

- Objective 3.5 (70-210.03.05)—Update drivers.

- Objective 3.6 (70-210.03.06)—Monitor and configure multiple processing units.

- Objective 3.7 (70-210.03.07)—Install, configure, and troubleshoot network adapters.

Objective Domain 4: Monitoring and Optimizing System Performance and Reliability

The objectives in Objective Domain 4 are as follows:

- Objective 4.1 (70-210.04.01)—Manage and troubleshoot driver signing.

- Objective 4.2 (70-210.04.02)—Configure, manage, and troubleshoot Task Scheduler.

- Objective 4.3 (70-210.04.03)—Manage and troubleshoot the use and synchronization of offline files.

- Objective 4.4 (70-210.04.04)—Optimize and troubleshoot performance of the Windows 2000 Professional desktop.

- Objective 4.5 (70-210.04.05)—Manage hardware profiles.

- Objective 4.6 (70-210.04.06)—Recover system state data and user data.

Objective Domain 5: Configuring and Troubleshooting the Desktop Environment

The objectives in Objective Domain 5 are as follows:

- Objective 5.1 (70-210.05.01)—Configure and manage user profiles.

- Objective 5.2 (70-210.05.02)—Configure support for multiple languages or multiple locations.

- Objective 5.3 (70-210.05.03)—Manage applications by using Windows Installer packages.

- Objective 5.4 (70-210.05.04)—Configure and troubleshoot desktop settings.

- Objective 5.5 (70-210.05.05)—Configure and troubleshoot fax support.

- Objective 5.6 (70-210.05.06)—Configure and troubleshoot accessibility services.

Objective Domain 6: Implementing, Managing, and Troubleshooting Network Protocols and Services

The objectives in Objective Domain 6 are as follows:

- Objective 6.1 (70-210.06.01)—Configure and troubleshoot the TCP/IP protocol.

- Objective 6.2 (70-210.06.02)—Connect to computers by using dial-up networking.

- Objective 6.3 (70-210.06.03)—Connect to shared resources on a Microsoft network.

Objective Domain 7: Implementing, Monitoring, and Troubleshooting Security

The objectives in Objective Domain 7 are as follows:

- Objective 7.1 (70-210.07.01)—Encrypt data on a hard disk by using Encrypting File System (EFS).

- Objective 7.2 (70-210.07.02)—Implement, configure, manage, and troubleshoot local security policy.

- Objective 7.3 (70-210.07.03)—Implement, configure, manage, and troubleshoot local user accounts.

- Objective 7.4 (70-210.07.04)—Implement, configure, manage, and troubleshoot local user authentication.

- Objective 7.5 (70-210.07.05)—Implement, configure, manage, and troubleshoot a security configuration.

Getting More Help

A variety of resources are available to help you study for the exam. Your options include instructor-led classes, seminars, self-paced kits, or other learning materials. The materials described here are created to prepare you for MCP exams. Each training resource fits a different type of learning style and budget.

Microsoft Official Curriculum (MOC)

Microsoft Official Curriculum (MOC) courses are technical training courses developed by Microsoft product groups to educate computer professionals who use Microsoft technology. The courses are developed with the same objectives used for Microsoft certification, and MOC courses are available to support most exams for the MCSE certification. The courses are available in instructor-led, online, or self-paced formats to fit your preferred learning style.

Self-Paced Training

Microsoft Press publishes self-paced training kits, which cover a variety of Microsoft technical products. The self-paced kits, which are based on MOC courses, feature self-paced lessons, hands-on practices, multimedia presentations, practice files, and demonstration software. They can help you understand the concepts and get the experience you need to prepare for the corresponding MCP exam.

To help you prepare for the Installing, Configuring, and Administering Microsoft Windows 2000 Professional 70-210 MCP exam, Microsoft has written the *MCSE Training Kit—Microsoft Windows 2000 Professional*. With this official self-paced training kit, you can learn the fundamentals of Microsoft Windows 2000 Professional.

MCP Approved Study Guides

MCP Approved Study Guides, available through several organizations, are learning tools that help you prepare for MCP exams. The study guides are available in a variety of formats to match your learning style, including books, compact discs, online content, and videos. These guides come in a wide range of prices to fit your budget.

Microsoft Seminar Series

Microsoft Solution Providers and other organizations are often a source of information to help you prepare for an MCP exam. For example, many solution providers will present seminars to help industry professionals understand a particular product technology, such as networking. For information on all Microsoft-sponsored events, visit *http://www.microsoft.com/events*.

Installing Windows 2000 Professional

Installing Microsoft Windows 2000 Professional is a complex task with many decision points along the way. The Installing Windows 2000 Professional Objective Domain encapsulates this complexity by categorizing installation into preparing for and performing two types: attended (manual) installation and unattended (automated) installation. A variety of automated installation methods exist using technologies such as the Remote Installation Service (RIS), the System Preparation (SYSPREP.EXE) utility, and WINNT.EXE or WINNT32.EXE with unattended answer files. An important factor in deciding on an appropriate installation method is determining whether installed operating systems and applications will be upgraded or removed and replaced with new installations. This Objective Domain includes questions about upgrading to Windows 2000 Professional, applying updates to installed applications, and deploying service packs. A task as complex as installation requires expertise with troubleshooting installation failures, the last objective in the Installing Windows 2000 Professional Objective Domain.

The Installing Windows 2000 Professional Objective Domain measures your ability to install Windows 2000 Professional on computers containing other operating systems, to install the operating system on computers in a variety of network environments, such as Novell NetWare and UNIX, and to troubleshoot installation failures. Expect a number of case studies on the exam that test your aptitude for choosing the ideal installation method when given detailed and often complex information on various computing environments.

Tested Skills and Suggested Practices

The skills you need to successfully master the Installing Windows 2000 Professional Objective Domain on Exam 70-210: Installing, Configuring, and Administering Microsoft Windows 2000 Professional include the following:

- **Verify that a computer meets all requirements for a new installation or upgrade to Windows 2000 Professional.**

    - Practice 1: Review the minimum hardware requirements for installing Windows 2000 Professional. (See the introduction to Objective 1.1.)

    - Practice 2: Check compatibility of computers by running the Microsoft Windows 2000 Readiness Analyzer. This tool is named CHKUPGRD.EXE and can be downloaded from *http://www.microsoft.com* by first searching for the title, Windows 2000 Readiness Analyzer. Additionally, run WINNT32 with the /checkupgradeonly switch. On a computer running Microsoft Windows 95 or Microsoft Windows 98, review *%windir%*\UPGRADE.TXT; on a computer running Microsoft Windows NT, review *%windir%*\WINNT32.LOG.

    - Practice 3: Check the system BIOS to verify that it is compatible with Windows 2000. If it isn't compatible, reconfigure the BIOS, update it, or complete both procedures.

- **Manually install Windows 2000 Professional.**

    - Practice 1: Observe the phases of installation by running several Windows 2000 Professional attended installation procedures on computers with no operating system and computers with existing Windows 32-bit operating systems.

    - Practice 2: Observe the phases of installation on a computer running MS-DOS by loading SMARTDRV.EXE and then running a 16-bit (WINNT.EXE) installation of Windows 2000 Professional.

- **Create and run automated installations of Windows 2000 Professional.**

    - Practice 1: Type **winnt32 /?** and study the installation switches.

    - Practice 2: Run Setup Manager to create an unattended installation file for a single computer. Run Setup Manager again, but this time, use a UDB for multi-computer automated computer setup. Run a Windows 2000 Professional installation using the answer file and UDB file that Setup Manager created.

- Practice 3: Build and run a RIS-based deployment structure by doing the following: install and configure RIS on a computer running Windows 2000 Server; install and configure Windows 2000 Professional; use the RIS image preparation tool, RIPrep (RIPREP.EXE), to prepare and upload the image to a Microsoft Windows 2000 Server RIS server; and create a Remote Boot Disk or use a PXE-capable computer to boot to the network and run a RIS-based installation.

- Practice 4: Prepare a computer running Windows 2000 Professional for cloning by running the System Preparation (SYSPREP.EXE) utility. Use the image prepared with the System Preparation utility (often called "SysPrep") to run a semiautomated installation.

- Practice 5: Use Setup Manager to further automate an image installation prepared with SysPrep. Use the answer file and the SysPrep supporting files to run a fully automated installation.

- Practice 6: Type **sysprep /?** and review the command parameters.

- **Upgrade to Windows 2000 Professional and deploy service packs.**

  - Practice 1: Run installation procedures to upgrade Windows 95, Windows 98, and Windows NT Workstation to Windows 2000 Professional.

  - Practice 2: Upgrade Windows $9x$ applications that use the migration DLL facility in the Windows 2000 Professional setup routine.

  - Practice 3: Run UPDATE.EXE to apply the latest Windows 2000 service pack and review the UPDATE.EXE switches.

- **Troubleshoot the Windows 2000 installation.**

  - Practice 1: Open and review the contents of log files contained in the boot partition's operating system folder (*%systemroot%*) so that you are familiar with their purpose.

  - Practice 2: Use the HCL to determine any hardware incompatibilities and to obtain any information on updates needed to meet compatibility requirements.

  - Practice 3: Visit computer hardware manufacturer Web sites to learn about BIOS update procedures to support an installation of Windows 2000 Professional.

Further Reading

This "Further Reading" section provides lists of important readings to supplement your current understanding of the skills tested within this Objective Domain. The lists are delineated into pertinent readings for each objective within this Objective Domain. If you feel that you need additional preparation prior to taking the exam, study these sources thoroughly.

Objective 1.1

Microsoft Corporation. *Windows 2000 Professional Upgrade Guide*. Redmond, Washington: Microsoft Press, 2000. This guide explains how to prepare for a Windows 2000 Professional operating system upgrade in a simple network environment. You can locate this document at *http://www.microsoft.com* by searching for the title.

Microsoft Corporation. *MCSE Training Kit—Microsoft Windows 2000 Professional*. Redmond, Washington: Microsoft Press, 2000. Read and complete the lessons and practices in Chapter 2, "Installing Windows 2000 Professional."

Microsoft Corporation. *Microsoft Windows 2000 Professional Resource Kit*. Redmond, Washington: Microsoft Press, 2000. Read Chapter 4, "Installing Windows 2000 Professional." Review Appendix C, "Hardware Support."

Objective 1.2

Microsoft Corporation. *MCSE Training Kit—Microsoft Windows 2000 Professional*. Redmond, Washington: Microsoft Press, 2000. Read the lessons and complete the practices in Lessons 1, 2, and 3 in Chapter 23, "Deploying Windows 2000."

Microsoft Corporation. *Microsoft Windows 2000 Professional Resource Kit*. Redmond, Washington: Microsoft Press, 2000. Read Chapter 5, "Customizing and Automating Installations," and review Appendix B, "Sample Answer Files for Windows 2000 Professional Setup."

Microsoft Corporation. *Microsoft Windows 2000 Server Resource Kit Deployment and Planning Guide*. Redmond, Washington: Microsoft Press, 2000. Read Chapter 6, "Windows 2000 Professional/Client Deployment."

Microsoft Corporation. Microsoft Windows 2000 Resource Kit Deployment Tools Help (DEPTOOL.CHM). Available on the Windows 2000 Professional CD-ROM in the \Support\Tools\DEPLOY.CAB file. This online help file explains how to use Setup Manager and SysPrep.

Objective 1.3

Microsoft Corporation. *MCSE Training Kit—Microsoft Windows 2000 Professional.* Redmond, Washington: Microsoft Press, 2000. Read Lesson 4, Chapter 23, "Deploying Windows 2000."

Microsoft Corporation. "Upgrading from Previous Versions of Windows." This Web page contains a number of documents detailing upgrade paths from other operating systems. You can find this resource by searching on the title at *http://www.microsoft.com/ windows2000.*

Objective 1.4

Microsoft Corporation. *MCSE Training Kit—Microsoft Windows 2000 Professional.* Redmond, Washington: Microsoft Press, 2000. Read Lesson 5, Chapter 23, "Deploying Windows 2000."

Objective 1.5

Microsoft Corporation. *Microsoft Windows 2000 Professional Resource Kit.* Redmond, Washington: Microsoft Press, 2000. Read Chapter 6, "Setup and Startup," and Chapter 31, "Troubleshooting Tools and Strategies."

OBJECTIVE 1.1

Perform an attended installation of Windows 2000 Professional.

Before installing Windows 2000 Professional, you must assess the computer's compatibility with the operating system. Compatibility falls into two categories: hardware and software. The hardware must meet the minimum requirements for running the operating system and while not mandatory, all hardware components should appear on the Windows 2000 Hardware Compatibility List (HCL).

You can find the latest edition of the HCL at *http://www.microsoft.com* by searching on the keywords, Windows 2000 HCL. You can find a local copy of the HCL in the HCL.TXT file contained in the \Support folder on the Windows 2000 Professional CD-ROM. Another important Internet location for assessing your computer's readiness for Windows 2000 Professional is the Windows 2000 home page at *http://www.microsoft.com/windows2000/*. From the Windows 2000 home page, locate the Hardware and Software Compatibility page. The Hardware and Software Compatibility page contains the Windows 2000 Readiness Analyzer program, links to information on basic input/output system (BIOS) compatibility, and summary information on upgrading from previous versions of Windows. Running the Windows 2000 Readiness Analyzer and typing **winnt32 /checkupgradeonly** at the command line verifies hardware and software compatibility.

Note Hardware compatibility does not guarantee that the Windows 2000 Professional installation CD-ROM contains all of the Windows 2000 drivers for your hardware. If the Windows 2000 Professional installation CD-ROM does not contain a required driver, contact the hardware manufacturer for a driver update.

The minimum resource requirements for a computer running Windows 2000 Professional are as follows:

- Pentium class 133-MHz processor

- 64 MB RAM

- 650 MB free space for the boot partition

- Disk space for the boot and system partitions that have not been compressed using technologies such as Windows 9*x* DriveSpace or DoubleSpace

---

Caution If an existing partition will be used for the system and boot partitions, the partition must be running a compatible file system.

After you have established hardware and software compatibility and properly configured the BIOS, you must plan how to install Windows 2000 Professional. Checking for viruses on the local computer and assessing whether existing files on the computer need to be backed up are the next critical steps you must perform prior to installation. After you back up any critical files, installation begins. Factors influencing how Windows 2000 Professional should be installed include but are not limited to the following:

- The presence or absence of an existing operating system

  If an operating system is running on the computer, assess whether it will be preserved, upgraded, or removed.

- The level of required security

- Any networks to which the computer will be connected

  The network and network service interactions will significantly affect operating system installation and configuration.

- The purpose of the installation

  You must understand how the computer running Windows 2000 Professional will be used.

To answer the questions in this objective, you must be proficient with manually installing Windows 2000 Professional on a variety of hardware platforms in various configuration states. For example, if the computer is connected to a network running Microsoft Windows NT Server or Windows 2000 Server and the computer will be joined to the domain, you must create a computer account in the domain.

Objective 1.1 Questions

70-210.01.01.001

You have acquired a new Pentium III computer with two blank hard disks, a 40x CD-ROM drive, an AGP display adapter, and a Fast Ethernet network adapter. All hardware is on the HCL. You want to achieve these results:

- Install Windows 2000 Professional on the computer.

- Minimize the time required to install Windows 2000 Professional.

- Choose a file system to enable maximum security of data on the computer.

- Have the computer join your domain.

Your proposed solution is to start the computer, access its BIOS, set the computer to boot from the CD-ROM drive, save the changes, and restart the computer. When Setup runs, complete the necessary tasks and specify the NTFS partition type. After restarting the computer again, restore the original boot disk configuration in the BIOS. When prompted, specify the appropriate domain name.

Which results does the proposed solution provide? (Choose three.)

A. Windows 2000 Professional is installed on the computer.

B. The time required to install Windows 2000 Professional is minimized.

C. The specified file system enables maximum security of data on the computer.

D. The computer joins your domain.

70-210.01.01.002

You have acquired a new Pentium III computer with two blank hard disks, a 40x CD-ROM drive, an AGP display adapter, and a Fast Ethernet network adapter. All hardware is on the HCL. You want to achieve these results:

- Install Windows 2000 Professional on the computer.

- Minimize the time required to install Windows 2000 Professional.

- Choose a file system to enable maximum security of data on the computer.

- Have the computer join your Windows 2000 domain.

Your proposed solution is to insert the Windows 2000 Professional installation CD-ROM into the CD-ROM drive and start the computer from the Setup Boot Disk. When installation runs, complete the necessary tasks, insert the other Setup Disks when prompted, and specify the NTFS partition type. When prompted, specify the appropriate domain name.Which results does the proposed solution provide? (Choose two.)

A. Windows 2000 Professional is installed on the computer.

B. The time required to install Windows 2000 Professional is minimized.

C. The specified file system enables maximum security of data on the computer.

D. The computer joins your domain.

70-210.01.01.003

You have acquired a new Pentium III computer with two blank hard disks, a 40x CD-ROM drive, an AGP display adapter, and a Fast Ethernet network adapter. All hardware is on the HCL. You want to achieve these results:

- Install Windows 2000 Professional on the computer.

- Minimize the time required to install Windows 2000 Professional.

- Choose a file system to enable maximum security of data on the computer.

- Have the computer join your domain.

Your proposed solution is to insert the Windows 2000 Professional installation CD-ROM and start the computer from the Setup Boot Disk. When Setup runs, complete the necessary tasks, insert the other Setup Disks when prompted, and specify the FAT32 partition type. When prompted, specify the appropriate domain name.

Which results does the proposed solution provide? (Choose one.)

A. Windows 2000 Professional is installed on the computer.

B. The time required to install Windows 2000 Professional is minimized.

C. The specified file system enables maximum security of data on the computer.

D. The computer joins your domain.

Objective 1.1 Answers

70-210.01.01.001

▶ **Correct Answers: A, B, and C**

A. **Correct:** The installation of Windows 2000 Professional is likely to succeed because it is being run on HCL-certified computer hardware. Installation is possible by starting the setup routine from the Windows 2000 installation CD-ROM on a computer with a bootable CD-ROM BIOS that supports the El Torito specification. After the BIOS is configured to boot from the CD-ROM drive, insert the Windows 2000 Professional installation CD-ROM into the drive bay, restart the computer, and Windows 2000 Professional installation proceeds. On computers that do not include bootable CD-ROM support, you can use the other Windows 2000 Professional installation methods: Setup Boot Disk, over-the-network, and automated installation.

B. **Correct:** By configuring the BIOS to boot from the CD-ROM drive, the four Setup Disks are unnecessary. Starting Windows 2000 Professional installation from the CD-ROM drive instead of the floppy drive reduces the installation time. Immediately after the first restart during setup, the boot from CD-ROM feature in the BIOS starts Windows 2000 Professional Setup again. The setup routine then pauses and prompts you to either continue the installation process by booting from the system partition on the fixed disk or starting the setup routine again from the CD-ROM. If no answer is provided in 30 seconds, the setup process continues from the fixed disk.

C. **Correct:** NTFS provides for local permissions at the folder and file levels. Local permissions secure the file system from both local and over-the-network access. The version of NTFS shipped with Windows 2000 Professional also supports the Encrypting File System (EFS). EFS is a security feature that enables a user to encrypt files so that others cannot read the data within them.

D. **Incorrect:** Before a computer can join a domain, you must create a computer object (previously known as a computer account in Windows NT 4 domains) in a container of the Windows 2000 domain. You can accomplish this step during the installation process if you have access to a user account with the Add Workstation To Domain privilege in the domain or the privilege to create computer objects in a container of the domain. Alternatively, an administrator or a user in a Windows 2000 domain who has been granted the necessary privilege can add the computer object to the domain prior to running the Windows 2000 Professional installation. Nothing in the proposed solution suggests that one of these procedures was completed.

70-210.01.01.002

▶ **Correct Answers: A and C**

A. **Correct:** The installation of Windows 2000 Professional is likely to succeed because it is being run on HCL-certified computer hardware. Installation is possible by booting from the Setup Boot Disk and inserting the other Setup Disks when prompted. You can create the four Setup Disks by using the MAKEBOOT.EXE or MAKEBT32.EXE utilities located in the \Bootdisk folder on the Windows 2000 Professional installation CD-ROM. MAKEBOOT.EXE creates the Setup Disks (3.5" high-density floppy disks) on computers running 16-bit operating systems and Windows 9*x*. MAKEBT32.EXE creates Setup Disks on computers running Windows NT or Windows 2000.

B. **Incorrect:** Installing Windows 2000 Professional using the Setup Boot Disk method is the most common manual installation method, but it's also the most tedious. Therefore, using this method does not minimize the time required to install the operating system.

C. **Correct:** NTFS provides for local permissions at the folder and file levels. Local permissions secure the file system from both local and over-the-network access. The version of NTFS shipped with Windows 2000 Professional also supports the Encrypting File System (EFS). EFS protects file data so that users without the proper decryption key cannot read it.

D. **Incorrect:** Before a computer can join a domain, you must create a computer object (previously known as a computer account in Windows NT 4 domains) in a container of the Windows 2000 domain. You can accomplish this step during the installation process if you have access to a user account with the Add Workstation To Domain privilege in the domain or the privilege to create computer objects in a container of the domain. Alternatively, an administrator or a user in a Windows 2000 domain who has been granted the necessary privilege can add the computer object to the domain prior to running the Windows 2000 Professional installation. Nothing in the proposed solution suggests that one of these procedures was completed.

70-210.01.01.003

► **Correct Answers: A**

A. **Correct:** The installation of Windows 2000 Professional is likely to succeed because it is being run on HCL-certified computer hardware. Installation is possible by booting from the Setup Boot Disk and inserting the other Setup Disks when prompted.

B. **Incorrect:** Installing Windows 2000 Professional using the Setup Boot Disk method is the most common manual installation method but it's also the most tedious. Therefore, using this method does not minimize the time required to install the operating system.

C. **Incorrect:** The FAT32 file system does not support local permissions at the folder and file levels. Like all file systems in Windows 2000, FAT32 supports Share permissions. Share permissions provide for over-the-network secure access at the folder level. Configuring permissions at the file level is not available, and local computer access is not affected by Share-level security. In addition, only NTFS supports EFS.

D. **Incorrect:** Before a computer can join a domain, you must create a computer object (previously known as a computer account in Windows NT 4 domains) in a container of the Windows 2000 domain. You can accomplish this step during the installation process if you have access to a user account with the Add Workstation To Domain privilege in the domain or the privilege to create computer objects in a container of the domain. Alternatively, an administrator or a user in a Windows 2000 domain who has been granted the necessary privilege can add the computer object to the domain prior to running the Windows 2000 Professional installation. Nothing in the proposed solution suggests that one of these procedures was completed.

O B J E C T I V E   1 . 2

Perform an unattended installation of Windows 2000 Professional.

Unattended installation, also known as **automated installation**, brings efficiencies to the installation process, making it possible to rapidly deploy Windows 2000 Professional and other applications in a large network environment.

This objective requires that you know how to *plan* for an automated installation, *prepare* the automated installation environment, *customize* the answer files, and *deploy* the operating system and applications to the network.

Note Operating system deployment techniques require that you are familiar with Windows 2000 Server technologies such as Remote Installation Service (RIS). You are more likely to succeed on Exam 70-210 if you understand how to use Windows 2000 Server technology to enhance deployment of Windows 2000 Professional.

Unattended installation has evolved with the operating system. As a result, a number of preparation methods are available for creating automated installation routines, and a number of distribution methods exist to deploy these packages to the network.

The preparation methods are the following:

- Install scripts to create a partially or fully automated setup.

    These scripts consist of an answer file named UNATTEND.TXT by default, a Uniqueness Database File (UDB) to support a multicomputer automated setup routine, and a CMDLINES.TXT file for running commands during the setup routine, such as a command that runs an automated application installation.

- Use the /syspart switch to complete the setup loader and text-mode phases of installation on a fixed disk.

- Use SysPrep to prepare an installation for imaging.

To use SysPrep, configure a reference computer exactly as the operating system should be configured for the target computers. Run SysPrep to prepare the operating system for imaging. Fully automate the installation routine with an answer file named SYSPREP.INF. You can create SYSPREP.INF by using Setup Manager. Then use an imaging utility to copy the image to a central location or removable media. From the central location, the image is distributed using a distribution method. This process demonstrates that deployment utilities can be combined to create an automated installation routine.

Note Know the purpose of the Sysprep switches: -quiet, -nosidgen, -pnp, and snf -reboot.

- Use images created with a third-party imaging tool or the RIS RIPrep utility.

Some common distribution methods are the following:

- A batch file with a distribution folder

- RIS

RIS supports CD-based and image-based installation preparation methods. Installation is automated using answer files, image download to Preboot Execution Environment (PXE)-compliant computers, or networked computers that support the RIS remote boot disk procedure.

- Microsoft Systems Management Server (SMS)

You use SMS for operating system upgrades prepared using answer files.

Objective 1.2 Questions

70-210.01.02.001

You want to use Setup Manager to automate the installation of Windows 2000 Professional. Which tasks must you perform to run the Windows 2000 Setup Manager? (Choose two.)

A. Copy the Windows 2000 deployment tools by extracting the files in the DEPLOY.CAB file on the Windows 2000 Professional installation CD-ROM.

B. Copy the Windows 2000 deployment tools by extracting the files in the WINSYS32.CAB file on the Windows 2000 Professional CD-ROM.

C. Run the SETUPCL.EXE application in the directory to which you extracted the .cab file.

D. Run the SETUPMGR.EXE application in the directory to which you extracted the .cab file.

70-210.01.02.002

You want to install Windows 2000 Professional on 25 computers with similar hardware configurations.

To use the System Preparation utility as part of the disk duplication process, which parts of the master (reference) and destination (target) computers must be identical or, at the very least, compatible? (Choose two.)

A. A sound card

B. A video adapter

C. A network adapter

D. A hard disk controller device driver

E. The hardware abstraction layer (HAL)

70-210.01.02.003

You are an administrator for a corporate network supporting 50 users running Windows NT Workstation 4. You want to perform RIS-based remote installations of Windows 2000 Professional on your network clients without using the remote installation boot floppy. Which conditions allow you to perform remote installations? (Choose two.)

A. The computers on your network are PXE compliant.

B. The computers on your network support operating system–level remote control.

C. You have a Windows 2000 Server infrastructure in place.

D. You have either a Windows NT Server 4 or Windows 2000 Server infrastructure in place.

Objective 1.2 Answers

70-210.01.02.001

▶ **Correct Answers: A and D**

A. **Correct:** To automate an installation by using Setup Manager, you must first copy the Windows 2000 deployment tools from the Windows 2000 Professional installation CD-ROM. Extract the files in the \Support\Tools folder named DEPLOY.CAB to a disk location. The DEPLOY.CAB file contains Setup Manager, a deployment help file, a sample answer file, and other useful deployment utilities.

B. **Incorrect:** The WINSYS32.CAB file is located in the \i386 folder on the Windows 2000 Professional installation CD-ROM. This .cab file contains two files, MWWAVE.SYS and MWWDM.SYS. These files are used to support IBM modem hardware. If you weren't sure whether A or B was correct, consider the filenames listed in these multiple-choice answers to select the most likely correct answer.

C. **Incorrect:** SETUPCL.EXE supports System Preparation utility (SysPrep) functions. SETUPCL.EXE generates a new security ID (SID) and starts the Mini Setup Wizard. The combination of SYSPREP.EXE and SETUPCL.EXE replaces the ROLLBACK.EXE utility used in automating deployment of Windows NT 4. SysPrep and Setup Manager are two different methods for preparing an automated installation. You can use Setup Manager to fully automate a SysPrep installation by generating a SYSPREP.INF file. SYSPREP.INF is called in the final stage of installation.

D. **Correct:** After Setup Manager is extracted to a folder on a disk, you start it by running SETUP-MGR.EXE. Setup Manager guides you through the process of generating an answer file to script an installation of Windows 2000 Professional. The generated script files are used for partially automated or fully automated installation.

70-210.01.02.002

▶ **Correct Answers: D and E**

A. **Incorrect:** Peripheral devices such as modems, sound cards, and network adapters can differ or be absent in the master computer and the destination computer. However, device driver installation files for all devices in the destination computer must be available in the SysPrep image. If the destination computer contains Plug and Play versions of these devices, they will be detected and installed automatically.

B. **Incorrect:** Video adapters can differ in the master computer and the destination computer. However, device driver installation files for all video adapter types in the destination computers must be available in the SysPrep image. If the destination computer contains Plug and Play versions of these devices, they will be detected and installed automatically.

C. **Incorrect:** Network adapters can differ or be absent in the master computer and the destination computer. However, device driver installation files for all network adapters in the destination computer must be in the SysPrep image. If the destination computer contains Plug and Play versions of these devices, they will be detected and installed automatically.

D. **Correct:** The disk controller device drivers in the master and destination computer must be identical. If they are not identical, you should not use SysPrep to automate the installation process. Instead, you can complete an unattended installation with an answer file. The answer file is passed to WINNT32.EXE using the /unattend:*num answer_file* switch. The *num* parameter specifies the number of seconds between finishing the setup routine and restarting the computer; the *answer_file* parameter specifies the name of the answer file. The /unattend switch without any parameters is used to perform an unattended operating system upgrade from Windows 9*x*, Windows NT 3.51, or Windows NT 4. WINNT.EXE uses the /u:*answer_file* /s:*source_path* switches for unattended installation from a 16-bit operating system such as MS-DOS or Windows 3.1. You can also use Windows 2000 Setup (WINNT32.EXE only) with the /syspart switch to complete the text phase of installation on a target disk.

E. **Correct:** The HAL on the computer where the disk image is generated must be compatible with the HAL on the target computer. (The HALs do not have to be identical.)

70-210.01.02.003

▶ **Correct Answers: A and C**

    A. **Correct:** Remote installation refers to the process of automatically booting to the network, connecting to a RIS server, and starting a clean installation of Windows 2000 Professional. To automatically connect to RIS, the computer must support or emulate PXE. PXE-compliant computers automatically boot to the network when an operating system isn't installed locally and the computer is configured to boot from the network. PXE support is provided in a number of ways. The PXE ROM is embedded on the network interface card (NIC), or the system BIOS contains the PXE-complaint, remote boot ROM code. A PXE-based remote boot ROM network adapter is included on computers that are Net PC-compliant or PC98-compliant systems.

    RIS can provide operating system installation services to non-PXE-complaint systems by emulating PXE using the remote installation boot floppy. The remote installation boot floppy is mentioned in the question. The remote installation boot floppy disk starts the process of remote operating system installation. The remote installation boot floppy is a PXE emulator that connects to the RIS server through a supported Peripheral Component Interconnect (PCI) network adapter. You use the RBFG.EXE utility to generate a remote installation boot floppy disk. The boot floppy disk contains many common PCI-based network adapters so that a separate network boot disk is not required. Non-PCI network adapters are not supported.

    B. **Incorrect:** Remote control is a feature that allows a computer called a viewer to control the keyboard, mouse, and monitor of a computer called a host. The host must be running a remote control agent and the viewer must be running remote viewer software. Other common features of a remote control package are remote chat, remote file transfer, and remote reboot. SMS and a number of third-party products include a remote control agent and a viewer. Terminal Services also includes a version of remote control that is configured and works differently than typical remote control software. Remote control is not required for RIS and does not play a role in a RIS-based installation.

C. **Correct:** RIS is a feature included with Windows 2000 Server and Windows 2000 Advanced Server. It is used to deploy new installations of Windows 2000 Professional. Therefore, a Windows 2000 Server infrastructure is integral to using RIS. Additionally, the PXE client uses Dynamic Host Configuration Protocol (DHCP) to initiate the process of remotely installing Windows 2000 Professional on a client.

When a PXE client performs a remote boot for the first time, the computer requests an Internet Protocol (IP) address and the IP address of an active RIS server through the DHCP protocol and its PXE extensions. As part of the initial request, the client sends out its globally unique identifier (GUID), which is used to identify the client in Active Directory directory services. The client receives an IP address from the DHCP server and the IP address of the RIS server that services the client. In the RIS server's response, the client is given the name of an installation command line or boot image that it must request when contacting the RIS server for initial service.

D. **Incorrect:** A Windows NT Server 4 infrastructure cannot support RIS because RIS is a new feature in Windows 2000. RIS is designed to run as a service on Windows 2000 Server and Windows 2000 Advanced Server to deploy scripted installations or images of Windows 2000 Professional to client computers.

OBJECTIVE 1.3

Upgrade from a previous version of Windows to Windows 2000 Professional.

The next step after assessing Windows 2000 hardware compatibility is performing a clean installation of Windows 2000 Professional, upgrading an existing operating system installation, or preserving the other operating system by installing Windows 2000 Professional in a separate folder.

When Windows 2000 Professional is installed to coexist with another operating system, the computer runs in a multiboot configuration (sometimes referred to as dual-boot.) In a multiboot configuration, it is important to consider Windows 2000 file system compatibility with the previous operating system. For example, the version of NTFS in Windows 2000 (version 5) isn't fully backward compatible with Windows NT, and Windows 9x cannot read NTFS partitions without the installation of a third-party utility. A local installation of Windows NT 4 requires Service Pack 4 (SP4) or later to read partitions formatted with NTFS version 5. If Windows NT 4 contains no service pack or a service pack prior to SP4, the Windows 2000 setup routine will warn you not to continue the installation. If the installation is continued, you will not be able to boot Windows NT 4 after Windows 2000 is installed.

You can upgrade an existing operating system to Windows 2000 Professional if the computer is running Windows 95, Windows 98, Windows NT Workstation 3.51, or Windows NT Workstation 4. In all cases, you run WINNT32.EXE to initiate the upgrade to these operating systems. Consequently, you can't use WINNT.EXE, the 16-bit version of the setup routine for computers running MS-DOS and Windows 3.x, to upgrade the operating system to Windows 2000 Professional. Although no other operating system can be upgraded to Windows 2000 Professional, a multiboot configuration is an option. Make sure to disable virus-scanning software before starting a Windows 2000 Professional installation upgrade.

You might need to upgrade Windows 9*x*-compatible applications to run in Windows 2000. To determine compatibility, check with the application vendor and review the Microsoft software compatibility list. The Microsoft software compatibility list is located by searching for the keywords "software compatibility" at *http://www.microsoft.com/ windows2000/*. Windows 16-bit applications that use virtual device driver (VxD) files will not run properly in Windows 2000. To aid in detecting known compatibility issues, run the Windows 2000 Readiness Analyzer (CHKUPGRD.EXE) or the /checkupgrade-only installation switch. On a computer running Windows 9*x*, the upgrade report generated with the /checkupgradeonly switch is automatically logged locally to *%windir%* as UPGRADE.TXT. Upgrade reports can also be logged to a central location using an automated answer file. For more information on compatibility logging, read the *Windows 2000 Professional Upgrade Guide*. (See the "Further Reading" section.)

The Windows 2000 Professional setup routine allows you to upgrade third-party application dynamic-link libraries (DLLs) written for Windows 9*x* using migration DLLs that the application vendor provides. Using migration DLLs and carefully testing before a widespread upgrade ensures that the upgraded applications will run on Windows 2000 Professional.

An upgrade is broken into two phases: a report phase and an installation phase. The report phase displays any known incompatibilities so that they can be addressed before upgrade proceeds, and this phase generates an installation script (answer file). The installation phase migrates registry settings, user accounts, and local profiles; installs Windows 2000 Professional in the same directory as the existing Windows installation; and runs any migration DLLs specified.

Caution If a computer running Windows 9*x* in a Windows NT or Windows 2000 domain will be upgraded to Windows 2000, make sure to create a computer account or a computer object in the domain prior to or during the upgrade.

Installation order is an important topic when configuring a computer for multiboot. For example, you should install Windows 2000 Professional only after you install Windows 98 on a multiboot computer. If you installed Windows 98 after Windows 2000 Professional, use the Emergency Repair Disk (ERD) to recover the system partition. For details on configuring a computer for multiboot, see the *Microsoft Windows 2000 Professional Resource Kit*, Chapter 6, "Setup and Startup," pages 259–261. (See this reference under Objective 1.5 in the "Further Reading" section.)

Objective 1.3 Questions

70-210.01.03.001

You are an administrator for a corporate network supporting 50 users. Their systems are running a variety of operating systems including Windows 95, Windows 98, Windows NT 3.1, Windows NT 3.5, Windows NT 3.51, and Windows NT 4. Which of these systems can be upgraded directly to Windows 2000 Professional? (Choose two.)

A. Windows 9x

B. Windows NT 3.1

C. Windows NT 3.5

D. Windows NT Workstation 3.51 or Windows NT Workstation 4

70-210.01.03.002

You are an administrator for a corporate network supporting 50 users running Windows NT Workstation 4. You are planning to deploy Windows 2000 Professional on 50 computers.

You need to ensure that the existing computer hardware is compatible with Windows 2000. Which two methods can you use to generate a hardware compatibility report? (Choose two.)

A. Download and run CHKUPGRD.EXE.

B. Run MKCOMPAT.EXE from the root of the Windows 2000 installation CD-ROM.

C. Open the Run dialog box and, including the path to the \i386 folder on the Windows 2000 installation CD-ROM, type **winnt32 /checkupgrade** in the Open text box.

D. Open the Run dialog box and, including the path to the \i386 folder on the Windows 2000 installation CD-ROM, type **winnt32 /checkupgradeonly** in the Open text box.

70-210.01.03.003

You are an administrator for a corporate network supporting 50 users running Windows NT Workstation 4. You are planning to deploy Windows 2000 Professional on 50 computers.

What is the most efficient way to determine whether any of your third-party applications require updates to operate properly in Windows 2000?

A. Connect to the Windows Update Web site.

B. Contact the vendor of each software application.

C. Generate a compatibility report using the SMS Crystal Reports snap-in.

D. Generate a compatibility report using the Windows 2000 Readiness Analyzer.

Objective 1.3 Answers

70-210.01.03.001

▶ **Correct Answers: A and D**

A. **Correct:** Windows 2000 Professional can upgrade Windows 95 and Windows 98 to Windows 2000 Professional. Note that it is not possible to upgrade Windows 9*x* to Windows 2000 Server.

B. **Incorrect:** You can't upgrade Windows NT 3.1 Workstation and Windows NT 3.1 Advanced Server to Windows 2000 Professional. You can upgrade Windows NT 3.1 Workstation to Windows NT 3.51 and then upgrade Windows NT 3.51 to Windows 2000 Professional. Server versions of Windows NT cannot be upgraded to Windows 2000 Professional.

C. **Incorrect:** You can't upgrade Windows NT 3.5 Workstation to Windows 2000 Professional. You can upgrade Windows NT 3.5 Workstation to Windows NT 3.51 Workstation or Windows NT 4 Workstation and then upgrade to Windows 2000 Professional.

D. **Correct:** You can upgrade Windows NT Workstation 3.51 or Windows NT Workstation 4 to Windows 2000 Professional.

70-210.01.03.002

▶ **Correct Answers: A and D**

A. **Correct:** The CHKUPGRD.EXE program is the Windows 2000 Readiness Analyzer self-extracting utility available for download from the Microsoft Web site. When run without any switches, CHKUPGRD.EXE expands files into a temporary working folder and then runs a minimal version of WINNT32.EXE designed specifically to check upgrade compatibility of the computer. This minimal version of WINNT32.EXE uses a data repository of ASCII and .htm files extracted to the temporary working folder to report any hardware and software incompatibilities found.

B. **Incorrect:** The MKCOMPAT.EXE program is a Windows 95 utility for troubleshooting problems running Windows 3.1-based programs in Windows 95.

C. **Incorrect:** The winnt32 /checkupgrade syntax is incorrect.

D. **Correct:** Typing the 32-bit Windows 2000 setup routine with the /checkupgradeonly switch included runs the Microsoft Windows 2000 Readiness Analyzer Wizard. On all operating systems capable of running the Microsoft Windows 2000 Readiness Analyzer Wizard, the upgrade report appears on the Report System Compatibility screen of the wizard. On a computer running Windows 9x, the wizard generates a log file in *%windir%* named UPGRADE.TXT. On a computer running Windows NT, the wizard generates a log file in *%systemroot%* named WINNT32.LOG. By running the 32-bit Windows 2000 setup routine with the /checkupgradeonly switch and an answer file, upgrade reports can be logged to a central location.

70-210.01.03.003

▶ **Correct Answers: D**

A. **Incorrect:** The Windows Update Web site provides updates in the form of operating system service packs, hot fixes, and drivers, not third-party applications.

B. **Incorrect:** Contacting a vendor to determine whether Windows 2000 is supported or whether updates are available or necessary is inefficient. First determine whether an update is required, and then contact the vendor to obtain an update.

C. **Incorrect:** You use the SMS Crystal Reports snap-in to create reports on data stored in the SMS database, not to generate Windows 2000 compatibility data. Instead, the SMS database is populated with Windows 2000 compatibility data using a number of SMS utilities that augment the Windows 2000 Readiness Analyzer program. These utilities allow for the easy distribution and automation of the Windows 2000 Readiness Analyzer. The output from the Windows 2000 Readiness Analyzer is then stored in the SMS 2 database. These results can then be reported by using Crystal Info for SMS.

D. **Correct:** From the list of answers, the Windows 2000 Readiness Analyzer is the most direct way to determine whether any third-party applications require updates (also called update packs) to operate properly in Windows 2000. For greater efficiency, augment the Windows 2000 Readiness Analyzer with SMS 2 or use the 32-bit Windows 2000 setup routine's /checkupgradeonly switch with an answer file so that the log it generates for each computer is centralized for easy access and analysis.

Don't use the report provided by the Windows 2000 Readiness Analyzer or /checkupgradeonly as a guarantee of compatibility because it tests only known software and hardware incompatibilities. Thorough application testing is a critical step in determining application readiness.

OBJECTIVE 1.4

Deploy service packs.

Microsoft uses service packs to distribute numerous updates and hot fixes to an operating system. You can locate service packs for Microsoft operating systems on the Windows Update Web site, a centralized, online resource for Windows updates, including service packs, hot fixes, and drivers.

A shortcut to the Windows Update Web site is located near the top of the Start menu unless Group Policy restrictions remove it. This shortcut points to the Windows Update program UPDMGR.EXE, located in *%systemroot%*\system32. Running this program starts Microsoft Internet Explorer and connects to the Windows Update Web site. This Web site uses Active Setup and Microsoft ActiveX controls to provide product enhancements. These controls are downloaded and installed on the computer the first time you establish a connection with the site. Windows Update automatically compares device drivers installed on the computer with a database of updated drivers on the server. Any drivers newer than those currently installed are offered for installation.

In a medium to large network, distributing updates locally from the intranet is more efficient than applying updates externally from the Internet. To prevent users from accessing Windows Update, configure the Windows 2000 group policy setting: disable and remove links to Windows Update to restrict access to the Windows Update site.

You apply local updates using service packs. For earlier versions of Windows 32-bit operating systems such as Windows NT, you must reapply a service pack every time you install operating system components from the operating system's installation CD-ROM or a distribution point. A **distribution point** is a network share containing the operating system source files. A distribution point is synonymous with a **distribution share**.

In Windows 2000 Professional, **slipstreaming** avoids the administrative overhead of service pack reapplication. Slipstreaming allows you to apply a service pack update to the source files in the Windows 2000 Professional distribution point. When the distribution point is the source for an installation of Windows 2000 Professional, the new installation contains the service pack. Any services or drivers added to the local installation come from the distribution point, thus avoiding the need to reapply the service pack.

You complete a manual, local installation of a service pack by running the service pack UPDATE.EXE utility. If, after applying the service pack, you add any services or drivers to the local installation, you must reapply the service pack. To avoid manual service pack reapplication, type **update -s:** *distribution_folder* (where *distribution_folder* is the location containing the operating system files) to slipstream a distribution point. Then use the distribution point rather than the Windows 2000 Professional installation CD-ROM to add services or drivers to the local installation.

Objective 1.4 Questions

70-210.01.04.001

You install Windows 2000 Professional on a new Pentium III computer that is not connected to an intranet. One week later, you want to apply a service pack. What should you do?

A. Type **update**.

B. Type **update -s:** *distribution_folder*.

C. Type **update /syspart**.

D. Type **update /cmdcons**.

70-210.01.04.002

You are an administrator for a corporate network supporting 50 users running Windows NT Workstation 4. You are planning to deploy Windows 2000 Professional on 50 computers.

You want to apply a service pack simultaneously during Windows 2000 deployment by integrating the service pack with an image of the Windows installation files. What should you do?

A. Type **update**.

B. Type **update -s:** *distribution_folder*.

C. Type **update /syspart**.

D. Type **update /cmdcons**.

70-210.01.04.003

You have a home office with a dial-up Internet connection. You install and configure all hardware and software yourself. You install Windows 2000 Professional on a new Pentium III computer. One week later, you apply a service pack. If you later add another service to the installation of Windows 2000 Professional using the Windows 2000 Professional installation CD-ROM as the file source, what other task should you perform?

A. Do nothing.

B. Type **setupcl**.

C. Run SETUPMGR.EXE.

D. Reapply the service pack.

Objective 1.4 Answers

70-210.01.04.001

▶ **Correct Answers: A**

A. **Correct:** To apply a service pack to an existing installation of Windows 2000, acquire the service pack from Microsoft via CD-ROM or by downloading from their Internet site, and then type **update** to run UPDATE.EXE. If new services or drivers are installed, reapply the service pack. Alternatively, you can visit the Windows Update site so that new updates are applied automatically.

B. **Incorrect:** When you type **update -s:** *distribution_folder*, the command updates a central distribution point of Windows 2000 source files. This distribution point is then used to update a computer running Windows 2000 Professional with the latest service pack. Because the computer described in the question is not connected to an intranet, a central distribution point is not available.

C. **Incorrect:** /syspart is a valid Windows 2000 setup switch used to complete the setup loader and text-mode phases of installation on a fixed disk. The disk is then moved to another computer to continue installation. This switch is not valid for the service pack update program, UPDATE.EXE.

D. **Incorrect:** /cmdcons is a valid switch for the 32-bit Windows 2000 setup routine, which is used to create a recovery command console startup option for Windows 2000. This switch is not valid for the service pack update program, UPDATE.EXE.

70-210.01.04.002

▶ **Correct Answers: B**

A. **Incorrect:** You use UPDATE.EXE to apply a service pack to a computer already running an installation of Windows 2000. You could include UPDATE.EXE at the end of an automated installation of Windows 2000 Professional, but this is an inefficient method of applying the service pack.

B. **Correct:** You use the -s: *distribution_folder* switch for service pack slipstreaming. Slipstreaming applies the service pack files to a distribution point containing the operating system source files. By adding the service pack to the operating system's distribution share, the service pack will be installed when Windows 2000 is installed.

C. **Incorrect:** /syspart is a valid Windows 2000 setup switch that you use to create a partial installation of Windows 2000 on a disk before you move the disk to another computer to continue installation. This switch is not valid for the service pack update program UPDATE.EXE.

D. **Incorrect:** /cmdcons is a valid Windows 2000 setup switch that you use to create a recovery command console startup option for Windows 2000. This switch is not valid for the service pack update program UPDATE.EXE.

70-210.01.04.003

▶ **Correct Answers: D**

A. **Incorrect:** When you add a new service using the Windows 2000 Professional installation CD-ROM, some files that the service pack updated may be replaced. As a result, Windows 2000 Professional contains a mixture of installation files from the original installation and the service pack installation. This hybrid installation is potentially unstable.

B. **Incorrect:** SETUPCL.EXE supports the functions of SysPrep, the System Preparation utility. SET-UPCL.EXE generates a new security ID (SID) and starts the Mini Setup Wizard. SETUPCL.EXE does not play a role in service pack updates.

C. **Incorrect:** Setup Manager is a utility for generating an answer file to script an installation of Windows 2000 Professional or to fully automate a SysPrep installation procedure.

D. **Correct:** Whenever you install a new service or driver using the Windows 2000 Professional installation CD-ROM, you must reapply a previously installed service pack.

OBJECTIVE 1.5

Troubleshoot failed installations.

When you troubleshoot a failed installation, you should always start by double-checking that all hardware in the computer is listed on the Hardware Compatibility List (HCL). You should remove any hardware component not on the HCL before repeating installation. Another important preinstallation or installation troubleshooting task is verifying that the basic input/output system (BIOS) is up-to-date. Vendor-provided BIOS updates and operating-specific BIOS configuration settings can resolve a number of installation failures. For example, disabling the Plug and Play Operating System (PnP OS) BIOS setting is important before installing Windows 2000 Professional on computers that don't support the Advanced Configuration and Power Interface (ACPI) specification. Additionally, you should reserve any legacy ISA device interrupt request (IRQ) settings in the BIOS on all computers before setup commences.

The next troubleshooting step is determining in which phase the installation failure is occurring. The three installation phases are the Setup Loader phase, the Text-Mode Setup phase, and the GUI-Mode Setup phase.

In the Setup Loader phase, preliminary installation files are copied from the source to the local disk. Setup Loader starts the installation process and loads a SCSI disk controller support driver, if required, and a hardware detection program. After base hardware is detected, a minimal version of the Windows 2000 kernel and additional hardware drivers are loaded. Finally the boot sector is modified to continue Windows 2000 installation.

The Text-Mode Setup phase is characterized by white text on a blue background. In this phase, installation and configuration of hardware driver detection continues. Next partitions are created and they are formatted or converted as necessary. Minimum system requirements are verified and most installation files are copied to the local disk.

GUI-Mode Setup phase marks the conclusion of the setup process. In this phase, additional devices are detected, installed, and configured; optional components are installed; additional installation files are copied; and dynamic-link library (DLL) files are registered. If installation fails in this phase, restarting the computer may resolve the failure, thus allowing setup to continue.

Four general information log files are created during setup to record the installation process: SETUPACT.LOG, SETUPERR.LOG, SETUPAPI.LOG, and SETUP-LOG.TXT. These files provide essential information about the installation process to assist in resolving installation failures.

Device-specific or component-specific log files are also generated during the setup process or when a new Plug and Play device is added. These log files are stored in *%systemroot%* (by default, C:\WINNT). The following is a list of some of the device-specific or component-specific log files generated during setup:

- COMSETUP.LOG—Logs Component Object Model (COM) setup routines

- MMDET.LOG—Logs multimedia installation and resource allocation

- NETSETUP.LOG—Logs network computer name, workgroup, and domain validation

- IIS5.LOG—Logs the installation and configuration of Internet Information Services (IIS) 5

For this objective, you must be familiar with the activities occurring in each setup phase, the purpose of the primary files or classes of files installed in each phase of setup, and the function of the installation log files. Log files are essential to troubleshooting a failed installation.

Objective 1.5 Questions

70-210.01.05.001

You attempt to install Windows 2000 Professional on a Pentium III computer, but the process fails. You suspect that a multimedia device caused the failure. Which log file should you view to determine the port ranges used by each multimedia device?

A. COMSETUP.LOG

B. MMDET.LOG

C. NETSETUP.LOG

D. WINNT32.LOG

70-210.01.05.002

You attempt to install Windows 2000 Professional on a Pentium III computer, but the process fails. Which log file should you view to determine the severity of a setup error?

A. COMSETUP.LOG

B. MMDET.LOG

C. NETSETUP.LOG

D. SETUPERR.LOG

70-210.01.05.003

You attempt to install Windows 2000 Professional on a Pentium III computer, but the process fails. Which log file should you view for an overview of all files that are copied during setup?

A. MMDET.LOG

B. NETSETUP.LOG

C. SETUPACT.LOG

D. SETUPERR.LOG

Objective 1.5 Answers

70-210.01.05.001

▶ **Correct Answers: B**

   A. **Incorrect:** Use COMSETUP.LOG to troubleshoot COM component installation. This and all log files mentioned in the answer choices are stored in *%systemroot%*.

   B. **Correct:** Use MMDET.LOG to troubleshoot multimedia device detection and resource allocation. It contains the port ranges for each multimedia device.

   C. **Incorrect:** Use NETSETUP.LOG to troubleshoot network computer name, workgroup, or domain detection errors.

   D. **Incorrect:** WINNT32.LOG is the output file generated on computers running Windows NT or Windows 2000 when you run the Microsoft Windows 2000 Readiness Analyzer or you type **winnt32 / checkupgradeonly**.

70-210.01.05.002

▶ **Correct Answers: D**

   A. **Incorrect:** Use COMSETUP.LOG to troubleshoot COM component installation.

   B. **Incorrect:** Use MMDET.LOG to troubleshoot multimedia device detection and resource allocation. It contains the port ranges for each multimedia device.

   C. **Incorrect:** Use NETSETUP.LOG to troubleshoot network computer name registration and workgroup or domain detection.

   D. **Correct:** Use SETUPERR.LOG located in *%systemroot%* to troubleshoot errors encountered during the installation process.

70-210.01.05.003

▶ **Correct Answers: C**

A. **Incorrect:** Use MMDET.LOG to troubleshoot multimedia device detection and resource allocation. It contains the port ranges for each multimedia device.

B. **Incorrect:** Use NETSETUP.LOG to troubleshoot network computer name registration and work-group or domain detection.

C. **Correct:** Use SETUPACT.LOG created in *%systemroot%* during the setup process; it records all files copied locally during setup.

D. **Incorrect:** Use SETUPERR.LOG located in *%systemroot%* to troubleshoot errors encountered during the installation process.

Implementing and Conducting Administration of Resources

The core operating system *resources* in Microsoft Windows 2000 Professional are the file system, the files and folders that the file system supports, and **shares**. The three primary share types in a Windows 2000 network are folder shares, Web shares, and printer shares.

Resource implementation tasks include preparing partitions with file systems; creating folders, shares, and Internet-accessible resources; and configuring access permissions to them. After implementation, these resources require regular administration. Administration tasks include removing unnecessary partitions, shares, folders, and files; reconfiguring permissions; and troubleshooting resource access problems.

Some implementation and administration tasks are unique to the type of resource. For example, **printer shares** require print job management and printing device configuration; **partitions or volumes** require capacity management and disk access optimization.

Windows 2000 natively supports a number of file systems. The two fixed-disk file systems it supports are **file allocation table (FAT)** and **New Technology File System (NTFS)**. The FAT file system is ideal for providing access compatibility for computers configured to multiboot operating systems. NTFS is a more robust and feature-rich file system for computers that exclusively run Microsoft Windows NT or Windows 2000.

Tested Skills and Suggested Practices

The skills you need to successfully master the Implementing and Conducting Administration of Resources Objective Domain on Exam 70-210: Installing, Configuring, and Administering Microsoft Windows 2000 Professional include the following:

- **Implement and administer Windows 2000 file system features.**

  - Practice 1: Automate an unattended installation of Windows 2000 Professional that converts a primary partition to NTFS.

  - Practice 2: Compress NTFS partitions, folders, and files using the Compact command-line utility and Microsoft Windows Explorer.

  - Practice 3: Review the various Compact switches by typing **compact /?**. Type **compact** with no switches to see the compression state of folders and files.

  - Practice 4: Use Windows Explorer and the CACLS.EXE utility to configure NTFS local permissions on partitions, folders, and files.

  - Practice 5: Type **net share** at the command line to view available shares, and then type **net share /?** to view the switches supported by this utility. Finally create and remove a share using this command-line utility.

  - Practice 6: Create a share, configure permissions for a share, and delete a share using Windows Explorer.

  - Practice 7: Install Microsoft Internet Information Services (IIS) and then create and configure security for Web sharing.

  - Practice 8: Stop the Server service and then attempt to create a share. Restart the Server service, and verify that you can successfully create a share.

  - Practice 9: Create a partition using the Disk Administrator snap-in.

  - Practice 10: Format a partition from the command line by using the Disk Administrator snap-in.

- **Implement and administer Windows 2000 printing.**

  - Practice 1: Create a printer and share it using the Add Printers Wizard.

  - Practice 2: Make sure that IIS is installed to support Internet printing.

  - Practice 3: Create a new port for printing.

  - Practice 4: Connect to a printer through a UNC name and using HTTP.

  - Practice 5: Complete all administration tasks available through the Printers window. For example, create a printer pool, prioritize printers, redirect documents for printing, and configure a separator page.

Further Reading

This "Further Reading" section provides lists of important readings to supplement your current understanding of the skills tested within this Objective Domain. The lists are delineated into pertinent readings for each objective within this Objective Domain. If you feel that you need additional preparation prior to taking the exam, study these sources thoroughly.

Objective 2.1

Microsoft Corporation. *MCSE Training Kit—Microsoft Windows 2000 Professional.* Redmond, Washington: Microsoft Press, 2000. Read and complete the practices in Chapter 14, "Securing Resources with NTFS Permissions."

Microsoft Corporation. *Microsoft Windows 2000 Server Resource Kit Windows 2000 Distributed Systems Guide.* Redmond, Washington: Microsoft Press, 2000. Read Chapter 12, "Access Control."

Objective 2.2

Microsoft Corporation. *Microsoft Windows 2000 Professional Help.* Redmond, Washington: Microsoft, 2000. Using the online help file included with Windows 2000 Professional, search for and read about the following topics: "Change permissions for a shared folder," "Securing shared drives," "Shared folder permissions," "Special shared folders," and "Using shared folders."

Microsoft Corporation. *MCSE Training Kit—Microsoft Windows 2000 Professional.* Redmond, Washington: Microsoft Press, 2000. Read and complete the practices in Chapter 15, "Administering Shared Folders."

Objective 2.3

Microsoft Corporation. *MCSE Training Kit—Microsoft Windows 2000 Professional.* Redmond, Washington: Microsoft Press, 2000. Read and complete the practices in Chapter 12, "Setting Up and Configuring Network Printers," and Chapter 13, "Administering Network Printers."

Microsoft Corporation. *Microsoft Windows 2000 Server Resource Kit Windows 2000 Server Operations Guide.* Redmond, Washington: Microsoft Press, 2000. Read Chapter 4, "Network Printing."

Objective 2.4

Daily, Sean. "NTFS5 vs. FAT32," *Windows 2000 Magazine.* Denver, Colorado: Duke Communications International, 2000. Sean Daily provides a comprehensive comparison of FAT32 and NTFS in Windows 2000 and how and when to use these file systems.

Microsoft Corporation. *Microsoft Windows 2000 Professional Resource Kit.* Redmond, Washington: Microsoft Press, 2000. Read Chapter 17, "File Systems."

Microsoft Corporation. *Microsoft Windows 2000 Professional installation CD-ROM.* Redmond, Washington: Microsoft, 2000. Read the release notes contained in README.DOC. You can find this file at the root of the CD-ROM.

O B J E C T I V E   2 . 1

Monitor, manage, and troubleshoot access to files and folders.

Large file types, such as multimedia files and application files that are hundreds of megabytes in size, drive greater and greater disk capacity requirements. A number of technologies are able to slow disk capacity use. The most common of these technologies is **compression**. Windows 2000 Professional includes built-in compression. Compression functions on **NTFS** partitions formatted with 4-KB cluster sizes or smaller and operates on **partitions**, **volumes**, folders, or files.

You apply compression either through Windows Explorer or from the command line with the COMPACT.EXE utility. Through Windows Explorer, you can compress an entire partition, folder, or file. Compression applied at the partition or folder level can be inherited by subfolders and files or just applied to the parent partition or folder. The COMPACT.EXE utility is ideal for running in a batch process. If the compression fails initially because a file targeted for compression is opened by another process, this utility will ensure that the compression procedure completes in the background.

Whether a file remains compressed when it is moved or copied depends on the target file system, the target partition, the target folder compression state, the file's compression state, and whether a file is moved or copied. The table on the following page shows the behavior of compression when a file is moved or copied.

Action from Source to Target	Copy	Move
Compressed file from an NTFS-formatted partition to any other file system partition	Decompressed	Decompressed.
Uncompressed file from any partition to an NTFS-formatted and compressed partition or compressed parent folder	Compressed	Compressed.
Compressed or uncompressed file from an NTFS-formatted partition to the same partition	Inherits compression state from parent folder or partition	Remains in original compression state regardless of parent folder or partition compression state.
Uncompressed or compressed file from an NTFS-formatted partition to another NTFS partition	Inherits compression state from parent folder or partition	Inherits compression state from parent folder or partition. A moved file inherits the compression state of the target parent folder or partition because a move to another partition is actually an automatic copy to the target partition and an automatic delete operation from the source partition.

The amount a file is compressed depends on the file type. ASCII, document, and bitmap files are highly compressible, whereas binary files, such as application executables, are not. Compression can affect system performance because it adds overhead to standard file I/O operations such as opening and saving a file. NTFS compression technology is convenient because compression and decompression is managed in the background. For example, when a compressed file is opened in Microsoft Word, the operating system decompresses the file before the word processor opens it. When the file is saved, the operating system returns the file to its original compressed state.

NTFS provides file system security with **local permissions**. Local permissions are stored in the **discretionary access control list (DACL)** as **access control entries (ACEs)**. The DACL is a table containing a set of configurable privileges. Each NTFS partition, folder, and file contains a DACL. Only NTFS provides this level of file system security to Windows 2000.

Note You will see DACL shortened to ACL in much of the documentation.

You configure local permissions either using Windows Explorer or from the command line using the CACLS.EXE utility. You must be able to navigate to and view or set security on partitions, folders, or files using Windows Explorer. You must also know how to use the CACLS.EXE utility to view or configure permissions from the command line. These tools can impact permissions throughout a folder hierarchy. Know how to control permission inheritance using both Windows Explorer and CACLS.EXE.

Local permission inheritance and certain **explicit rights**, such as allowing the Take Ownership permission or denying the Full Control permission, can influence user or group effective permissions. **Effective permissions** are the actual rights a user is granted to a resource, whether they are inherited or explicitly assigned. Combinations of user and group permissions configured for an NTFS resource will influence effective permissions. For example, if a user is granted the Read permission to a folder and a group in which the user is a member is granted the Write permission, then the user's effective permissions are Read and Write.

Two types of permissions exist: general permissions, such as Full Control and Read, and permission entries, such as Change permissions and Delete. General permissions are a combination of permission entries. For example, the Full Control permission means that all permission entries are allowed. The Read permission configured for a folder means that the following permission entries are allowed:

- List Folder / Read Data

- Read Attributes

- Read Extended Attributes

- Read Permissions

Copying and moving folders and files can change their DACL. NTFS permissions are affected in much the same way that compression attributes are affected by move-and-copy operations. A Resource Kit utility that is used to preserve permissions when copying NTFS files is ROBOCOPY.EXE. This utility preserves NTFS permissions when a file is *moved* or *copied* from one NTFS partition to another or when it is *copied* from one NTFS folder to another. NTFS file permissions are not changed when a file is moved from one location on a partition to another location on the same partition. Local permissions are removed when a file is moved or copied to any other file system.

Optimizing access to file resources requires careful organization of partitions, folders, and files. For example, the following practices will help to optimize file resource access:

- Protect the operating system files from file activity, such as application installation or user data storage that could cause the boot partition to run out of available disk capacity.

- A boot partition that is filled to capacity will cause the operating system to fail. Consider placing PAGEFILE.SYS on a separate partition. Other procedures to control the use of the boot partition include the following: placing user profiles in a location other than the boot partition and moving the Offline Files cache to another partition. Moving the Offline Files cache is explained in Objective Domain 4 and user profile management is explored in Objective Domain 5.

- Place application folders and data folders on a partition separate from the boot partition.

- Separate the application folders and the data folders from each other.

- Consider placing application and user data on separate partitions.

These easy practices will optimize file resource availability, simplify backup procedures, and simplify application upgrades and permission assignment.

Objective 2.1 Questions

70-210.02.01.001

You are assigned to help desk support for your corporate network. A user reports that she is unable to compress a folder on an NTFS partition. What are the two most likely causes? (Choose two.)

A. The volume is corrupt.

B. The user has been denied access to the disk volume.

C. The Encrypting File System (EFS) attribute has been applied.

D. When the volume was formatted, a cluster size greater than 4 KB was specified.

70-210.02.01.002

You set NTFS permissions on a folder named \Download on your computer running Windows 2000 Professional. The \Download folder contains several nested subfolders. By default, which folder or folders inherit the permissions you set on the \Download folder?

A. \Download

B. \Download and first-tier subfolders

C. \Download, first-tier subfolders, and second-tier subfolders

D. All subfolders

70-210.02.01.003

You have been hired to deploy a Windows 2000 network for a small business. You must also plan and establish NTFS permissions for all users. You want to simplify administration and backup operations. What should you do? (Choose two.)

A. Place applications and shared data in each user's home folder on the server.

B. Create separate folders for applications, shared data, and individual user data (home folders) on the server.

C. Place home folders and shared data beneath public folders on the server volume where your applications and operating system reside.

D. Place home folders and shared data folders beneath public folders on a server volume separate from your applications and the operating system.

Objective 2.1 Answers

70-210.02.01.001

▶ **Correct Answers: C and D**

   A. **Incorrect:** From the user's report, it appears that she can access the folder, so it is unlikely that the volume is corrupt. Additionally, although NTFS volume corruption is possible, it is unlikely because of the protections built into this file system, such as transaction logging and cluster remapping.

   B. **Incorrect:** If local permissions to the disk volume were the problem, a message box stating that access is denied would appear to the user. Because the user did not report that this message appeared, it is unlikely that the inability to compress the folder has anything to do with permissions.

   C. **Correct:** Folder and file compression and encryption are mutually exclusive attributes. Thus, a compressed file cannot be encrypted and an encrypted file cannot be compressed. This is demonstrated in Windows Explorer through the Advanced Attributes dialog box. To navigate to this dialog box, access the Properties dialog box of a folder or file and then click the Advanced button. The Advanced Attributes dialog box displays check boxes, one for compression and one for encryption. Unlike traditional check boxes, you can select only one advanced attribute at a time. Note that these check boxes operate like radio buttons.

   D. **Correct:** NTFS compression is designed to support cluster sizes up to 4 KB. Larger cluster sizes do not support NTFS compression. If compression is required, back up all files on the partition and reformat the partition using a cluster size of 4 KB or smaller. After the partition is reformatted, restore the files.

70-210.02.01.002

▶ **Correct Answers: D**

   A. **Incorrect:** The question states that you applied NTFS permissions to the \Download folder. This is an explicit assignment. Inherited assignments flow from a disk to folders, subfolders, and files beneath it and from a parent folder to subfolders and files beneath it.

   B. **Incorrect:** First, an explicit assignment was made to the \Download folder so inheritance was not involved in this assignment. Second, by default, inheritance flows from the parent folder to all subfolders beneath it, not just the first-tier subfolders.

C. **Incorrect:** First, an explicit assignment was made to the \Download folder so inheritance was not involved in this assignment. Second, by default, inheritance flows from the parent folder to all sub-folders beneath it, not just the first-tier and second-tier subfolders.

D. **Correct:** By default, when local permissions for a folder on an NTFS partition are modified, all sub-folders beneath it inherit those permissions. You can disable this inheritance property in the Security tab of a disk's or folder's Properties dialog box. At the bottom of the Security tab, the Allow Inheritable Permissions From Parent To Propagate To This Object check box is enabled by default.

70-210.02.01.003

▶ **Correct Answers: B and D**

A. **Incorrect:** Placing applications in each user's home folder is an inefficient use of disk space. Most applications that are run from the server should be installed only on the server, and all users should access the application from this central location. Home folder data should not be mixed with application data. If the application must be upgraded or removed, home folder data might be lost.

B. **Correct:** To simplify administration, group files into separate folders for applications, shared data, and individual user data. This is also the most efficient way to optimize access to these folder and file resources. For example, application, home, and shared data folders require different permissions because of how they are used.

C. **Incorrect:** Placing home folders and shared data folders beneath public folders does provide a manageable structure for configuring permissions. However, placing these folders on the same drive containing your applications and operating system is dangerous because user data could fill the partition to capacity and cause the operating system to fail.

D. **Correct:** Centralizing home folders and public folders on a volume that is separate from applications and the operating system is an ideal structure for administration. For example, you could choose to compress the partition containing the user data while leaving the application and operating system partition uncompressed.

O B J E C T I V E 2 . 2

Manage and troubleshoot access to shared folders.

In Windows 2000, you can make disk resources network-accessible in two ways: through **sharing** or **Web sharing**. Sharing opens in a Windows Explorer window and uses the following **Universal Naming Convention (UNC)** syntax: *computer-name\sharename*. Web sharing opens in a browser window and uses the following **Hypertext Transfer Protocol (HTTP)** syntax: *http://computername/alias*.

Sharing is a critical step in making a folder and its contents (files and subfolders) available over the network. Additionally, sharing provides a limited form of network security using **share permissions**. These permissions are configured similarly to **NTFS** permissions, but they are limited in two important ways: First, share permissions do not provide local security, meaning that a user can log on locally and access folders regardless of the assigned share permissions. Second, you apply shares and share permissions only at the drive or folder level. In contrast, you apply NTFS local permissions at the drive, folder, or file level and provide local and network security. Sharing functions on all file systems supported in Windows 2000.

Each fixed disk in the computer is automatically assigned a hidden share name of *drive letter*$. For example, the hidden share name of drive C is C$. A share is hidden if the last character in the share name is a dollar ($) sign. The permissions assigned to these hidden shares cannot be changed. There are additional hidden shares such as Admin$ and Print$.

You create and remove shared folders by using Windows Explorer or from the command line by using the Net Share command-line utility. You can also create shares by using the Microsoft Windows Scripting Host (WSH).

Note SHARE.VBS is a WSH sharing administration script sample. See the Windows 2000 Server Resource Kit, "Remote Administration Scripts Help" file to view the syntax for SHARE.VBS.

The Server service manages sharing and share permissions. Therefore, sharing functions only if the Server service is running. The World Wide Web Publishing Service manages Web sharing and Web share permissions. Therefore, Web sharing functions only if the World Wide Web Publishing Service component of Internet Information Services (IIS) is running.

Sharing and Web sharing permissions are different. Share permissions are Full Control, Read, and Write. When a share is created, the Everyone group is granted Full Control and the number of users allowed to connect to the share—the user access limit—is set to the maximum allowed. The maximum number of concurrent connections allowed to a computer running Windows 2000 Professional is 10. The following table shows rights granted based on assigned permission:

Right to	Full Control	Change	Read
View filenames and subfolder names	x	x	x
Navigate to subfolders	x	x	x
View data in files and running programs	x	x	x
Add files and subfolders to the shared folder	x	x	
Change data in files	x	x	
Delete subfolders and files	x	x	
Change permissions (when the share is located on an NTFS partition)	x		
Take ownership (when the share is located on an NTFS partition)	x		

Sharing permissions, user access limits, and share caching are configurable settings for sharing.

The security settings for IIS enforce access to Web shares. A Web share is also called an **alias**. The security settings for IIS are categorized by access permissions and application permissions. Access permissions are Read, Write, Script Source Access, and Directory Browsing. Application permissions are None, Scripts, and Execute (includes scripts).

The inability to configure sharing or Web sharing is commonly associated with the state of its supporting service. Sharing depends on the Server service; Web sharing depends on the World Wide Web Publishing Service. Inability to access a shared resource is usually caused by improperly configured permissions, NTFS and share permission conflicts, share names that are too long for client computers running legacy operating systems, or network access problems.

Objective 2.2 Questions

70-210.02.02.001

You recently installed Windows 2000 Professional on a Pentium III computer, and then you shared the \Download folder. By default, which share permissions does Windows 2000 assign to the Everyone group? (Choose three.)

A. Full Control

B. Change

C. Read

D. List Folder Contents

70-210.02.02.002

You create the \Reports folder on a computer running Windows 2000 Professional. You share the \Reports folder, assign the Read share permission to user TonyV, and assign the Change share permission to the Developers group. TonyV is a member of the Developers group. Which effective share permission does TonyV have to the \Reports folder when accessing it from a remote Windows 2000 computer?

A. Read

B. Change

C. Full Control

D. No Access

70-210.02.02.003

You create and share the \Sales folder on a computer running Windows 2000 Professional. During the next two weeks, various users save Microsoft Excel files to the \Sales folder. You later decide to move the \Sales folder to a more powerful computer. Now users are calling you because they are unable to access the \Sales folder. What is the most likely cause of this problem?

A. The disk signature on the target volume is corrupt.

B. When you move a shared folder, Windows 2000 stops sharing the folder.

C. Users must log off and log back on before being able to access a shared folder that was moved.

D. To be able to move a shared folder, you must download the Microsoft Windows 2000 High Encryption Pack and apply it from the Windows Update site.

70-210.02.02.004

You are the Windows 2000 administrator for your small business. Five Pentium III computers running Windows 2000 Professional are connected in a workgroup network configuration. Which Windows 2000 user groups have the ability to share folders on computers running Windows 2000 Professional? (Choose two.)

A. Administrators

B. Backup Operators

C. Power Users

D. Server Operators

Objective 2.2 Answers

70-210.02.02.001

▶ **Correct Answers: A, B, and C**

A. **Correct:** By default, the Everyone group is assigned Full Control permissions to the share. All accounts are assigned membership to this special group by the operating system. It is not possible to revoke membership to this group.

B. **Correct:** The Full Control permission is a superset of the Change permission and the Read permission. When the operating system automatically assigns Full Control permission, the Change permission Allow check box is selected.

C. **Correct:** The Full Control permission is a superset of the Change permission and the Read permission. When the operating system automatically assigns Full Control permission, the Read permission Allow check box is selected.

D. **Incorrect:** The List Folder Contents permission is an NTFS local permission, not a share permission.

70-210.02.02.002

▶ **Correct Answers: B**

A. **Incorrect:** The user account TonyV is directly assigned the Read share permission to the \Reports folder. Through group membership, the TonyV account inherits the Change share permission. Thus, the effective share permission of TonyV is the sum of explicitly assigned permissions and permissions inherited through group membership.

B. **Correct:** Effective rights are the sum of user permissions and group permissions. TonyV is granted Read share permission to the \Reports folder and as a member of the Developers group, Change share permission to the same folder. Therefore, his effective right is Change. The Change permission is a superset of the Read permission.

C. **Incorrect:** The Full Control permission is equivalent to the Change permission on FAT volumes. However, when the Full Control permission is a user's effective right to a share on an NTFS volume, the user is able to modify NTFS local permissions and take ownership of the share folder and its sub-folders and files.

D. **Incorrect:** No Access is a user's effective right to a share only if the Full Control Deny check box is selected or if the user and any groups to which the user belongs have not been granted any rights to the share.

70-210.02.02.003

▶ **Correct Answers: B**

A. **Incorrect:** A disk signature is written to a disk when the Windows 2000 Disk Administrator snap-in is used to view a disk for the first time. A corrupted disk signature suggests potential disk problems.

B. **Correct:** When a shared folder is moved, the Windows 2000 operating system automatically stops sharing the folder. This automatic share removal by the operating system avoids error messages that the Server service generates because a share cannot be recreated on operating system startup. When a folder is moved, it must be shared from its new location.

C. **Incorrect:** Logging on and logging off will not make the share accessible after it has been moved.

D. **Incorrect:** The Windows 2000 High Encryption Pack applies 128-bit encryption for secure access. The High Encryption Pack is available only to computer users in the United States because of export restrictions. This encryption pack will not make a moved share accessible.

70-210.02.02.004

▶ **Correct Answers: A and C**

A. **Correct:** In a Windows 2000 workgroup, members of the built-in Administrators local group have complete and unrestricted access to the computers where the Administrators local group resides. Therefore, any member of the Administrators local group can share folders on the local computer.

B. **Incorrect:** Members of the Backup Operators group can override security restrictions for the sole purpose of backing up or restoring files. This does not allow members of this group to create shares.

C. **Correct:** Members of the Power Users group possess most administrative privileges with some restrictions. One of those privileges is the right to share folders on the computer where the group resides.

D. **Incorrect:** The Server Operators group is found only in a Windows NT or Windows 2000 domain.

Connect to local and network print devices.

A **printer** is the software that provides local computer access to a **printing device**. A **printer share** is the facility that provides network access to a printing device. A printer accessible over the network through a **Universal Naming Convention (UNC)** name is called a **shared printer**; a printer accessible via **Hypertext Transfer Protocol (HTTP)** is called an **Internet printer**. The Server service makes the printer available through a UNC share name: *computername**printsharename*. The World Wide Web Publishing Service component of Internet Information Services (IIS) makes the printer available through a Web browser. Unlike the Server service, IIS services are not installed if you accept the default installation options when installing Windows 2000 Professional. You must install IIS and the World Wide Web Publishing Service component on the computer to support Internet printing.

A printing device attached directly to a computer is local to the computer. Attachment is usually through an LPT or COM port. Printer connections available on the computer are called **local ports**. A computer can host a printing device on other local port types besides LPT or COM ports. For example, a printer attached through an Infrared Data Association (IrDA) port uses the IR local port, and a printer attached through a universal serial bus (USB) port uses the USB local port. These local ports appear in the local port list for printers if Windows 2000 detects a printing device attached to them. After you configure the printing device as a local printer using the **Add Printer Wizard** and sharing is configured, the local computer is a **print server**. Other computers attach to the printing device over the network by choosing the Network Printer option on the Add Printer Wizard screen.

Tip You can also configure ports in the Print Server Properties dialog box by clicking File and then choosing the Server Properties option. The Printer Server Properties dialog box provides additional configuration capabilities not available in the Add Printer Wizard.

A computer can act as a print server for network-attached printers. The local computer must support the protocol running on the network-attached printer. For example, if the network-attached printer runs TCP/IP (Transmission Control Protocol/Internet Protocol), TCP/IP must be installed on the print server. Client computers running Windows operating systems can attach to the shared printer and automatically download the printer driver if the printer driver is installed on the print server.

Windows 2000 Professional print servers provide printing support to computers running MS-DOS, Windows, and UNIX operating systems. All editions of Windows 2000 support advanced printing features such as **printer pools** and **printing priority**.

After a printer is configured, you manage it using the Printers window. Management tasks are categorized by print server, printer, and document. You complete most print server management tasks by choosing Server Properties from the File menu. You complete most printer management tasks by choosing Properties from a printer's context menu. You complete most document management tasks by opening a printer in the Printers window.

A printer's Properties dialog box includes a Security tab used for configuring printer permissions. The three general permissions are Print, Manage Printers, and Manage Documents. Like **NTFS** permissions, these primary permissions are a combination of permission entries.

For this objective, you must be familiar with print server, printer, and print job management. You must also be able to delegate printer management tasks and control access to print servers and printers using permissions. Finally, you must be able to establish connections to shared printers and Internet printers.

Objective 2.3 Questions

70-210.02.03.001

You are the administrator of your computer running Windows 2000 Professional. You want to connect to a network-interface printing device using the Add Standard TCP/IP Printer Port Wizard. What can you specify to identify the port? (Choose two.)

A. A TCP/IP host name

B. An IP address

C. A Media Access Control (MAC) address

D. A Windows Internet Naming Service (WINS) computer name

70-210.02.03.002

Assuming that Microsoft Internet Print Services has not been installed, which type of client computer can use a Web browser to connect to a network printer?

A. Microsoft Windows 95

B. Microsoft Windows 98

C. Windows NT 4

D. Windows 2000

70-210.02.03.003

You are the administrator of your Windows 2000 Professional computer. Your network environment includes a Windows 2000 Server domain. The Microsoft Windows 9x client computers are not running the Windows 2000 Directory Service client or the Microsoft Internet Print Services. Considering this environment, which methods can clients running Windows 9x use to connect to a network printer when using the Add Printer Wizard?

A. Enter a UNC name.

B. Browse the network.

C. Use the URL name.

D. Search Active Directory directory services.

70-210.02.03.004

You are the administrator of a Windows 2000 Professional computer named WIN2KPRO. An HP DeskJet 540 printing device is connected to the LPT1 port and shared as HPDJ540. The user of an MS-DOS client computer calls you to ask how she can connect to the network printer. Which syntax should you instruct her to use?

A. Net use lpt1: \\win2kpro\hpdj540

B. Net use lpt1: \\hp deskjet 540\win2kpro

C. Net print lpt1: \\win2kpro\hpdj540

D. Net print lpt1: \\hp deskjet 540\win2kpro

Objective 2.3 Answers

70-210.02.03.001

▶ **Correct Answers: A and B**

   A. **Correct:** A TCP/IP-based network-interface printing device uses a network interface card (NIC) and TCP/IP to connect directly to the local area network (LAN). If the printer's host name is registered on the network, it can be used to locate and connect to the port using the Microsoft Windows 2000 Standard TCP/IP Port Monitor (SPM).

   B. **Correct:** All TCP/IP-based network-interface printing devices must be assigned a valid IP address. This IP address can be used to locate and connect to the port using SPM.

   C. **Incorrect:** A printer's MAC address is not used to establish a port connection to a network-interface printing device running the TCP/IP protocol. The Hewlett-Packard Network Port monitor uses the MAC address to communicate with network-interface printing devices running the Data Link Control (DLC) protocol.

   D. **Incorrect:** SPM uses either an IP address or IP host name to establish a port connection to a TCP/IP-based network-interface printing device.

70-210.02.03.002

▶ **Correct Answers: D**

A. **Incorrect:** Unless Microsoft Internet Print Services is installed, Windows 95 cannot connect to a printer through the Internet printing facility. A Windows 95 client computer can use standard UNC syntax *computername**printersharename* to connect to the printer. The connection is established either from the command line using the Net Share command or by using the Add Printer Wizard.

B. **Incorrect:** Unless Microsoft Internet Print Services is installed, Windows 98 cannot connect to a printer through the Internet printing facility. A Windows 98 client computer can use standard UNC syntax *computername**printersharename* to connect to the printer. The connection is established either from the command line using the Net Share command or by using the Add Printer Wizard.

C. **Incorrect:** Windows NT cannot connect to a printer through the Internet printing facility. A Windows NT client computer can use standard UNC syntax *computername**printersharename* to connect to the printer. The connection is established either from the command line using the Net Share command or by using the Add Printer Wizard.

Service Pack 7 for Windows NT 4 might provide Internet Printing Services to Windows NT 4. However, this service pack was not released before this book was published.

D. **Correct:** Client computers running Windows 2000 can connect to a printer through the Internet printing facility. The Windows 2000 computer hosting the printer, the print server, must be running IIS. When a printer is shared on a Windows 2000 computer running IIS, a Printers virtual directory is created below the default Web site. You can connect a client computer to the printer by first accessing a list of printers using the following syntax: http://*computername*/printers. After selecting a printer, click the Connect link appearing in the left frame of the Web page.

70-210.02.03.003

▶ **Correct Answers: A and B**

A. **Correct:** When a client computer running a down-level operating system such as Windows 98 or Windows NT runs the Add Printer Wizard, you can enter a UNC name. If you know the print server computer name and the printer share name, entering the UNC name saves time because the browser function is not involved in making the connection.

To streamline the printer installation process, install Windows 9x and Windows NT printer drivers from the Windows 2000 Server installation CD-ROM onto the Windows 2000 print server so that computers running Windows 9x or Windows NT will automatically download and install the printer driver. You can install additional printer drivers by running the Add Printer Driver Wizard. You start this wizard by clicking Add in the Drivers tab in the Print Server Properties dialog box. Intel-based Windows NT 4 and Windows 2000 printer drivers are installed by default.

B. **Correct:** If you don't know the network path or queue name of a printer on the network, clicking the Browse button displays the Browse For Printer window. Here you can select a print server and printer share.

C. **Incorrect:** Windows 9x cannot connect to a printer through the Windows 2000 Internet printing facility unless Microsoft Internet Print Services is installed. However, a Windows 9x client is able to use the Internet printing facility to view the properties of a printer through a Web browser. Windows NT is able to view the properties of an Internet printer, but it is unable to connect to the printer through this facility.

D. **Incorrect:** Windows 9x cannot connect to a printer by browsing the Active Directory store unless the Windows 2000 Directory Services client is installed.

70-210.02.03.004

▶ **Correct Answers: A**

A. **Correct:** The Net Use command-line utility allows a computer running a Network Driver Interface Specification (NDIS) client to establish a connection with a folder or printer share. The correct syntax for connecting to a printer share is net use lpt$x$: *printservername**sharename*, where x is the port number, *printservername* is the NetBIOS computer name of the print server, and *sharename* is the name of the shared printer.

B. **Incorrect:** Running the Net Use command is correct, but the computer name always precedes the share name.

C. **Incorrect:** Print is not a valid parameter for the NET.EXE command.

D. **Incorrect:** Print is not a valid parameter for the NET.EXE command.

O B J E C T I V E   2 . 4

Configure and manage file systems.

Windows 2000 supports the **CD-ROM File System (CDFS), Universal Disk Format (UDF)**, **FAT**, and **NTFS** file systems. You use CDFS for CD-ROM access and UDF primarily for **digital video disk (DVD)** access. Use FAT and NTFS for fixed and removable disk access. The implementation of UDF in Windows 2000 does not support writing to UDF volumes. Instead, you must use proprietary methods to write to UDF volumes in Windows 2000.

Three implementations of FAT exist in Windows 2000: FAT12, **FAT16**, and **FAT32**. FAT12 is for small volume formatting, such as formatting floppy disks; FAT16 and FAT32 support larger volumes. FAT16 is ideal for small disk volumes no larger than 511 MB. A volume up to 4 GB in size is supported on FAT16 but not recommended. The minimum format size of FAT32 in Windows 2000 is 512 MB, and its maximum format size is 32 GB. However, a FAT32 volume created in Windows 98 that is larger than 32 GB can be mounted by Windows 2000. FAT32 provides a higher degree of fault tolerance than FAT16, and its cluster-sizing algorithm makes more efficient use of disk space. You should use FAT16 on volumes that a multiboot computer running MS-DOS, Windows 3.*x*, or Windows 95 must access, and it shouldn't be larger than 2 GB to maintain backward compatibility. You should use FAT32 on volumes that a multiboot computer running Windows 95 OSR2 or Windows 98 must access.

NTFS supports the following features not available to FAT running in Windows 2000: local permissions, compression, encryption, disk quotas, reparse points, directory junctions, volume mount points, sparse files, volume change journals, POSIX application compatibility, distributed link tracking, and cluster remapping. The maximum theoretical size allowed for an NTFS volume is 16 exabytes, but 2 terabytes (2048 gigabytes) is the practical limit. (One exabyte is 1024 petabytes, and 1 petabyte is 1024 terabytes.)

Tip Don't worry about memorizing exactly how much an exabyte is; just know that it's much bigger than a terabyte and that even a terabyte is an enormous amount of storage capacity!

You can use the **Disk Administrator** snap-in to create or delete a partition during or after a Windows 2000 installation. You configure FAT and NTFS partitions using the Disk Administrator snap-in or from the command line using the Format command. If you run the Windows 2000 installation routine on a computer running the Windows NT version of NTFS, any mounted NTFS volumes are converted to NTFS version 5. Windows 2000 does not support previous versions of NTFS. Therefore, any time a previous version of NTFS is mounted on the computer, Windows 2000 automatically converts it to NTFS version 5. FAT volumes are manually converted to NTFS using the CONVERT.EXE command-line utility. Type **convert /?** at the command line to see the syntax for this command. Conversion is one way: After a partition is converted from FAT to NTFS, it cannot be converted back to FAT without first deleting the partition. After a partition is converted to NTFS version 5, the only way to return the partition to the previous file system is to back up the data, delete the partition, reformat the partition to the previous file system, and restore the data.

For this objective, you must be proficient with configuring and administering the NTFS and FAT file systems. You must also understand how conversion works in Windows 2000 and how to convert FAT to NTFS.

Objective 2.4 Questions

70-210.02.04.001

You have a Pentium III computer on which you want to run Windows 2000 Professional. You want to be able to set permissions on individual files. You do not need to run any other operating system on the computer. Which file system should you use on the first hard disk?

A. FAT

B. NTFS

C. CDFS

D. FAT32

70-210.02.04.002

You have a Pentium III computer with two 6-GB fixed disks on which you want to run Windows 2000 Professional. You also want to have the ability to dual-boot Windows 98. You will create a single system volume that is the size of this first fixed disk. Which file system should you use on the first hard disk?

A. FAT

B. NTFS

C. CDFS

D. FAT32

70-210.02.04.003

You are planning to deploy Windows 2000 Professional on 12 Pentium II computers running Windows 98. You want to configure Windows 2000 Setup to convert existing FAT32 file systems automatically to NTFS. What should you do?

A. Add the FileSystem = NTFS entry to SYSPREP.INF.

B. Add the FileSystem = ConvertNTFS entry to SYSPREP.INF.

C. Add the FileSystem = NTFS entry to the [Unattended] section of your answer file.

D. Add the FileSystem = ConvertNTFS entry to the [Unattended] section of your answer file.

Objective 2.4 Answers

70-210.02.04.001

▶ **Correct Answers: B**

A. **Incorrect:** The FAT file system provides operating system compatibility to support multiboot computer configurations. This legacy file system does not include advanced file system features such as local permissions. Local permissions are necessary to implement file-level access protection. You can configure folder shares to provide limited over-the-network access to folders and their contents. Share-level permissions are possible because the Server service provides the security, not the file system.

B. **Correct:** NTFS supports local permissions. Local permissions are stored as a **security descriptor** with each folder and file on an NTFS partition. The security descriptor contains a discretionary access control list (**DACL**).

   The DACL is a table of access control entries (**ACEs**) that define user and group access. The security subsystem checks the folder's or file's DACL for ACEs that apply to the user and group security identifiers (SIDs). Many objects in Windows 2000, including user and group objects, contain SIDs. A SID uniquely identifies the object to the operating system. By comparing the ACEs on the file object with the SID or SIDs attempting to access it, the operating system can grant or deny access to the user.

C. **Incorrect:** CDFS is an implementation of ISO 9660 for Windows 2000. This file system does not support file-level security.

D. **Incorrect:** The FAT32 file system is an improvement over the legacy FAT file system. It supports larger disk partitions, minimal fault tolerance for file system recovery, and better performance for large files. FAT16 supports volumes up to 4 GB, whereas FAT32 can manage much larger volume sizes. A Windows 2000 computer running FAT32 can be configured for multiboot with Windows 95 OSR2 or Windows 98. The FAT32 features in Windows 2000 are similar to those in Windows 95 OSR2 and Windows 98.

70-210.02.04.002

▶ **Correct Answers: D**

A. **Incorrect:** The largest FAT volume supported in Windows 2000 is 4095 MB or 4 GB. A volume formatted with FAT is allocated in clusters. The default cluster size is determined by the volume size and can be as large as 64 KB. A volume of 2048 MB to 4095 MB will contain a cluster size of 64 KB. To specify a different cluster size when formatting a volume, run the Format command with the /a:*size* switch, where the size is the number of clusters or allocation units for the volume.

FAT12 is supported for small volumes such as floppy disks. When FAT is written without a designated number of bits, assume the 16-bit version of FAT, FAT16.

B. **Incorrect:** Microsoft supports NTFS on Windows NT and Windows 2000, but not on Windows 98. If the system volume is formatted with NTFS, it will not be possible to start Windows 98 from this volume.

Note that to dual-boot Windows NT and Windows 2000, Windows NT must be running Service Pack 4 to mount a volume converted to NTFS version 5.

C. **Incorrect:** This file system is not designed to house a functioning operating system. CDFS is supported in both Windows 98 and Windows 2000 to provide access to CD-ROM media.

D. **Correct:** This is the ideal file system for a multiboot configuration containing both Windows 98 and Windows 2000. The FAT32 format and features in Windows 2000 are similar to those of Windows 95 OSR2 and Windows 98. FAT32 allows for much larger volumes than is possible using FAT16. However, Windows 2000 imposes minimum (512 MB) and maximum (32 GB) volume size limits on FAT32. Windows 2000 can still mount a FAT32 volume created in Windows 98 that is not within Windows 2000 formatting size limits.

Cluster sizes are more flexible using FAT32 than they are using FAT16. For example, a FAT32 volume of 512 MB to 8 GB can be created using a cluster size as small as 4 KB.

70-210.02.04.003

▶ **Correct Answers: D**

A. **Incorrect:** SYSPREP.INF is the mini-setup answer file used to further automate installation of images prepared using SysPrep. NTFS conversion occurs during text-mode setup. A SysPrep installation using the SYSPREP.INF file starts in GUI-mode.

B. **Incorrect:** ConvertNTFS does not work in SYSPREP.INF because NTFS conversion happens in text mode and SysPrep begins in GUI-mode. If an installation to be prepared using SysPrep is automated before SysPrep is used, the FileSystem = ConvertNTFS entry is used in the automated installation answer file. SYSPREP.INF supports ExtendOemPartition = 1 (or additional size in megabytes) to extend the active system partition. Only NTFS supports the ExtendOemPartition command. ExtendOemPartition allows for the creation of an image no larger than is required to accommodate the image containing the operating system and applications. The ExtendOemPartition command then increases the size of the system partition to the entire available disk space or the size in megabytes that you specify.

C. **Incorrect:** NTFS conversion is possible during an automated installation routine, but FileSystem = NTFS is not the correct syntax.

D. **Correct:** In a scripted installation of Windows 2000, the FileSystem = ConvertNTFS entry in the [Unattended] section of the answer file converts the primary partition to NTFS during the text-mode phase of installation.

Implementing, Managing, and Troubleshooting Hardware Devices and Drivers

Implementing new hardware in a computer is a two-step process. First, the hardware is connected to the computer's bus and then a device driver is installed so that the operating system can communicate with it. After the hardware is operational, it must be *managed*. Management tasks vary by hardware type. For example, a hard disk is managed by configuring **volumes** and monitoring available space; a display device is managed by configuring the display adapter resolution and color depth. A device that isn't functioning properly or a failure in the operating system requires *troubleshooting*.

Troubleshooting is the process of isolating the source of a system error and correcting it. At first glance this may sound simple, but effective troubleshooting requires tenacity, creativity, and a thorough technical understanding of the system. Troubleshooting is a critical part of administering Microsoft Windows 2000 Professional.

Tested Skills and Suggested Practices

The skills that you need to successfully master the Implementing, Managing, and Troubleshooting Hardware Devices and Drivers Objective Domain on Exam 70-210: Installing, Configuring, and Administering Microsoft Windows 2000 Professional include the following:

- **Perform hardware troubleshooting using tools provided with Windows 2000 Professional and with the tools included in the Windows 2000 Professional Resource Kit.**

  - Practice 1: Run Device Manager to view driver settings. In particular, view resource allocation of various hardware devices such as a modem, a PCMCIA controller, and a USB host controller.

- Practice 2: Using Device Manager, create an All Devices And System Summary report and review the output.

- Practice 3: Run the Add/Remove Hardware Wizard to add, remove, or trouble-shoot a device.

- Practice 4: Run DRIVERS.EXE to view a list of running drivers. This utility is contained in both the *Microsoft Windows 2000 Server Resource Kit* and *Windows 2000 Professional Resource Kit*.

- Practice 5: Run DXDIAG.EXE and review the screens in this utility.

- Practice 6: Run the System Information snap-in (MSINFO32.EXE), and query the System Summary node. Run the various system tools available from the System Information snap-in. To access these tools, click Windows on the Tools menu and then click the tool you want to run.

- Practice 7: Run the Windows 2000 Display, Hardware, Modem, Multimedia And Games, Print, and Sound troubleshooters. You can find these troubleshoot-ers on line in Windows 2000 Help under Troubleshooting And Maintenance.

- Practice 8: Navigate through all interfaces described in the answer explanations accompanying the questions.

- **Perform hardware installation, configuration, and upgrade procedures.**

  - Practice 1: Run Device Manager, access the properties of installed devices, and then run the Upgrade Device Driver Wizard available from the Update Driver button in the Driver tab of each device.

  - Practice 2: Visit the Windows Update site by clicking Windows Update on the Start menu.

  - Practice 3: Install Plug and Play hardware, and observe the detection and instal-lation process.

  - Practice 4: Install non-Plug and Play hardware, install supporting device driv-ers, and allocate system resources required by the hardware.

  - Practice 5: Install a second video adapter and display, and configure the com-puter for multiple monitor support.

- **Install and configure network adapters, protocols, and services.**

  - Practice 1: Install TCP/IP on a network adapter, and configure it with static addressing. Switch to dynamic addressing to activate APIPA.

  - Practice 2: Install the DHCP Server service on a computer running Windows 2000 Server. Configure a client computer for dynamic addressing, and verify that a dynamic address was assigned to the client computer.

- Practice 3: Use ipconfig to release and renew a DHCP assigned address.

- Practice 4: Install NWLink and CSNW, and modify the frame_type, network number, and internal network number for the adapter bound to NWLink and CSNW.

- Practice 5: Configure a computer with an APM BIOS for APM support using the Power Options program.

- Practice 6: View the Power Options dialog box on an ACPI-compliant computer, and compare the settings to a non-ACPI-compliant computer.

- Practice 7: Install a PC Card, and then stop the card's services and eject the card.

- Practice 8: Install a second processor in an APIC-compatible computer, and use Device Manager to install a multiprocessor-compatible HAL.

- Practice 9: Run the Performance snap-in to log counters contained in the Processor, System, Job Object, Process, and Thread objects. Analyze the collected data, and read the explanations included with the counters.

Further Reading

This "Further Reading" section provides lists of important readings to supplement your current understanding of the skills tested within this Objective Domain. The lists are delineated into pertinent readings for each objective within this Objective Domain. If you feel that you need additional preparation prior to taking the exam, study these sources thoroughly.

Objective 3.1

Microsoft Corporation. *Microsoft Windows 2000 Professional Resource Kit*. Redmond, Washington: Microsoft Press, 2000. Read Chapter 30, "Examining and Tuning Disk Performance," Chapter 31, "Troubleshooting Tools and Strategies," Chapter 32, "Disk Concepts and Troubleshooting," and Appendix C, "Hardware Support."

Microsoft Corporation. *Microsoft Windows 2000 Server Manual*. Redmond, Washington: Microsoft Corporation, 2000. Read the section entitled "Storing Data."

Microsoft Corporation. *MCSE Training Kit—Microsoft Windows 2000 Professional*. Redmond, Washington: Microsoft Press, 2000. Read and complete the practices in Chapter 6, "Managing Disks."

Objective 3.2

Microsoft Corporation. *Microsoft Windows 2000 Professional Resource Kit*. Redmond, Washington: Microsoft Press, 2000. Read pp. 836–843, Chapter 19, "Device Management."

Objective 3.3

Microsoft Corporation. *Microsoft Windows 2000 Professional Resource Kit*. Redmond, Washington: Microsoft Press, 2000. Read Chapter 10, "Mobile Computing"; read pp. 830–835, Chapter 19, "Device Management"; read Chapter 20, "Power Management."

Microsoft Corporation. *MCSE Training Kit—Microsoft Windows 2000 Professional*. Redmond, Washington: Microsoft Press, 2000. Read and complete the practices in Chapter 24, "Configuring Windows 2000 for Mobile Computers."

Microsoft Corporation. *Microsoft Windows 2000 Professional installation CD-ROM*. Redmond, Washington: Microsoft, 2000. Read the "Advanced Power Management" section of the README.DOC file.

Objective 3.4

Microsoft Corporation. *Microsoft Windows 2000 Professional Resource Kit*. Redmond, Washington: Microsoft Press, 2000. Read Chapter 11, "Multimedia," Chapter 12, "Telephony and Conferencing," and Chapter 15, "Scanners and Cameras."

Microsoft Corporation. *Windows 2000 Help*. Redmond, Washington: Microsoft Corporation, 2000. Read the *Troubleshooting and Maintenance* book.

Objective 3.5

Microsoft Corporation. *Device Manager Help*. Redmond, Washington: Microsoft Corporation, 2000. This file is located on line in *%systemroot%*\Help\Devmgr.chm. Read the entire contents of this help file, and navigate to the features outlined in the help file by running Device Manager.

Microsoft Corporation. *MCSE Training Kit—Microsoft Windows 2000 Professional*. Redmond, Washington: Microsoft Press, 2000. Read and complete the practices in Chapter 25, "Implementing, Managing, and Troubleshooting Hardware Devices and Drivers."

Objective 3.6

Microsoft Corporation. *Microsoft Windows 2000 Professional Resource Kit*. Redmond, Washington: Microsoft Press, 2000. Read Chapter 29, "Analyzing Processor Activity."

Objective 3.7

Microsoft Corporation. *Microsoft Windows 2000 Professional Resource Kit*. Redmond, Washington: Microsoft Press, 2000. Read pp. 880–905, Chapter 21, "Local and Remote Network Connections."

Microsoft Corporation. *MCSE Training Kit—Microsoft Windows 2000 Professional*. Redmond, Washington: Microsoft Press, 2000. Read and complete the practices in Chapter 7, "Installing and Configuring Network Protocols."

Implement, manage, and troubleshoot disk devices.

Windows 2000 supports a variety of storage media technologies. The most common media types are fixed disks, such as Intelligent Drive Electronics or Integrated Drive Electronics (IDE), Advanced Technology Attachment (ATA) or Advanced Technology Attachment Packet Interface (ATAPI), and Small Computer Systems Interface (SCSI) drives; and removable media, such as **digital video disc** or **digital versatile disc** (DVD), compact disc read-only memory (CD-ROM), and tape devices. Storage media is physically connected to the computer's bus by a controller. A software device driver provides the communication between the controller and the operating system. Following hardware installation, storage media is managed and configured in the operating system.

To manage and configure disks and the partitions or volumes that they contain, use the Disk Administrator snap-in. For viewing and troubleshooting devices, including storage media and controllers, use Device Manager. To troubleshoot device and media failures, view the System and Application logs created by the Event Logging service. To monitor system resources, such as fixed disk activity, run the Performance snap-in and use the System Monitor and Performance Logs and Alerts nodes.

Note Use the Diskperf command-line utility to enable and disable physical and logical disk performance counters. By default, the physical disk performance counters are enabled and the logical disk performance counters are not. Type **diskperf /?** at the command line for details on using this utility. Modifications to the performance counters take effect after you restart the operating system.

Windows 2000 supports two disk storage types: **basic disks** (also known as basic storage) and **dynamic disks** (also known as dynamic storage). Basic disks use the traditional method of dividing a physical disk into primary or extended partitions with logical drives. A partition on a basic disk is called a **basic volume**. Basic volumes support other operating systems such as Microsoft Windows NT. Therefore, you must configure a computer configured for multiboot as a basic volume for the system partition. Dynamic disks are divided into **dynamic volumes**. This storage type allows for a number of advanced disk configuration features such as unlimited volumes per dynamic disk, volume spanning, volume extending, **mirroring**, **striping**, and **striping with parity**. Only Windows 2000 supports dynamic disks.

Note Striping with parity and mirroring are not supported in Windows 2000 Professional but are supported in the other editions of Windows 2000. Windows 2000 supports advanced disk configurations created on basic disks when running Windows NT. For example, a volume set created in Windows NT can be read from and written to in Windows 2000.

Installing and configuring tape devices for operation in Windows 2000 is similar to installing and configuring other media types. Windows 2000 includes an optional backup and restore utility, Windows Backup (NTBACKUP.EXE), to make use of the tape device. Windows Backup is run interactively through a graphical interface; by using a variety of switches, it can run without any user interaction. To review the switches that Windows Backup supports, in the Open text box of the Run dialog box, type **ntbackup /?**. The Windows 2000 version of Windows Backup is not limited to tape devices as its target backup media—it supports backup to any writable media type.

You can schedule backups when creating a backup job in Windows Backup or manually by using Windows 2000 Task Scheduler. You configure Task Scheduler by opening the Scheduled Tasks program in Control Panel and then from the Scheduled Task window, opening the Add Scheduled Task icon to start the Scheduled Task Wizard. The Scheduled Task window is also available by clicking the Scheduled Task program in the System Tools program group.

Objective 3.1 Questions

70-210.03.01.001

You are planning to install Windows 2000 Professional on a new Pentium III computer with two 10-GB hard disks. You want the ability to extend a volume on the second hard disk without restarting Windows. Which characteristics define the appropriate type of disk storage for use in this scenario? (Choose two).

A. A basic disk

B. A dynamic disk

C. A simple volume

D. A striped volume

70-210.03.01.002

You have a Pentium III computer running Windows 2000 Professional. You add an Iomega parallel port Zip drive to the system using the Add/Remove Hardware program in Control Panel, but Windows 2000 does not detect the Iomega parallel port Zip drive. What should you do to enable use of your Iomega parallel port Zip drive?

A. Return the Iomega parallel port Zip drive for one with a universal serial bus (USB) interface.

B. Use Registry Editor to enable a communications port for the Zip drive.

C. Use Device Manager to detect the Iomega parallel port Zip drive.

D. Contact Iomega for an updated Zip device driver that will function in Windows 2000.

70-210.03.01.003

You are responsible for deploying Windows 2000 on several computers and want to be able to apply disk quotas to limit disk space used. Which file system is required to support disk quotas?

A. FAT

B. FAT32

C. NTFS

D. Universal Disk Format (UDF)

70-210.03.01.004

You have a computer running Windows 2000 Professional with the following hard disk drive configuration:

- Disk 0: NTFS Layout: Partition (System)

- Disk 1: FAT32 Layout: Partition

- Disk 2: NTFS Layout: Simple

- Disk 3: FAT32 Layout: Partition

Which disk can be extended?

A. Disk 0

B. Disk 1

C. Disk 2

D. Disk 3

Objective 3.1 Answers

70-210.03.01.001

► **Correct Answers: B and C**

A. **Incorrect:** The default disk storage type when a disk is initialized by Windows 2000 is basic storage. This storage type is available to support disk access by Windows 2000 and legacy operating systems that coexist on a computer. A basic disk can contain up to four partitions, either four primary partitions or three primary partitions and an extended partition divided into logical drives. A partition on a basic disk cannot be part of a spanned volume and cannot be extended in Windows 2000. However, a spanned volume (known as a volume set in Windows NT) created or extended in Windows NT can be read and written to by Windows 2000.

B. **Correct:** A spanned volume is composed of 2 to 32 regions of disk space on 2 to 32 dynamic disks. All drives in the set are configured as dynamic disks to support volume spanning. Only volumes created *after* upgrading a basic disk to a dynamic disk can be spanned. The result of this limitation is that the system volume and the boot volume on a dynamic disk cannot be part of a spanned volume. Because volume spanning is not fault tolerant, this spanned volume limitation increases system reliability. A spanned volume is created in the Disk Management snap-in by first selecting a region of unallocated space on a dynamic disk and then starting the Create Volume Wizard. After a spanned volume is created, it can be extended. To extend a spanned volume, the volume must be formatted to the New Technology File System (NTFS). Restarting Windows 2000 is not necessary after extending a volume.

C. **Correct:** A simple volume is spanned on multiple dynamic disks. A volume is considered spanned when it contains two or more simple volumes on two or more disks. Volume spanning supports up to 32 disks. A simple volume can be a part of a volume set only if you create it after you upgrade the disk that contains it to a dynamic disk. After you create a spanned volume, you can extend it if it contains no file system or is formatted for NTFS. File allocation table (FAT) and FAT32 volumes cannot be extended. Do not confuse extended partitions with extended volumes. An **extended partition** is contained on a basic disk and can contain logical drives. An **extended volume** is a simple or spanned volume extended into additional space.

D. **Incorrect:** Like spanned volumes, striped volumes (Level 0 Redundant Array of Inexpensive Disks or RAID 0) are not fault tolerant. However, they provide significantly improved disk I/O performance because data is accessed across the striped dynamic disks. A striped volume requires at least 2 dynamic disks and supports up to 32 dynamic disks. Striping volumes is mutually exclusive of spanning volumes or extending spanned volumes. You start creating a striped volume in the same way as you create a spanned volume, by selecting a region of unallocated space in the Disk Management snap-in and starting the Create Volume Wizard.

70-210.03.01.002

▶ **Correct Answers: C**

A. **Incorrect:** Windows 2000 supports USB devices, and although returning the Iomega parallel port Zip drive for a USB Zip drive is one solution, it is not the most cost-effective or efficient way to remedy an unrecognized device problem in Windows 2000. If you are unsure whether a device is supported in Windows 2000, check the Windows 2000 Hardware Compatibility List (HCL). Also, check the README.DOC file included on the root of the Windows 2000 Professional installation CD-ROM for any fixes found close to the time that the operating system was released for distribution.

B. **Incorrect:** The Iomega parallel port Zip drive uses a standard LPT port as its interface to the system. LPT ports are automatically detected when Windows 2000 is installed. Check Device Manager to verify that the LPT ports are recognized by the operating system.

C. **Correct:** The Iomega parallel port Zip drive is considered a legacy Plug and Play device. Windows 2000 will detect this device if you locate the parallel port it is attached to in Device Manager and then, in the Port Settings tab, select the Enable Legacy Plug And Play Detection check box. This is the type of detailed information that could appear on Exam 70-210. Thus, be sure you thoroughly review the contents of the README.DOC file on the Windows 2000 Professional installation CD-ROM.

D. **Incorrect:** According to the HCL included on the installation CD-ROM, the Iomega parallel port Zip drive is supported in Windows 2000 and a driver for this device is included. This device is listed in the HCL.TXT file under the section titled "Storage/Removable Drive."

70-210.03.01.003

▶ **Correct Answers: C**

A. **Incorrect:** The FAT file system (FAT12 and FAT16) does not support advanced features such as disk quotas. It was originally designed for relatively small disk partitions and simple folder structures. In Windows 2000, the maximum size for a FAT partition is 4096 MB (4 GB). Windows 2000 supports FAT to make upgrading from other operating systems to Windows 2000 simpler and for computers that will multiboot other operating systems such as MS-DOS or Windows 3.*x* and Windows 2000.

B. **Incorrect:** The FAT32 file system is an improvement over FAT for a number of reasons. First, FAT32 supports a much larger partition size. Windows 2000 can be used to create a partition up to 32 GB in size, and larger FAT32 partitions created in other operating systems such as Windows 98 can be mounted, read, and written to in Windows 2000. Second, FAT32 supports more flexible cluster sizing and a larger cluster size within the FAT. A feature not supported on FAT32 is disk quotas.

C. **Correct:** NTFS provides performance improvements, reliability enhancements, and new features not found in FAT. A number of features in Windows 2000, such as the storage management based on reparse points and disk quota management, are available only on volumes formatted with NTFS. An important part of supporting disk quotas is the ability to identify file ownership. NTFS is the only file system in Windows 2000 that supports this feature. Disk quotas are applied at the volume level. It is not possible to set per-folder quota limits when using Windows 2000 disk quota management.

D. **Incorrect:** UDF is a new file system standard supported by Windows 2000 for removable disk formats such as DVD, write once, read many (WORM), and compact disc–recordable (CD-R) media. UDF is the successor to CD-ROM File System (CDFS). Like CDFS, Windows 2000 does not support writing to UDF volumes. Third-party software is necessary to write to UDF media. UDF in Windows 2000 does not support disk quotas.

70-210.03.01.004

▶ **Correct Answers: C**

A. **Incorrect:** The system partition contains the operating system startup files. This might or might not be the same partition containing the boot partition. The boot partition contains the operating system files. A layout type of partition means that Disk 0 is a basic disk. Regardless of the disk storage type, basic or dynamic, the system partition cannot be extended.

B. **Incorrect:** Disk 1 is formatted as a FAT32 partition. FAT32 cannot be extended. Additionally, a layout type of partition means that this is a basic disk storage type containing basic volumes. Basic disks and basic volumes do not support volume spanning or volume extending.

C. **Correct:** Disk 2 is a simple volume formatted as NTFS, and it is not serving as the boot or system partition. Because the question doesn't specify whether the volume was created before or after upgrading the storage type from basic to dynamic, you should assume that the volume creation occurred *after* the storage type was upgraded.

These conditions must be met to extend a volume: the volume *does not* host the boot or system partition; the volume was created after an upgrade to a dynamic disk; the dynamic volume is not striped (RAID 1 or RAID 5) or mirrored; a simple disk must contain unallocated space for the extension; and the simple or spanned volume to be extended must be running NTFS or no file system at all. An unformatted volume to be extended will be formatted as NTFS.

By definition, a volume is extended into some or all unallocated space on the disk containing the dynamic volume or another dynamic disk. To extend the simple volume, start the Disk Management snap-in, right-click the simple or spanned volume to be extended, and click Extend Volume.

D. **Incorrect:** Like Disk 1, Disk 3 is running FAT32 on a basic disk, so it cannot support extending the volume.

Implement, manage, and troubleshoot display devices.

Like Windows 98, Windows 2000 includes **multiple monitor support**. When Windows 2000 multiple monitor support is operational, it spans a single desktop over 2 to 10 monitors, effectively expanding the workspace by the number of monitors in operation.

To support this feature, a computer must contain a **Peripheral Component Interconnect (PCI)** or **Accelerated Graphics Port (AGP)** video adapter for each monitor or a distinct output channel on a single adapter for each monitor. A single video adapter with multiple outputs is common in laptop computers, but in most cases, it does not support the multiple monitor feature because the video adapter contains two video outputs on a single channel.

A video adapter embedded on the motherboard to be used for multiple monitor support must be set to Video Graphics Adapter (VGA) in the basic input/output system (BIOS). The BIOS detects the VGA device based on slot order unless the BIOS offers an option for choosing which video adapter is to be treated as the VGA device. Typically, an embedded adapter will be the first detected video adapter device. By default, Windows 2000 recognizes the first detected device as the **primary adapter**. In the case of a motherboard adapter, after installing a second video adapter, the onboard adapter becomes a **secondary adapter**.

The primary adapter displays the Logon dialog box when starting the computer. In addition, most programs will appear on the monitor connected to the primary adapter when they are first opened. Each monitor and adapter set can have a unique configuration based on its combined capabilities. For example, one set can run 800 × 600 resolution with 16-bit color at 60 Hz, while another set can run 1024 × 768 resolution with 24-bit color at 75 Hz.

After you have installed the second video adapter or output channel and it is detected, you configure multiple monitor support using the Settings tab in the Display Properties dialog box.

Note Some video adapter manufacturers include third-party software for configuring multiple monitor support.

Installing a single video adapter is similar to but simpler than installing several adapters for multiple monitor support. It is simpler because resource conflicts are less likely when only a single video adapter is installed. Windows 2000 supports most legacy video adapters that connect to an Industry Standard Architecture (ISA) bus and more modern PCI or AGP video adapters, which are required for multiple monitor support. To configure multiple monitor support, install Windows 2000 before installing another video adapter. This step will avoid the possibility of Windows 2000 Setup disabling one of the video adapters during installation.

Non-Plug and Play video adapters may require that you determine available system resources to make them function properly in Windows 2000. Required system resources to support a video adapter vary by adapter model. Common system resources to support video adapters include memory and I/O ranges, direct memory access (DMA), and interrupt requests (IRQs).

Video adapter reset failure, or memory, I/O, DMA, IRQ, and BIOS (video and system BIOS) conflicts can cause the display to fail or be skewed after a restart. An IRQ sharing conflict is the most likely cause of this behavior. BIOS conflicts are likely if cold-booting the computer resolves the video problem. To resolve this problem, reconfigure the adapter driver to use available resources.

An unreadable display or no video output is commonly caused by a video adapter and monitor configuration mismatch. For example, the display adapter may support 1280 × 1024 resolution, but the monitor may not support this resolution. Another cause of an unreadable display or no video output is the installation of an incompatible video adapter driver. Windows 2000 does not support adapter drivers built for Windows NT.

To troubleshoot an unreadable display or no video output, restart the computer in **Safe Mode** and either select the Last Known Good Configuration option or the Enable VGA Mode option on the Windows 2000 Advanced Options boot menu. If VGA mode is enabled, use the Display program in Control Panel to reconfigure the device and then restart the computer. A restart is not necessary if you use the Last Known Good Configuration option.

For this objective topic, you should be proficient in the following skills:

- Installing multiple video adapters

- Changing the primary monitor

- Arranging multiple monitor behavior

- Moving items between monitors

- Using Device Manager and the Add/Remove Hardware Wizard to configure and troubleshoot a video adapter

- Configuring and troubleshooting legacy and Plug and Play devices for operation in Windows 2000

Objective 3.2 Questions

70-210.03.02.001

You install Windows 2000 Professional on a Pentium 166 computer with an ISA-based display adapter. Windows 2000 Setup fails to detect the ISA-based display adapter. What can you do to use the ISA-based display adapter with Windows 2000?

A. Use REGCLEAN.EXE.

B. Use Registry Editor to enable use of the ISA-based display adapter.

C. Locate and manually install the correct driver for the display adapter.

D. Because Windows 2000 does not support ISA-based display adapters, you must replace it with a compatible PCI or AGP display adapter.

70-210.03.02.002

You have assembled a new Pentium III computer with an AGP video adapter. You run Windows 2000 Professional Setup, and the adapter is automatically configured. You later want to change the refresh frequency of the display. What should you do?

A. Use the Adapter tab in the Display Adapter Advanced Options dialog box.

B. Use the Monitor tab in the Display Adapter Advanced Options dialog box.

C. Open the Computer Management console and access Device Manager.

D. Open the Computer Management console and access the Services and Applications node.

70-210.03.02.003

You are planning to purchase a new Pentium III computer to run Windows 2000 Professional. The motherboard on your new computer will have a built-in display adapter. You want to extend your desktop across two monitors. What should you do? (Choose two.)

A. Install Windows 2000 after installing the second video adapter.

B. Install Windows 2000 before installing the second video adapter.

C. Ensure that the motherboard adapter is multiple-display compatible.

D. Ensure that the motherboard adapter is configured as the primary adapter.

Objective 3.2 Answers

70-210.03.02.001

▶ **Correct Answers: C**

A. **Incorrect:** The RegClean utility is designed to remove unnecessary Windows Registry entries located in HKEY_CLASSES_ROOT. RegClean does not fix every known problem with the registry. For example, it can't fix a corrupt registry. The RegClean utility was originally supplied with Microsoft Visual Basic version 4 for Windows and has since been updated.

B. **Incorrect:** In previous versions of Windows, it was sometimes necessary to use the registry to solve software configuration issues. You can still use the registry for this purpose, but new features in Windows 2000 are specifically designed to deal with unrecognized hardware devices. Therefore, this is not the recommended approach to solving a device configuration failure.

C. **Correct:** ISA devices do not support Plug and Play features available in other bus specifications such as PCI and AGP. Windows 2000 does contain detection routines designed for legacy hardware, but sometimes the operating system will not detect a device and install a driver to support it. To manually install a device driver, run the Add/Remove Hardware Wizard in Control Panel and, on the Choose A Hardware Task screen, select Add/Troubleshoot A Device and click Next. Follow the instructions that appear to install the device driver.

D. **Incorrect:** Windows 2000 supports a wide variety of legacy device drivers. If the device driver does not appear in the list of supported devices displayed through the Add/Remove Hardware Wizard, check the Windows 2000 Hardware Compatibility List (HCL) and check with the hardware vendor.

70-210.03.02.002

▶ **Correct Answers: B**

A. **Incorrect:** Use the Adapter tab to see detailed adapter hardware information, the list of video modes supported by the adapter, and the properties of the adapter. The properties of the adapter show the status of the device, the drivers loaded to support the device, and the system resources allocated to the device. This information is also shown in Device Manager.

B. **Correct:** The question states that you want to modify the monitor's refresh frequency. You configure display settings in the Monitor tab, which provides information on the model or type of monitor detected and the monitor's properties. You also configure the refresh frequency and Mode Pruning in this tab. You enable Mode Pruning by selecting the Hide Modes That This Monitor Cannot Display check box.

Mode Pruning removes display modes that the display and video adapters in combination cannot support. Only the modes that are common to both devices are made available to the system. This feature requires that the operating system know specifically which monitor and video adapter are connected to the computer. When both devices are known because they are Plug and Play compatible or they are manually specified, Mode Pruning is available. Click the List All Modes button in the Adapter tab to see a list of all modes.

Note that this question focuses on knowing how to navigate the Windows 2000 interface to configure settings. You must be able to proficiently navigate in the graphical user interface (GUI) before taking many of the Microsoft certification exams.

C. **Incorrect:** The properties of the adapter and the monitor are accessible through Device Manager. You complete system resource configuration or modification from here but not other monitor and adapter settings.

D. **Incorrect:** The Services and Applications node shows installed software below it, such as the Windows Management Instrumentation (WMI) service and other services. This interface provides a central location to configure and manage the services.

70-210.03.02.003

▶ **Correct Answers: B and C**

A. **Incorrect:** If Windows 2000 Setup detects both a motherboard video adapter and another adapter in a PCI or AGP bus slot, it will disable the motherboard video adapter. Additionally, the BIOS on some computers will detect a video adapter in a card slot and automatically disable the motherboard video adapter. If this occurs, attempt to modify the BIOS configuration so that the motherboard adapter is not disabled. Some BIOS utilities will not allow you to change this configuration setting.

B. **Correct:** When Windows 2000 is installed on a computer with a single video adapter on the motherboard, a video adapter driver will be loaded for the onboard device. After Windows 2000 is set up, shut down Windows 2000, power off the computer, and install a second PCI or AGP video adapter. Upon Windows 2000 startup, the video adapter card will be detected and the appropriate driver will be installed to support it. As long as the BIOS does not disable the motherboard video adapter, it will be possible to configure the computer to support multiple displays.

C. **Correct:** Some onboard video adapters do not support multiple displays. This is usually indicated if the motherboard video adapter is automatically disabled when a video adapter card is installed. Laptop computers contain onboard video adapters that are often disabled when connected to a docking station containing a video adapter card.

D. **Incorrect:** In a multiple monitor configuration, the onboard video adapter becomes the secondary video source. There is always one primary video source and one or more (up to nine) additional secondary video sources. The primary adapter should not be stopped in a multiple monitor configuration.

OBJECTIVE 3.3

Implement, manage, and troubleshoot mobile computer hardware.

Mobile computing often involves using battery power as an energy source. Many technological advances have been made to extend battery life. There are two ways this is accomplished: by improving battery technology and by reducing power consumption. The operating system and the computer hardware can play a significant role in the latter. Reduced power consumption technology has also crossed over into desktop computer systems.

Windows 2000 supports two power management specifications: **Advanced Power Management (APM)** and **Advanced Configuration and Power Interface (ACPI)**. ACPI-compliant computers can take full advantage of reduced power consumption by controlling power requirements for Plug and Play hardware and applications. ACPI is a more advanced form of power management supported by both the operating system and the computer system hardware.

If a computer is ACPI compliant, it is indicated in Device Manager under the Computer node. ACPI support is provided by the ACPI driver (ACPI.SYS) and the ACPI embedded controller driver (ACPIEC.SYS). These drivers are loaded upon operating system startup and are located in the *%systemroot%*\System32\Drivers folder.

In ACPI systems, the operating system—not the hardware—is tasked with managing hardware power consumption. The operating system controls power consumption of the ACPI-compliant system board and all connected Plug and Play devices. To optimize power efficiency, consider replacing any legacy hardware with Plug and Play devices.

You configure APM using the Power Options program in Control Panel. Power Options will display only power management features that match the hardware's power management specifications. For example, if a computer is ACPI compliant, the APM tab will *not* appear because power management is controlled entirely by ACPI.

For this objective topic, you must be able to use the Power Options program to do the following:

- Choose or create a new power scheme and customize the power scheme settings.

- Enable or disable **Hibernation** mode.

- Configure power alarms, **Standby** mode, and advanced settings.

- Configure APM on non-ACPI-compliant computers that support APM.

Windows 2000 supports disk and monitor power level control and hibernation on all computer hardware. APM- and ACPI-compliant hardware is not necessary for these features. Standby mode requires APM- or ACPI-compliant hardware.

Hibernation requires enough disk capacity to create a file named HIBERFIL.SYS on the root of the boot partition. The file size is equal to the amount of RAM in the computer. After you enable hibernation in Power Options, Hibernate is an available option in the Shut Down Windows dialog box. Hibernation and standby activation are usually associated with a hardware controlled key or key sequence on APM or ACPI computer hardware. You use the Power Options program to configure the operating system to react to hardware events such as pressing a standby key or closing the lid.

If you will be upgrading a computer to Windows 2000 that is running third-party power management software, consider disabling it so that Windows 2000 power management support is installed.

PC Card support, previously known as **Personal Computer Memory Card International Association (PCMCIA)**, is another important enhancement, particularly for mobile computers. On a mobile computer, PC Cards plug into a PC Card slot. Windows 2000 includes CardBus support so that the 32-bit PC Card hardware can perform high-bandwidth I/O operations such as video image playback.

Note To use a network adapter in the PC Card slot, both the PC Card socket driver and network driver must be Plug and Play compatible.

To support Plug and Play capability, a PC Card contains identifying information that Windows 2000 uses to create a unique device ID called the Card Information Structure (CIS). After creating the CIS, Windows 2000 installs a driver to support the card. The three types of drivers are the following: standard Plug and Play device drivers for PC Cards, such as Network Driver Interface Specification (NDIS) version 5.*x* drivers for network adapters and miniport drivers for Small Computer Systems Interface (SCSI) cards; generic device drivers for modems and disk drives; and vendor-supplied device drivers.

If a Plug and Play device driver is contained in the DRIVER.CAB file, it is automatically installed for the device. DRIVER.CAB is copied by the Windows 2000 setup routine into the *%systemroot%*\Driver Cache\i386 folder. If the driver is not contained in the DRIVER.CAB file, the Add/Remove Hardware Wizard starts automatically.

You should be familiar with how to navigate PC Card and PC Card controller properties in Device Manager. For example, use the PCMCIA Adapters node in Device Manager to view and troubleshoot the properties of the card bus controller. Also, from the Unplug or Eject Hardware icon on the taskbar, stop a card's operation before removal.

Objective 3.3 Questions

70-210.03.03.001

You are thinking about installing Windows 2000 on your laptop computer. Your laptop computer has an APM-based BIOS, and you want to know whether the BIOS has any known problems. What should you do?

A. Use Device Manager.

B. Run the Dxdiag support tool.

C. Run the Apmstat utility.

D. Obtain a diagnostic utility from the original equipment manufacturer (OEM).

70-210.03.03.002

You install Windows 2000 Professional on a Pentium III computer. You open the Power Options program in Control Panel, but no APM tab is displayed. Which conditions are most likely to cause the absence of the APM tab from the Power Options Properties dialog box? (Choose two.)

A. APM is disabled in the BIOS.

B. The computer does not have an APM-based BIOS.

C. The computer has an ACPI-compliant system board.

D. The computer does not have a smart uninterruptible power supply (UPS) device connected to the serial port.

70-210.03.03.003

Which condition allows Windows 2000 Professional to automatically install and configure a PC Card for your laptop computer?

A. The PC Card vendor has supporting drivers for the socket.

B. The PC Card vendor has supporting drivers for the PC Card.

C. The PC Card vendor has supporting drivers for the PC Card and socket.

D. Windows 2000 Professional includes supporting drivers for the socket.

E. Windows 2000 Professional includes supporting drivers for the PC Card.

F. Windows 2000 Professional includes supporting drivers for the PC Card and socket.

Objective 3.3 Answers

70-210.03.03.001

▶ **Correct Answers: C**

A. **Incorrect:** Device Manager might display status information on the function of APM, but known problems with an APM-based BIOS will not appear in this interface. APM may appear under Device Manager's Batteries node or System Devices node, or it might not appear at all in Device Manager.

B. **Incorrect:** You use DXDIAG.EXE, located in the *%systemroot%*\System32 folder, to report detailed information on all installed Microsoft DirectX multimedia components and to troubleshoot any errors occurring in them. This utility tests sound, graphics output, and DirectPlay service providers, and it disables some hardware acceleration features. It has no purpose related to the Windows 2000 power management facility.

C. **Correct:** The Advanced Power Management Status (APMSTAT.EXE) utility is specifically designed for testing a computer's APM-based BIOS for compatibility with Windows 2000 APM support. This tool is located on the Windows 2000 Professional installation CD-ROM in the \Support\Tools\Support.cab file. You can extract APMSTAT.EXE from SUPPORT.CAB or run SETUP.EXE from the \Support\Tools folder to install all support utilities.

APM is a pre-ACPI standard for power management. This utility will not diagnose an ACPI-compliant system because APM is irrelevant to this platform. If a portable computer has an APM-based BIOS, Apmstat determines whether the BIOS has any known problems. If Apmstat does not report known problems, use APM to manage power on the portable computer. To accomplish this, select APM in the APM tab. This tab is part of the Power Options program in Control Panel.

D. **Incorrect:** Windows 2000 Professional includes the Apmstat utility for this purpose. Therefore, it is not necessary to contact the hardware manufacturer for a diagnostic utility. If APM does not appear to be functioning properly, check the Windows 2000 Hardware Compatibility List (HCL) and contact the manufacturer for any recommended BIOS updates.

70-210.03.03.002

▶ **Correct Answers: B and C**

A. **Incorrect:** In an APM system, the BIOS provides power management functions unless the operating system is able to supersede this role. As a result, power management can be disabled in the BIOS and APM will continue to function in the operating system. Windows 2000 Professional provides operating system–level power management if the APM 1.2 specification is supported in the BIOS.

B. **Correct:** A computer without an APM-based BIOS, a computer containing multiple processors, or a computer that supports ACPI will not show an APM tab in the Power Options Properties dialog box. Windows 2000 Professional can still provide limited power management features, specifically disk and monitor power control and hibernation, to computers without BIOS-level power management support. You configure power to the disk and monitor on the Power Schemes tab in the Power Options dialog box; you configure hibernation in the Hibernate tab. Standby mode and advanced battery management features are available only on APM and ACPI systems.

C. **Correct:** An ACPI-based computer does not contain an APM tab in the Power Options Properties dialog box. On an APM-based system, you use the APM tab to enable and disable APM support. In contrast, ACPI functions are automatic and fully controlled by the operating system. You can change individual power management settings in the Power Options Properties dialog box, but you cannot enable and disable operating system ACPI support. In an ACPI-compliant computer system, ACPI manages power consumption of all installed Plug and Play hardware, the operating system, and application software.

D. **Incorrect:** A desktop computer running Windows 2000 Professional will display a UPS tab in the Power Options Properties dialog box. You configure a Component Object Model (COM) port, UPS manufacturer, and UPS settings appropriate to the manufacturer on the UPS tab. You also view the status of the UPS service from this location.

70-210.03.03.003

▶ **Correct Answers: F**

A. **Incorrect:** PC Card vendors do not create drivers to support the socket where their cards are installed. Socket driver creation is the responsibility of the PC Card socket vendor. Manual socket driver installation is necessary for operating systems that do not include native PC Card socket driver support, such as MS-DOS.

B. **Incorrect:** PC Card vendors create the drivers to support their hardware in various operating systems. These drivers are required for device classes that Windows 2000 Professional does not natively support and devices that are not supported by the drivers included with the operating system. If the PC Card contains configuration information, the operating system initializes the device and passes the configuration information to the driver. The PC Card driver alone does not initiate an automatic installation and configuration.

C. **Incorrect:** The PC Card vendor creates drivers for the PC Card. The PC Card socket vendor creates drivers for the PC Card socket.

D. **Incorrect:** Windows 2000 Professional ships with many supporting drivers for the socket. A PC Card socket is called a CardBus Controller in the operating system. To see a list of bundled CardBus Controller drivers, run the Add/Remove Hardware Wizard and select PCMCIA Adapters from the list of hardware types. The appropriate driver bundled with Windows 2000 Professional is automatically installed when Windows 2000 Setup runs. To see if a CardBus Controller is installed and functioning properly, run Device Manager and, from the default view, select the PCMCIA Adapters node and then open the properties of the CardBus Controller appearing under this node. The PC Card socket driver alone does not initiate automatic installation and configuration of a PC Card.

E. **Incorrect:** Windows 2000 Professional ships with a number of PC Card drivers created by the PC Card vendors. The presence of the driver on the Windows 2000 Professional installation CD-ROM does not guarantee that a driver is automatically installed and configured in the operating system. The PC Card socket driver must be installed before the PC Card driver is installed.

F. **Correct:** If Windows 2000 Professional includes supporting drivers for the PC Card and for the socket, detection, installation, and configuration are automatic. If drivers are not available on the Windows 2000 Professional installation CD-ROM, the operating system might detect the devices, but you are prompted to supply an alternate location for the necessary drivers.

OBJECTIVE 3.4

Implement, manage, and troubleshoot input and output (I/O) devices.

Windows 2000 supports a variety of **input/output (I/O)** hardware devices, each requiring driver installation, configuration, management, and, in some cases, troubleshooting to achieve optimal or proper operation. The first three objectives in this Objective Domain were concerned with disk, display, and **Personal Computer Memory Card International Association (PCMCIA)** device configuration. All of these devices use I/O operations to move data from one location to another. This objective focuses on the following hardware devices, which are also involved in I/O operations:

- Multimedia hardware

- **Modems**

- Wireless hardware, primarily **Infrared Data Association (IrDA) devices**

- **Universal serial bus (USB) devices**

- **Smart Card devices** (readers and cards)

Typical multimedia hardware includes CD, **digital video disc or digital versatile disc (DVD)**, camera, **Musical Instrument Digital Interface (MIDI)**, and scanner devices. DVD media is a relatively new standard for digital storage and delivery of audio, video, and data, popularized for its enormous media capacity. DVD media can hold 8 to 40 times more data than traditional CD media. Each DVD format is intended for a specific purpose. **DVD-video** is designed for video playback of **Moving Pictures Experts Group v2 (MPEG-2)** video; DVD-audio is designed for audio playback of Dolby Digital (AC-3) or MPEG-2 audio; DVD read-only memory (DVD-ROM) and DVD-recordable (DVD-R) are replacements for CD-ROM and are designed to read data; DVD-write once (DVD-WO) is designed for data archiving; and DVD-random access media (DVD-RAM) and digital versatile disc+Read/Write (DVD+RW) formats are for rewritable storage. Windows 2000 supports DVD through the **Universal Disk Format (UDF)** 1.5 file system. UDF 1.5 in Windows 2000 does *not* support recording capabilities for those DVD formats that support write operations. Instead, third-party software is necessary to record to DVD media in Windows 2000.

Any installed devices appear in Device Manager. You use this interface to perform device troubleshooting, device driver updates, and operating system resource allocation. Administrative privileges are required to modify device settings in Device Manager. If an installed device does not appear in Device Manager, this might be caused by a missing device driver or an improperly configured basic input/output system (BIOS).

Use the Add/Remove Hardware Wizard to add any device drivers for devices that Windows 2000 doesn't automatically detect. Hardware detection is usually followed by automatic device driver installation. You also use this wizard interface to remove, unplug, or troubleshoot hardware. You use the Scanners and Cameras program in Control Panel to install a digital camera, scanner, or other still image device that was not detected by Plug and Play enumeration. If running a hardware installation wizard fails to install a device, check the BIOS to make sure the device class is enabled. For example, if an installed USB controller does not appear in Device Manager, make sure that USB support is enabled in the BIOS.

Drivers for **Personal Computer/Smart Card (PC/SC)**-compliant Plug and Play smart cards and readers are included with the operating system. Smart cards typically connect through an RS-232 cable (serial connection) or in a **PC Card** socket. You use smart cards for domain authentication, remote dial-up network access, and other applications that require secure logon. Windows 2000 does not support non-PC/SC-compliant or non-Plug and Play smart card readers. To use smart cards, the network must support a **public key infrastructure (PKI)** and an **Enterprise Certification Authority (CA)**, and each computer that will use smart card logon requires a smart card reader.

If a device controlled by the BIOS appears in Device Manager but is not functioning properly (usually indicated by a yellow warning icon or red failure icon), update the BIOS. Yellow warning and red failure icons might appear in Device Manager if resource conflicts occur between I/O devices. Resource conflicts are unlikely between Plug and Play-compatible devices but are more common when non-Plug and Play drivers are installed. Use the Resource By Type and Resources By Connection Device Manager views to see how all system resources are allocated.

Devices connected to an I/O port such as a USB controller might appear in different locations in Device Manager. For example, in the Device By Type Device Manager view, USB game controllers are listed under Human Interface Devices. If a device can't be located, go to the View menu in Device Manager and then click Show Hidden Devices. You can view, delete, or uninstall devices not currently connected to the computer (phantom devices) in Device Manager by typing the following environment variable at the command line: **set devmgr_show_nonpresent_devices=1**. Next run Device Manager at the command line by typing **devmgmt.msc**. After Device Manager is running, click the Show Hidden Devices option on the View menu so that the phantom devices appear.

Tip To be able to permanently view devices not currently connected in Device Manager, select the System program in Control Panel, click the Advanced tab, click the Environment Variables button, and add the phantom devices environment variable as a new system variable.

Other important tools for troubleshooting I/O errors are the **DirectX Diagnostic Tool** (DXDIAG.EXE) and the **System Information snap-in** (MSINFO32.EXE). You use Dxdiag to report detailed information on all installed DirectX multimedia components and to troubleshoot errors occurring in any installed DirectX components. The System Information snap-in is a Microsoft Management Console (MMC) interface to hardware, system components, and software configuration data.

Device Manager and the System Information snap-in are nodes of the Computer Management snap-in. You can also start these tools independently of the Computer Management snap-in.

After a device appears in Device Manager, you configure and troubleshoot using a variety of Control Panel programs. To configure multimedia hardware, use the Scanners and Cameras program, or the Sounds and Multimedia program depending on the multimedia hardware requiring configuration. To configure and troubleshoot modems, run the Phones and Modems program, and to configure and troubleshoot IrDA devices, run the Wireless Link program.

If a DVD device appears to be set up properly, make sure that the appropriate decoding hardware or software is installed to play back or record to the media. If a supported decoder is installed, check that the display adapter and monitor can support $800 \times 600 \times 16$ bits per pixel (BPP) graphics or better. If the DVD Player is used to play back DVD-Video, it searches all local drives for the Video_TS folder. The file in this folder is run and video streaming begins. If the same folder name exists on another local drive, the DVD Player will fail to play the DVD.

To demonstrate your proficiency with this objective, you must be able to use Device Manager and the Add/Remove Hardware Wizard to implement, manage, and troubleshoot I/O devices, and you must be able to use the individual device configuration programs in Control Panel as well.

Objective 3.4 Questions

70-210.03.04.001

You connect a legacy scanner device to a computer running Windows 2000 Professional, but the operating system does not automatically install the scanner. What should you do to install the device under Windows 2000?

A. Use Device Manager to add the scanner.

B. Use the Computer Management console to add the scanner.

C. Use the Administrative Tools program in Control Panel to add the scanner.

D. Use the Scanners and Cameras program in Control Panel to add the scanner.

70-210.03.04.002

You acquire a Pentium III computer running Windows 2000 Professional. You connect a digital camera to one of the USB ports on the computer, but Windows does not install the device. What is the most likely cause?

A. USB support is disabled in the BIOS.

B. USB support is disabled in Windows.

C. The USB port is physically damaged.

D. The device is not supported by Windows 2000. You might be able to obtain an updated driver from the device manufacturer.

70-210.03.04.003

You want to view a list of installed multimedia devices, determine driver versions, and perform diagnostics. Which interfaces should you use?

A. The Audio tab of the Sounds and Multimedia program.

B. The Sounds tab of the Sounds and Multimedia program.

C. The Hardware tab of the Sounds and Multimedia program.

D. The Sound, Video, and Game Controllers node in Device Manager.

70-210.03.04.004

Your Pentium III computer running Windows 2000 Professional has a 40× CD-ROM drive with a head-phone jack. You insert your favorite audio CD into the drive and plug a new pair of headphones into the jack on the front of the CD-ROM drive, but there is no audible sound. What is the most likely cause?

A. Windows 2000 does not support the sound card.

B. Digital CD Playback is enabled for the CD-ROM drive.

C. The CD-ROM drive is not connected to the sound card.

D. Digital CD Playback is disabled for the CD-ROM drive.

70-210.03.04.005

Which three methods can you use to install a modem under Windows 2000 Professional? (Choose three.)

A. Use Device Manager.

B. Plug in a Plug and Play modem.

C. Use the Mail and Fax program in Control Panel.

D. Use the Add/Remove Hardware program in Control Panel.

E. Use the Add/Remove Programs program in Control Panel.

F. Use the Phone and Modem Options program in Control Panel.

70-210.03.04.006

You attach an IrDA device transceiver to a serial port on your computer running Windows 2000 Professional, but Windows does not automatically install the device. What should you do to install the IrDA device?

A. Use the Wireless Link program in Control Panel.

B. Use the Add/Remove Hardware program in Control Panel.

C. Use the Add/Remove Programs program in Control Panel.

D. This is not possible because Windows 2000 does not support an IrDA device connected to a serial port.

Objective 3.4 Answers

70-210.03.04.001

▶ **Correct Answers: D**

A. **Incorrect:** Device Manager is the proper tool to use to troubleshoot devices that are known by Windows 2000 Professional. The devices that appear in Device Manager are detected either automatically by the operating system or through the manual installation of a device driver. You can use Device Manager to scan for Plug and Play-compliant hardware, but it won't detect and install legacy devices.

B. **Incorrect:** The Computer Management console contains a number of snap-ins designed to manage the operating system and hardware. Computer Management contains utilities for managing the system, storage devices, services, and applications. There is no facility in this console for installing legacy devices.

C. **Incorrect:** Double-clicking the Administrative Tools program in Control Panel displays the same list of administrative tools that are available by clicking the Start menu, pointing to Programs, and pointing to Administrative Tools. The Administrative Tools option is not available from the Start menu by default. It is enabled by selecting the Display Administrative Tools check box on the Advanced tab in the Taskbar And Start Menu Properties dialog box. There is no facility within Administrative Tools to install legacy devices.

D. **Correct:** Running the Scanners and Cameras program displays the Scanners And Cameras Properties dialog box. Clicking Add in this dialog box runs the Scanners and Cameras Installation Wizard. After a scanner or camera device driver is installed, additional configuration of the device is completed from the Scanners And Cameras Properties dialog box.

70-210.03.04.002

▶ **Correct Answers: A**

A. **Correct:** When a USB device is plugged into a port for the first time, Windows 2000 Professional detects and installs a device driver for the device. For detection and driver installation to occur, USB must be enabled in the BIOS on computers that include a USB enable/disable BIOS feature. However, many computers containing USB ports do not contain this setting in the BIOS. If USB support is provided through a USB hub card, the BIOS is not involved in enabling or disabling USB activities.

B. **Incorrect:** It is possible to disable a USB bus controller, USB hub, or USB device in Windows 2000 through Device Manager. However, to disable any of these devices using Device Manager, the device drivers must first be installed for the devices. USB bus controller and the USB hub drivers are automatically installed when Windows 2000 is installed. You could argue that one or both of these drivers were manually disabled using Device Manager, but this is less likely than USB support being disabled in the BIOS.

C. **Incorrect:** This is possible but unlikely. If a USB port (hub) is damaged, Device Manager should indicate this with a yellow warning or red failure icon next to the device.

D. **Incorrect:** This is also possible but less likely than BIOS support being disabled in the BIOS. Through Plug and Play enumeration, Windows 2000 will detect a new device even if a corresponding device driver doesn't exist for it. If you suspect that the USB device doesn't have a Windows 2000 device driver, check with the manufacturer.

70-210.03.04.003

▶ **Correct Answers: C**

A. **Incorrect:** You use the Audio tab to select the preferred device, control the volume, and configure advanced settings for sound playback, sound recording, and MIDI message playback. You also use this tab to configure Windows 2000 Professional to use only preferred devices selected in this interface.

B. **Incorrect:** You use the Sounds tab to associate sound (.wav) files with Windows events such as receiving an e-mail message or starting Windows. You also use this interface to select or create and save a sound scheme, to adjust the volume, and to indicate whether the volume control should or shouldn't appear on the taskbar.

C. **Correct:** The Hardware tab lists all installed sound and multimedia devices, such as DVD/CD-ROM drives and sound cards. Individual device and multimedia software components are shown here as well: for example, sound card game ports, legacy audio drivers, and audio codecs. If you select the item appearing in the Devices box, summary properties of each device will appear in the Hardware tab. You access detailed properties of a device by double-clicking the item listed in the Devices box or selecting the item and clicking the Properties button. You start troubleshooting by selecting the item and clicking the Troubleshooting button.

D. **Incorrect:** Some but not all multimedia devices appear under the Sound, Video, and Game Controllers node in Device Manager. For example, DVD/CD-ROM drives do not appear under this node. Double-clicking any of the items that do appear under this node shows their properties. This is the same dialog box that appears when you select the item from the Hardware tab of the Sounds And Multimedia Properties dialog box and click the Properties button.

70-210.03.04.004

▶ **Correct Answers: B**

A. **Incorrect:** It is unlikely that the sound card is part of the audio playback facility available from the headphone jack on the front of the CD-ROM drive.

B. **Correct:** If Digital CD Playback is enabled for a CD-ROM drive, audio output from the headphone jack on the CD-ROM drive is disabled. You enable/disable this property from the Properties menu of the CD-ROM drive. To view the properties, double-click the CD-ROM device in the Hardware tab of the Sounds And Multimedia Properties dialog box. In the Properties tab of the device is the Enable Digital CD Audio For This CD-ROM Device check box. Clear this check box to disable Digital CD Playback.

C. **Incorrect:** The headphone jack on the front of a CD-ROM drive will function as long as the CD-ROM drive is connected to an internal or external power source and the play instruction can be sent to the device. You should assume that the CD-ROM is playing the audio CD because the question doesn't say that the CD isn't playing, just that nothing is heard through the headphone jack.

D. **Incorrect:** Disabling Digital CD Playback will enable the headphone jack output as explained earlier.

70-210.03.04.005

▶ **Correct Answers: B, D, and F**

A. **Incorrect:** You use Device Manager to check the properties of installed devices and to scan for hardware changes. You use the Scan For Hardware Changes option if a Plug and Play device is not automatically detected after uninstalling it.

B. **Correct:** After connecting a Plug and Play modem to the computer, the Install New Modem screen of the Add/Remove Hardware Wizard appears and automatically detects the modem or allows you to manually select a modem from the list of known devices. The detection option queries the modem to configure it. If it cannot detect the modem, it prompts you to select the appropriate manufacturer and model.

C. **Incorrect:** The Mail and Fax functions are separate programs in the Windows 2000 Professional Control Panel. You use the Mail program to create and configure e-mail and fax accounts. You use the Fax program to configure fax properties such as cover page information, to obtain fax status information, and to configure advanced fax options such as adding a fax printer to the list of installed printers.

D. **Correct:** From the Add/Remove Hardware Wizard, navigate to the Add A New Device option on the Choose A Hardware Device screen. After selecting this option and clicking Next, you can either search for new hardware or select the hardware from a list. If a new modem is detected from this wizard or you select the Modems hardware type and click Next, the Install New Modem screen appears. From this screen, detection or manual installation is the same as outlined earlier.

E. **Incorrect:** You use the Add/Remove Programs program to install, remove, or update windows components and third-party software installed on the computer. Any programs listed in the Currently Installed Programs box are listed in the registry under HKEY_LOCAL_MACHINE\SOFTWARE\Microsoft\Windows\CurrentVersion\Uninstall. Each program's key data contains display name and uninstall information used by the Add/Remove Programs program. This program is not used to install a modem.

F. **Correct:** Clicking Add in the Modems tab in the Phone And Modem Options dialog box opens the Install New Modem screen of the Add/Remove Hardware Wizard. From this screen, detection or manual installation is the same as outlined earlier.

After a modem is installed, you can configure the following settings by using the Phone and Modem Options program: modem dialing rules, modem configuration, troubleshooting (diagnostics and logging), and adding or configuring existing telephony providers.

70-210.03.04.006

▶ **Correct Answers: B**

A. **Incorrect:** You use the Wireless Link program to configure file transfer, to configure photo image transfer, to view hardware properties, and to troubleshoot installed infrared port (device transceiver) hardware. This question specifically states that a device transceiver is connected to a Component Object Model (COM) port. If the transceiver is part of the computer's system board and the Wireless Link program does not appear in Control Panel, check the BIOS to confirm that the port is enabled and that a COM port is assigned to the device.

B. **Correct:** Unlike a USB port connection, it is likely that Windows 2000 Professional will not detect a Plug and Play device connected to a COM port without first running the Add/Remove Hardware Wizard. Instruct the Add/Remove Hardware Wizard to detect the hardware. Detection using the wizard occurs in two phases. Phase 1 runs Plug and Play detection; phase 2 runs more invasive detection routines to locate legacy devices. If the hardware is not detected, select Infrared Devices from the Hardware Type screen and click Next to select and install an infrared device. If the manufacturer and model of the infrared device does not appear, choose Serial Cable Using IrDA Protocol from the list of standard infrared ports.

C. **Incorrect:** You use the Add/Remove Programs program to install, remove, or update Windows components and third-party software installed on the computer. This program is not used to install new hardware.

D. **Incorrect:** The Windows 2000 Infrared Monitor service supports data transfer over infrared connections with computers, printers (IrLPT), cameras (IrTran-P), cellular phones, organizers, and other devices that use IrDA protocols supported by the service.

OBJECTIVE 3.5

Update drivers.

Windows 2000 maintains a list of installed hardware and the device drivers that support the hardware in the HKEY_LOCAL_MACHINE registry key. When a new device driver is needed, the device driver's key is queried to determine the current version of the installed driver.

A number of procedures exist for updating installed drivers. The simplest way to update drivers is by using the Windows Update tool. This tool is located on the Start menu unless network policies restrict access to it. It is also accessible through Device Manager's Upgrade Device Driver Wizard or from the Add Printer Wizard interface. If it is available, selecting Windows Update opens *http://windowsupdate.microsoft.com/*. The first visit to this site installs the Microsoft Active Setup ActiveX components. These components customize the online product update catalog for the computer running the update.

If a driver update needs to be removed, you can connect to the Windows Update site and follow the instructions to restore the previous configuration or run the Update Wizard Uninstall tool. This is a system tool available in the System Information snap-in.

Individual updates are available through a number of interfaces in Windows 2000 Professional. You update a printer driver by accessing the properties of a printer in the Printers window, clicking the Advanced tab, and clicking New Driver to start the Add Printer Driver Wizard.

Note The Windows Update button is not available in the Add Printer Driver Wizard, but it is available in the Add Printers Wizard.

You update other device drivers by accessing the properties of the device in Device Manager, clicking the Driver tab, and clicking Update Driver to start the Upgrade Device Driver Wizard. The Driver tab also includes name, location, and version information on currently installed device drivers.

The Add Printer Driver Wizard and the Upgrade Device Driver Wizard allow you to install a driver from the Windows 2000 Professional installation CD-ROM or from an alternate location. Administrator privileges are required to manually install device drivers. Plug and Play devices that are detected and automatically installed *do not* require Administrator privileges.

Objective 3.5 Questions

70-210.03.05.001

You administer a Pentium III computer running Windows 2000 Professional. Which interface should you use to upgrade drivers?

A. Device Manager.

B. The Add/Remove Hardware Wizard.

C. Environment variables.

D. The Component Services console.

70-210.03.05.002

You administer a Pentium III computer running Windows 2000 Professional. You suspect that an outdated driver is causing intermittent problems while running an application. You want to display a list of all drivers running. What should you do?

A. Use Device Manager.

B. Use the Add/Remove Hardware Wizard.

C. Use the CIPHER.EXE command-line utility.

D. Use the DRIVERS.EXE command-line utility.

70-210.03.05.003

A hard disk on your computer running Windows 98 fails, and you decide to install Windows 2000 Professional on the computer after replacing the hard disk and checking the Windows 2000 Hardware Compatibility List (HCL). You replace the hard disk and install Windows 2000 on the computer. One driver is not automatically installed by Windows 2000. Which conditions might require manual installation of drivers? (Choose all that apply.)

A. An error occurs during installation.

B. The driver package is not digitally signed.

C. The driver installation process requires a user interface to be displayed.

D. The driver package does not contain all files required to complete the installation.

70-210.03.05.004

By default, members of which group can manually install a driver on a computer running Windows 2000 Professional?

A. Administrators

B. Backup Operators

C. Power Users

D. Users

Objective 3.5 Answers

70-210.03.05.001

▶ **Correct Answers: A**

A. **Correct:** A number of methods exist to upgrade device drivers, but Device Manager is the only valid method listed in the answer choices. The Windows Update tool is another option for upgrading device drivers. To update a specific device, access the properties of the device from Device Manager and then click the Driver tab. In the Driver tab, click Update Driver to start the Upgrade Device Driver Wizard.

B. **Incorrect:** You use the Add/Remove Hardware Wizard to install new hardware and to remove, unplug, and troubleshoot existing hardware.

C. **Incorrect:** You configure environment variables from the command line or set them globally in the Environment Variables dialog box. This dialog box opens when you click the Environment Variables button located in the Advanced tab in the System Properties dialog box.

D. **Incorrect:** You use the Component Services console to install and configure Component Object Model (COM) components and COM+ applications, to view logs created by the Event Logging service, and to view, configure, and troubleshoot installed services.

70-210.03.05.002

▶ **Correct Answers: D**

   A. **Incorrect:** Device Manager does display the driver or drivers associated with each installed device, and you can use it to print reports on installed devices. However, there is no facility for displaying a list of installed drivers.

   B. **Incorrect:** You use the Add/Remove Hardware Wizard to install new hardware and to remove, unplug, and troubleshoot existing hardware. There is no facility for displaying a list of installed device drivers.

   C. **Incorrect:** The CIPHER.EXE command-line utility is an Encrypting File System (EFS) tool that you use to display and encrypt or decrypt files and folders and create a new encryption key.

   D. **Correct:** The DRIVERS.EXE command-line utility lists all of the drivers in the *%system-root%\System32\Drivers* folder that are currently running. You can use this tool to identify a driver that might be causing problems because of corruption or because it is missing, not loaded, or outdated. This tool is part of both the Windows 2000 Professional and Windows 2000 Server Resource Kits.

70-210.03.05.003

▶ **Correct Answers: A, B, C, and D**

   A. **Correct:** Errors occurring during installation could cause a driver installation to be skipped. After installation has completed, use the Add/Remove Hardware Wizard to run the Plug and Play process to find Plug and Play devices and the hardware detection process for other devices not recognized through Plug and Play. If hardware detection fails to find the device, manually install the supporting device driver from the Add/Remove Hardware Wizard. Manual installation of a driver requires Administrator privileges.

   B. **Correct:** The Windows 2000 Setup routine will not install unsigned device drivers. A driver that is signed contains a digital signature that is recognized by Windows 2000. A driver is signed after it has passed all Windows Hardware Quality Labs (WHQL) tests. Driver signing is a feature of Windows 98 and Windows 2000. After installation is complete, it is possible to manually install an unsigned driver, but this is not recommended.

   By default, the user who is installing an unsigned device driver is warned but not blocked from installing an unsigned device driver. File signature verification can be configured to block unsigned driver installations (Block mode), warn the user before installing the driver (Warn mode), or provide no warning of an impending unsigned driver installation (Ignore mode). You configure File Signature Verification mode in the Driver Signing Options dialog box. Open this dialog box by clicking the Driver Signing button in the Hardware tab of the System Properties dialog box.

C. **Correct:** Some devices use a device driver with a configuration interface that is separate from the Windows 2000 Setup routine. In this case, device driver installation is completed after Windows 2000 is installed.

D. **Correct:** If a hardware vendor does not provide a unique Plug and Play device identifier, Windows 2000 will not know that it needs a special driver, so a generic driver may be installed. This limits the special features available for the device. This is common for video adapters and monitors. After the operating system installation is complete, you can install the vendor-supplied driver in place of the generic driver.

70-210.03.05.004

▶ **Correct Answers: A**

A. **Correct:** After the operating system is installed, the Administrators group is the only group able to *manually* install device drivers on a computer running Windows 2000 Professional. Administrators can perform any and all functions supported by the operating system. Members of the Administrators group are able to grant themselves any rights that they do not already have by default. Administrative access is required to install, update, or configure the operating system and components, such as device drivers.

B. **Incorrect:** By default, the Backup Operators local group contains the privileges required to back up and restore files and folders. Members of this group can perform backup and restore operations regardless of folder or file ownership, access permissions, or encryption settings. Members of this group are not able to install device drivers.

C. **Incorrect:** By default, members of the Power Users local group are granted fewer system-level privileges than the Administrators group but more than the Users group. Power Users can install and uninstall applications locally that do not install system services and can customize systemwide resources such as display settings, shares, and power options. Members of the Power Users group cannot manually install device drivers.

D. **Incorrect:** By default, members of the Users group cannot manually install device drivers. The Users group has fewer privileges than the Power Users group. However, most Plug and Play devices can be automatically installed without Administrator privileges. If Plug and Play cannot fully configure a device, then Administrator privileges are necessary to complete the installation.

OBJECTIVE 3.6

Monitor and configure multiple processing units.

The Windows 2000 operating system kernel is able to use multiple processors to run processes and threads. Windows 2000 Professional includes support for one or two central processing units (CPUs). Support for multiple processors is provided by the **hardware abstraction layer (HAL)**, a hardware-specific operating system component that isolates the rest of the Windows 2000 operating system from the underlying hardware. Upgrading the HAL depends on the presence or absence of **Advanced Configuration and Power Interface (ACPI)** and **Advanced Programmable Interrupt Controller (APIC)** hardware on the computer. The HAL for a computer containing both ACPI and APIC hardware is upgradable to a multiprocessor system or downgradable to a uniprocessor system. The same rule applies to the hardware-specific HAL for a non-ACPI computer containing APIC hardware. Uniprocessor computers contain the simpler programmable interrupt controller (PIC) hardware, referred to as a Standard PC in Device Manager. The HAL for a computer containing ACPI and PIC hardware is not upgradable to the HAL for a PIC computer that is not ACPI compliant.

Use the Upgrade Device Driver Wizard to upgrade the HAL. This wizard is available in Device Manager. Upgrading to an incompatible HAL is likely to cause a critical system failure.

Use the Performance snap-in to monitor system resource use. Performance monitoring starts by establishing a baseline of satisfactory performance and then continuing to monitor the system to identify bottlenecks that are impacting performance. The System Monitor node in this snap-in has a number of important objects that contain counters for monitoring processor activity. The primary processor-specific objects to monitor are the following:

- Processor—Contains counters that monitor each processor individually (as individual instances).

- System—Contains counters that monitor all processors as a unit (single instance).

- Process—Contains counters that monitor each application running on the processors.

- Thread—Contains counters that monitor each unit of application execution on the processors.

- Job Object and Job Object Details—Contains groups of processes to be managed and manipulated as a unit (single instance) by one or multiple processors. You can view Web application activity counters through the Job object to determine an application's overall CPU use.

You use the Performance Logs and Alerts node of the Performance snap-in to collect performance data over time and to configure notification of exceeded activity thresholds.

Objective 3.6 Questions

70-210.03.06.001

You administer a Pentium III computer running Windows 2000 Professional. The computer has a single processor. You later decide to upgrade the hardware configuration to include two processors. How can you configure Windows 2000 Professional to distribute processing tasks across both processors?

A. Upgrade the HAL driver from Device Manager.

B. Reinstall Windows 2000 Professional.

C. Windows 2000 Professional does not support multiple processors.

D. No action is necessary because Windows 2000 will automatically begin using both processors.

70-210.03.06.002

You install Windows 2000 Professional on a computer with two processors. After installing the appropriate applications for your business, you decide to find a baseline for monitoring processor performance. While running multiple applications causing high processor activity, what is the expected range for the processor queue length?

A. 1–4

B. 2–6

C. 3–6

D. 4–7

70-210.03.06.003

Which multiprocessor configuration does Windows 2000 Professional support?

A. None

B. Symmetric multiprocessing (SMP)

C. Asymmetric multiprocessing (ASMP)

D. Both SMP and ASMP

Objective 3.6 Answers

70-210.03.06.001

▶ **Correct Answers: A**

A. **Correct:** From the question, you can infer that the computer running Windows 2000 Professional is capable of supporting a second processor. To change the installed HAL, start Device Manager and expand the Computer node to select and access the Properties dialog box for the computer. Click the Driver tab, and then click the Update Driver button to start the Upgrade Device Driver Wizard. Follow the instructions in the wizard to install the appropriate multiprocessor device driver.

B. **Incorrect:** In most cases, the Windows 2000 Professional Setup routine will detect a multiprocessor system and install a multiprocessor HAL to support it. However, this is not the most efficient choice for performing a HAL upgrade.

C. **Incorrect:** Windows 2000 Professional is capable of supporting two CPUs in a single computer.

D. **Incorrect:** The HAL that the Windows 2000 Setup routine installs on a computer with one processor is designed specifically for a uniprocessor configuration. A multiprocessor HAL must be installed to take advantage of both CPUs.

70-210.03.06.002

▶ **Correct Answers: B**

A. **Incorrect:** The System object's Processor Queue Length counter on a uniprocessor system with little activity will maintain a queue length average between 1 and 2. Therefore, a range of 1–4 does not accurately represent the activity expected on a dual-processor system displaying heavy processor use.

B. **Correct:** You observe overall processor activity by monitoring the processor queue length and processor use. A sustained queue of several waiting processor requests, combined with consistently high CPU use rate, signals a processor bottleneck. View the System object's Processor Queue Length counter to determine overall processor use on a system. Evidence of a processor bottleneck is indicated by a sustained or recurring queue of more than two threads. Therefore, a range of 2–6 threads waiting for processing is the expected range for the system described in the question.

C. **Incorrect:** A range of 3–6 suggests that the computer is heavily overused. This range is unacceptable for sustained periods. Note that the default scale for the System object's Processor Queue Length is 10. Therefore, a Processor Queue Length of 3 will appear as 30 in the Performance snap-in unless you change the scale to 1.

D. **Incorrect:** A range of 4–7 is unacceptable for sustained periods. At this range, the processor or processors might be the bottleneck. Some other reasons for this excessive queue length could be that a device in the computer is raising too many interrupts because of a hardware malfunction, or the computer does not contain enough physical RAM to service the running applications.

70-210.03.06.003

▶ **Correct Answers: B**

A. **Incorrect:** Windows 2000 Professional ships with HALs to support up to two processors.

B. **Correct:** SMP is a multiprocessor architecture in which all processors share the same memory containing a single copy of the operating system and one copy of each running application. The Windows 2000 kernel divides the workload into tasks, called threads, that are assigned to each processor.

C. **Incorrect:** ASMP is a multiprocessor architecture in which each processor serves a specific function. The operating system running on ASMP always selects the same processor to execute its instructions, while other processors service application requests.

D. **Incorrect:** The Windows 2000 operating system supports uniprocessor and multiprocessor SMP systems. ASMP is not supported by the operating system. However, it is possible for specialized hardware to support processors serving specific functions, such as disk I/O, but Windows 2000 is not involved in providing this support.

Install, configure, and troubleshoot network adapters.

Windows 2000 Professional supports many network adapter models as well as protocols and services that use the adapter hardware. A device driver for a Plug and Play network adapter, like many other hardware devices, is installed automatically when the operating system detects the device and the device driver is contained in the DRIVER.CAB file. Installing a device driver for a network adapter that is not Plug and Play compatible is typically completed by using the Add/Remove Hardware Wizard. After a device driver is installed for a network adapter, protocols and services are *bound* to the adapter so that it can communicate on the network.

A **protocol** allows the network adapter to establish communications with the network. Windows 2000 Professional supports the Transfer Control Protocol/Internet Protocol (TCP/IP), NWLink, NetBEUI, Data Link Control (DLC), and AppleTalk protocols. Each protocol is designed to communicate with network-accessible devices that support the same protocol. For example, a computer running NWLink, Microsoft's implementation of Internetwork Packet Exchange/Sequenced Packet Exchange (IPX/SPX), can communicate with NetWare servers running IPX/SPX. The most widely used protocol is TCP/IP.

A **protocol suite** is a combination of software services that run on top of the base protocol. For example, the TCP/IP protocol suite contains File Transfer Protocol (FTP) services to support TCP/IP file transfer. Protocols must be configured to operate properly in Windows 2000. For example, TCP/IP must be configured with IP addressing information. Configuration can be manually assigned or dynamically assigned by network services such as the DHCP Server service. For small networks, IP addressing can be dynamically assigned by Automatic Private IP Addressing (APIPA).

A critical service that must run on client computers to use file and print services is the client redirector. The client redirector for accessing a Windows 2000 server is the Microsoft Client. The client redirector for accessing a NetWare server is Client Services for NetWare (CSNW).

If a network adapter is not able to communicate on the network, check Device Manager to verify that a device driver is installed and operational. If so, check that the adapter is correctly connected to the network. Next run protocol-specific configuration utilities designed to test network connections, such as ping and ipconfig. For example, if the network adapter is running TCP/IP, type **ping *ip_address***, where ***ip_address*** is a valid host address on the network. If ping is unable to resolve an IP address on the network but pinging the local loopback address of 127.0.0.1 works, type **ipconfig** to verify that an address has been assigned to the network adapter. Configuration and protocol testing varies from one protocol to the next.

Objective 3.7 Questions

70-210.03.07.001

What is the most frequent cause of TCP/IP connection problems?

A. Unsupported network adapters.

B. Incorrect network adapter driver.

C. Incorrectly entered IP address data.

D. Failure of other networking components such as the hub and cables.

70-210.03.07.002

You are the administrator for a small local area network (LAN) supporting Windows NT, Windows 98, and Windows 2000. You currently use APIPA to obtain IP addresses for clients. You are considering using the DHCP Server service instead of APIPA. How should you configure Windows 2000 Professional to obtain an IP address from a computer running the DHCP Server service?

A. At a command prompt, type **ipconfig /dhcp** and press Enter.

B. No action is required because Windows 2000 Professional will automatically detect the DHCP Server service.

C. At a command prompt, type **ipconfig /release** and press Enter. Then type **ipconfig /renew** and press Enter.

D. At a command prompt, type **ipconfig /renew** and press Enter. Then type **ipconfig /release** and press Enter.

70-210.03.07.003

You are the administrator of a corporate LAN supporting a Novell NetWare server and various clients. You are planning to deploy some new computers running Windows 2000 Professional. Which conditions require you to manually assign a unique internal network number to the network adapter when using NWLink? (Choose three.)

A. An application is using the DLC protocol.

B. An application on the client computer is using the NetWare Service Advertising Protocol (SAP).

C. CSNW is installed, and multiple frame types are used on a single adapter.

D. CSNW is installed, and NWLink is bound to multiple adapters in the computer.

E. Gateway Services for NetWare (GSNW) is installed, and multiple frame types are used on a single adapter.

F. GSNW is installed, and NWLink is bound to multiple adapters in the computer.

Objective 3.7 Answers

70-210.03.07.001

▶ **Correct Answers: C**

A. **Incorrect:** Windows 2000 Professional supports hundreds of network adapters. Windows 2000 attempts to automatically detect the network adapter during operating system installation. If the network interface card (NIC) is installed after installation, Windows 2000 attempts to detect and install a driver for the adapter. You can initiate hardware detection routines after operating system installation by using the Add/Remove Hardware Wizard.

B. **Incorrect:** In most cases, if an incorrect driver is installed, Windows 2000 will not load it.

C. **Correct:** Each computer on a network running TCP/IP must be assigned a unique IP address and a valid subnet mask for the network segment in which the computer is connected. In a routed network, a default gateway address is required to communicate with computer resources on other networks. Additional IP addressing information—such as the IP addresses of Domain Name System (DNS) hosts on the network—might be required. Addressing information can be manually configured or automatically assigned. Automatic, centralized assignment is achieved by the DHCP Server service. In a simple network not running the DHCP Server service, you can avoid manual configuration by using APIPA.

D. **Incorrect:** It is possible to experience a network failure separate from the computer. However, this is not the most frequent cause of TCP/IP connection problems.

70-210.03.07.002

▶ **Correct Answers: B**

A. **Incorrect:** Ipconfig is a command-line TCP/IP configuration utility specifically designed for configuring dynamically assigned IP addressing information and for viewing IP address settings. To see a list of switches supported by ipconfig, type **ipconfig /?** at the command prompt. The /DHCP switch specified in the answer is not a valid ipconfig switch.

B. **Correct:** By default, the client computer periodically checks for a computer running the DHCP Server service with a valid address scope for the network in which the client is connected. Until such a server is located, the client computer will use APIPA. Additionally, when the computer is restarted, it will broadcast a modified Bootp request to the network in search of a computer running the DHCP Server service. If a host running the DHCP Server service answers, it will dynamically assign IP addressing information to the computer making the request.

C. **Incorrect:** Typing **ipconfig /release** at the command line will fail with a message stating that all adapters bound to DHCP do not have DHCP addresses and that all addresses were automatically configured and cannot be released.

D. **Incorrect:** If the DHCP Server service is running and it has a valid address scope for the client computer, typing **ipconfig /renew** will initiate IP addressing delivery by the DHCP Server service to the client computer. However, typing **ipconfig /release** afterward releases the IP address assigned by the DHCP Server service.

70-210.03.07.003

▶ **Correct Answers: B, C, and D**

    A. **Incorrect:** You use the DLC protocol for network-connected Hewlett-Packard printers that depend on DLC and to access Systems Network Architecture (SNA) hosts over an SNA network running DLC. This protocol is not used to access NetWare resources.

    B. **Correct:** NWLink uses a nonzero eight-digit hexadecimal internal network number for routing purposes. This network number is internal because NWLink uses it inside the computer. The internal network number must not be confused with the network number (also known as the external network number) that is used to uniquely identify an IPX/SPX network segment. If the client computer is acting as an application server by running a SAP application such as Microsoft SQL Server, the internal network number uniquely identifies the computer to the network so that other clients can access the application.

    C. **Correct:** CSNW is the client redirector used by Windows 2000 Professional to communicate over NWLink with network-accessible NetWare resources. A frame type defines how network packets are formatted before being sent over the network. Each frame type supported on a single adapter requires a unique internal network number to avoid internal collisions with packets using a different frame type.

    D. **Correct:** NWLink is Microsoft's implementation of the IPX/SPX protocol. Each network adapter in the computer running this protocol requires a unique internal network number so that packets created by the computer are internally routed to the appropriate adapter.

    E. **Incorrect:** GSNW is installed on Windows 2000 Server, not Windows 2000 Professional. GSNW enables a computer running Windows 2000 Server to connect to computers running the NetWare 3.*x* or 4.*x* network operating system. GSNW contains the client redirector software in CSNW, and you use it to create gateways to NetWare resources. Creating a gateway allows computers running the Microsoft client redirector to gain access to NetWare resources through the gateway.

    F. **Incorrect:** GSNW is a service available in Windows 2000 Server, as described earlier.

Monitoring and Optimizing System Performance and Reliability

Two important goals in the design of Microsoft Windows 2000 Professional were to create an operating system with performance and reliability that rivaled that of Microsoft Windows 98 and Microsoft Windows NT.

To improve reliability, Windows 2000 and Windows NT separate user processes from system processes, which protects critical operating system functions from errant applications. For the majority of user applications, memory space is separated to decrease the possibility of one application failure affecting other running applications. The only exception to this is running Windows 16-bit applications, which share the same memory space; however, each Windows 16-bit application can run in its own memory space if configured to do so. Because of these improvements, most operating system failures in Windows NT occur because of misbehaving device drivers.

Driver signing in Windows 2000 addresses this problem by helping to ensure the quality of device drivers and other critical system files before they are installed. Microsoft places a digital signature on a device driver or other critical system file after it has met a certain level of testing in the Microsoft Windows Hardware Quality Lab (WHQL). The operating system detects and maintains signed files to block or warn the installers of critical system files that are unsigned.

A reliable system is one that makes user data and applications highly available and system configuration flexible. The former is accomplished by the **Offline Files** feature. Files and programs can be made available to the user even when the primary network storage location of the data is off line. Flexible configuration is achieved by **hardware profiles**. Hardware profiles maintain unique driver and service configurations for the computer. They are created automatically during the Windows 2000 Setup routine, and they can be created manually from the Hardware Profiles dialog box.

Recoverability is an important part of system reliability. A system characterized as reliable must contain tools and techniques for recovery in the event of system failure. Windows 2000 includes a number of important recovery tools such as the **Advanced Options menu**, the **Recovery Console**, **Emergency Repair**, and **Windows Backup**.

Windows Backup as well as any command that can run in Windows 2000 can be scheduled. You can create schedules using either the Scheduled Tasks window or the AT command-line utility.

Monitoring how the system uses resources is an important step in optimizing operating system and application performance. The **Performance console** and **Task Manager** are important tools for monitoring the system.

Tested Skills and Suggested Practices

The skills you need to successfully master the Monitoring and Optimizing System Performance and Reliability Objective Domain on Exam 70-210: Installing, Configuring, and Administering Microsoft Windows 2000 Professional include the following:

- **Troubleshoot system operations and recover from system failures.**

  - Practice 1: Run the File Signature Verification utility (SIGVERIF.EXE) to view unsigned files. Adjust the advanced settings to scan for files in other folders and to adjust log file settings. View the log file.

  - Practice 2: Run the System File Checker utility using the /scannow and /scanonce switches. Reset WFP using the /enable switch.

  - Practice 3: Run a System State backup. Restore System State files that are allowed to be redirected to an alternate location. Review the contents of *%systemroot%*\Repair\Regback after running a System State backup.

  - Practice 4: Create an ERD using Windows Backup. Compare the contents of the Emergency Repair Disk to the contents of *%systemroot%*\Repair to verify that the registry files were *not* copied to the disk.

  - Practice 5: Review the Emergency Repair options available from the Text mode of the Windows 2000 Setup routine.

  - Practice 6: Open the Advanced Options Menu by pressing F8 during system startup. Run the various Safe Mode options, and perform a normal boot logging procedure. After each startup, review the contents of *%systemroot%*\Ntbtlog.txt.

  - Practice 7: Open the Advanced Options Menu by pressing F8 when a computer in Hibernate mode is coming out of hibernation. Compare the options appearing here to the Advanced Options Menu options appearing during a system startup.

- Practice 8: Install the Recovery Console to the system partition. Start the Recovery Console from the boot menu.

- Practice 9: Start the Recovery Console from the Windows 2000 Setup routine.

- Practice 10: In the Recovery Console, type **help** to see a list of commands. Type the name of each command followed by **/?** to learn about the purpose of each command.

- Practice 11: Restore the registry from a recent backup stored in the *%system-root%*\Repair\Regback folder.

- Practice 12: Start the Local Security Settings console by clicking the Local Security Policy icon in the Administrative Tools program group. Enable the two Recovery Console policies appearing under the Security Settings-Local Policies-Security Options node. Next start the Recovery Console, use the Set command to access all files and folders, and use another Set command to allow files to be copied to removable media.

- **Schedule tasks.**

  - Practice 1: Open the Windows 2000 Command Reference from Windows 2000 Help. Locate and read about the AT command. Read the AT notes page available from the Related Topics link at the bottom of the AT command Help page.

  - Practice 2: Use the AT command to schedule a task. View the AT command and compare it to a task scheduled using the Scheduled Task Wizard.

  - Practice 3: Copy a task created on one computer to another computer in a workgroup. Review the changes to task privileges and the changed user context of the copied task. Attempt to manually run a task from the task's context menu.

- **Configure and troubleshoot Offline Files.**

  - Practice 1: Enable Offline Files and configure synchronization for a folder and its contents.

  - Practice 2: Configure a share for automatic file caching. On the client computer configured for Offline Files, select and open a file contained below the share and then check the Client Side Cache in the Offline Files Folder window to verify that the file was synchronized.

  - Practice 3: Test manual file caching on the client computer by running the Offline Files Wizard to pin files.

  - Practice 4: Open the Synchronization Settings dialog box, and for the LAN connection, schedule synchronization, configure idle synchronization, and configure logon and logoff synchronization behavior.

■ **Monitor system performance.**

■ Practice 1: Run Task Manager and view the columns not appearing by default on the Processes tab. Sort the columns to determine which process has created the most page faults, which process has spawned the most threads, and which processes have a base priority of high.

■ Practice 2: View Kernel Times on Task Manager's Performance tab.

■ Practice 3: Pause and resume the Task Manager display.

■ Practice 4: In the Windows 2000 Professional Resource Kit, Chapter 27, locate the "Getting the Most from System Monitor," "Getting the Most from Performance Logs and Alerts," and "Working with Task Manager" sections. Open the corresponding tools in Microsoft Windows 2000 Professional, and navigate to all the items discussed in these three sections.

■ Practice 5: Create a Trace log and then use the TRACEDMP.EXE tool in the Windows 2000 Professional or Server Resource Kit to extract the log data. Open and review the resulting text file in Microsoft Notepad and the resulting comma-delimited file in Microsoft Excel.

■ Practice 6: Save a Counter log as an .html file and view it using Microsoft Internet Explorer. Change the System Monitor control in Internet Explorer so that it collects real-time data.

■ Practice 7: Insert the System Monitor Microsoft ActiveX control into an Excel worksheet using the Other Controls button on the Control Toolbox toolbar.

■ Practice 8: Run both System Monitor and Task Manager. Next find Table 27.6 in Chapter 27 of the Windows 2000 Professional Resource Kit. Then using the table and the two monitoring applications, compare Task Manager counters to System Monitor counters.

■ Practice 9: Create a performance baseline in the Performance console using Table 27.7 in Chapter 27 of the Windows 2000 Professional Resource Kit as your guide. Create the baseline using data collected over several weeks of normal activity. Compare the collected data to threshold data provided in Table 27.8.

■ Practice 10: Using the Alerts feature of the Performance Logs and Alerts snap-in, create an alert that sends your user account a network message when free space on any fixed disk in the computer has dropped below 15 percent.

Further Reading

This "Further Reading" section provides lists of important readings to supplement your current understanding of the skills tested within this Objective Domain. The lists are delineated into pertinent readings for each objective within this Objective Domain. If you feel that you need additional preparation prior to taking the exam, study these sources thoroughly.   ·

Objective 4.1

Microsoft Corporation. *Microsoft Windows 2000 Professional Resource Kit*. Redmond, Washington: Microsoft Press, 2000. Read pp. 1419–1428, "Maintenance and Update Tools," pp. 1429–1437, "System File and Driver Tools," and pp. 1467–1478, "Troubleshooting Procedures" in Chapter 31, "Troubleshooting Tools and Strategies."

Microsoft Corporation. *MCSE Training Kit—Microsoft Windows 2000 Professional*. Redmond, Washington: Microsoft Press, 2000. Read and complete the practices in Lesson 2, Chapter 25, "Implementing, Managing, and Troubleshooting Hardware Devices and Drivers."

Objective 4.2

Microsoft Corporation. *MCSE Training Kit—Microsoft Windows 2000 Professional*. Redmond, Washington: Microsoft Press, 2000. Read and complete the practices in Lesson 3, Chapter 3, "Using Microsoft Management Console and Task Scheduler."

Objective 4.3

Microsoft Corporation. *Microsoft Windows 2000 Professional Resource Kit*. Redmond, Washington: Microsoft Press, 2000. Read pp. 373–383, "Using Offline Files and Folders" in Chapter 9, "Managing Files, Folders, and Search Methods," and pp. 406–417, "Configuring Offline Files for Portable Computers" in Chapter 10, "Mobile Computing."

Microsoft Corporation. *MCSE Training Kit—Microsoft Windows 2000 Professional*. Redmond, Washington: Microsoft Press, 2000. Read and complete the practices in Lesson 1, Chapter 24, "Configuring Windows 2000 for Mobile Computers."

Objective 4.4

Microsoft Corporation. *Microsoft Windows 2000 Professional Resource Kit*. Redmond, Washington: Microsoft Press, 2000. Read Chapter 27, "Overview of Performance Monitoring," Chapter 28, "Evaluating Memory and Cache Usage," Chapter 29, "Analyzing Processor Activity," and Chapter 30, "Examining and Tuning Disk Performance."

Microsoft Corporation. "Windows 2000 Performance Tuning." This article can be downloaded from *http://www.microsoft.com/windows2000* by searching on the article title.

Objective 4.5

Microsoft Corporation. *Microsoft Windows 2000 Professional Resource Kit*. Redmond, Washington: Microsoft Press, 2000. Read pp. 435-445, "Managing Hardware on Portable Computers" in Chapter 10, "Mobile Computing."

Objective 4.6

Microsoft Corporation. *Microsoft Windows 2000 Professional Resource Kit*. Redmond, Washington: Microsoft Press, 2000. Read pp. 797–813, "Overview of Backups" in Chapter 18, "Removable Storage and Backup," and pp. 1398–1419, "Startup and Recovery Tools" in Chapter 31, "Troubleshooting Tools and Strategies."

Microsoft Corporation. *MCSE Training Kit—Microsoft Windows 2000 Professional*. Redmond, Washington: Microsoft Press, 2000. Read and complete the practices in Lessons 1, 3, and 5 in Chapter 19, "Backing Up and Restoring Data," and read Chapter 22, "The Windows 2000 Boot Process."

OBJECTIVE 4.1

Manage and troubleshoot driver signing.

Thousands of system files are installed when the Windows 2000 Setup routine and application installation routines are run. The files that are installed support all aspects of operating system and application functions. Service pack updates, hot fixes, and application updates replace targeted system files. In Windows operating systems prior to Windows 2000, operating system updates and numerous application installations are much more likely to cause an operating system failure or application failure than in Windows 2000.

Windows 2000 includes a number of important features and tools to manage system files and troubleshoot failures in drivers and other critical system files. **Windows File Protection (WFP)** protects against the replacement of critical system files and reduces file version mismatches. Before a system file is replaced, the operating system notifies WFP of an impending replacement. WFP checks the file's digital signature and compares it to the signature of the installed version of the file. If the digital signature doesn't match, a notification of the file replacement event is logged to the System event log and then the original file is restored from the *%systemroot%*\System32\Dllcache folder or, if it is not contained in this folder, from the Windows 2000 Professional installation CD-ROM.

The WFP facility is automatic; the System File Checker (SFC) utility is run manually to augment WFP. The SFC utility scans protected files, checks for version mismatches, reinstalls the correct system files to the *%systemroot%*\System32\Dllcache folder, repairs this folder if it becomes corrupted or unusable, and provides scan-scheduling capability.

If you suspect that a signed driver is not functioning properly, run **Driver Verifier Manager** (VERIFIER.EXE). This utility contains both a command-line and Windows interface. Typing **verifier /?** at the command line shows the switches this utility supports. Running verifier without any switches starts the Driver Verifier Manager Windows interface. After configuring a driver for verification by Driver Verifier Manager, restart the computer and then run procedures that access the device driver. Driver problems appear during startup or in the Windows interface. After a driver is verified, use Driver Verifier Manager to disable driver verification.

The Windows 2000 **signature checking** facility verifies that a driver is signed before it is installed. Three settings exist for signature checking: Level 0 (ignore) essentially disables signature checking; Level 1 (warn) prompts the installer of an impending unsigned driver installation; and Level 2 (block) prevents the installation of unsigned drivers. The default setting is Level 1. You set signature checking in the Driver Signing Options dialog box. To open this dialog box, click the Driver Signing button on the Hardware tab in the System Properties dialog box.

Signature checking is automatic, but the **File Signature Verification** (SIGVERIF.EXE) Windows utility allows for manual signature verification. This utility provides the following information: whether files are signed, the publisher of signed files, the date the file was modified, file version information, and which catalog holds a matching signature for the file. Catalogs are stored in a folder below *%systemroot%*\System32\Catroot. The primary catalog for Windows 2000 system files is NT5.CAT.

Objective 4.1 Questions

70-210.04.01.001

You are the chief administrator for your local area network (LAN), and you configure an unattended setup of Windows 2000 Professional. You need to install unsigned drivers during the installation of Windows 2000 Professional. When you run the unattended setup routine on a test computer, a prompt is displayed warning of impending unsigned driver installation. How can you disable the prompt?

A. Add the following entry to the [Data] section of UNATTEND.TXT: DriverSigningPolicy = Ignore.

B. Add the following entry to the [Unattended] section of UNATTEND.TXT: DriverSigningPolicy = Ignore.

C. Add the following entry to the [SetupParams] section of UNATTEND.TXT: DriverSigningPolicy = Ignore.

D. Add the following entry to the [GuiUnattended] section of UNATTEND.TXT: DriverSigningPolicy = Ignore.

70-210.04.01.002

You want to troubleshoot driver signing on your computer running Windows 2000 Professional. Which command-line utility can you use to check the signature of files?

A. EFSINFO

B. MCAST

C. SFC

D. SIGVERIF

70-210.04.01.003

You want to ensure that unsigned drivers are not installed on your computer running Windows 2000 Professional. What should you do?

A. No action is required.

B. Change the File Signature Verification setting to Ignore.

C. Change the File Signature Verification setting to Warn.

D. Change the File Signature Verification setting to Block.

Objective 4.1 Answers

70-210.04.01.001

▶ **Correct Answers: B**

A. **Incorrect:** The [Data] section of an answer file is required when performing an unattended installation by booting directly from the Windows 2000 Professional installation CD-ROM. The value names it supports are AutoPartition, MsDosInitiated, UnattendedInstall, and UseBIOSTo-Boot. You can find an explanation of these values in the UNATTEND.DOC file located in the \Support\Tools\DEPLOY.CAB file on the Windows 2000 Professional installation CD-ROM.

B. **Correct:** The [Unattended] section of an answer file is a required section of an answer-file-based installation of Windows 2000. This section contains the DriverSigningPolicy setting. The value of DriverSigningPolicy determines how unsigned drivers are processed during an unattended installation of Windows 2000 Professional. A value of *block* instructs the installation routine not to install the unsigned driver. A value of *warn* instructs the installation to display a prompt before allowing the installation of an unsigned driver. Each unsigned driver will cause the prompt to reappear. A value of *ignore* instructs the installation to continue even if the driver is not signed. A value of *ignore* is inadvisable unless the unsigned drivers have been thoroughly tested on the computers where they will be installed.

C. **Incorrect:** The [SetupParams] section is added to an answer file to specify a command to run when Windows 2000 installation completes but before the system settings are saved. This section requires a single value name of UserExecute, which is set equal to a path and program name. This section is equivalent to the WINNT command-line switch of /e and the WINNT32 command-line switch of /cmd:.

D. **Incorrect:** The [GuiUnattended] section of an answer file is used to specify GUI-mode setup behavior for both an answer-file-based setup of Windows 2000 and an automated setup of Windows 2000 using SYSPREP.EXE. For a list of the value names used in this section, review the UNATTEND.DOC file, located in the \Support\Tools\DEPLOY.CAB file on the Windows 2000 Professional installation CD-ROM.

70-210.04.01.002

▶ **Correct Answers: D**

A. **Incorrect:** EFSINFO.EXE is a troubleshooting tool used to view information about encrypted files, including information about the Encrypting File System (EFS) user account and the recovery agent accounts. This tool is part of the Windows 2000 Server and Windows 2000 Professional Resource Kits.

B. **Incorrect:** MCAST.EXE is a tool used to diagnose and resolve problems with audio and video multi-casting. This tool is part of the Windows 2000 Server and Windows 2000 Professional Resource Kits.

C. **Incorrect:** SFC is a command-line utility that scans protected system files and replaces any protected files that were overwritten after the installation of Windows 2000 Professional. The SFC utility checks the catalogs to determine correct file versions. A Windows Update procedure automatically updates the catalog so that SFC doesn't overwrite files that are properly updated.

D. **Correct:** SIGVERIF.EXE is a GUI-based utility that provides feedback on signed and unsigned files. After this utility runs, a list of unsigned drivers appears. A log file named SIGVERIF.TXT is created in the *%systemroot%* folder. This log file contains a detailed list of all signed and unsigned drivers. By default, SIGVERIF scans the system files, but you configure this setting and other settings from the Advanced File Signature Verification Settings dialog box. This dialog box opens when you click the Advanced button in the File Signature Verification dialog box. Additionally, you can view log files by clicking the View Log button in the Advanced File Signature Verification Settings dialog box.

70-210.04.01.003

▶ **Correct Answers: D**

A. **Incorrect:** You configure file signature verification in the Driver Signing Options dialog box. Level 1 (warn) is the default setting for file signature verification. As a result, a user is prompted about any impending unsigned driver installation. Therefore, it is possible to install an unsigned driver if no action is taken to reconfigure this setting.

B. **Incorrect:** This setting disables file signature verification so that any driver, whether it is signed or not, can be installed.

C. **Incorrect:** This is the default setting for file signature checking, as explained earlier. As a result, it is possible for a user to install an unsigned driver.

D. **Correct:** Changing the File Signature Verification setting to Level 2 (block) ensures that unsigned drivers cannot be installed on the computer when running Windows 2000 Professional. You configure this setting in the Driver Signing Options dialog box.

Configure, manage, and troubleshoot Scheduled Tasks.

Windows 2000 includes the Scheduled Task Wizard and the AT command-line utility for configuring operation schedules for processes that run in Windows 2000, such as a program or script. Scheduled tasks depend on the accuracy of the computer's clock. Make sure that the system clock is accurate.

A task scheduled using the AT utility appears in the Scheduled Tasks window but is managed from the AT command-line utility. Using either interface (the wizard or command-line utility), you can schedule, reschedule, disable, or remove a task. Task configuration allows for controlling exactly how the task will operate. For example, setting the user context for the task, stopping the task if it runs too long, allowing the task to run only when the computer is idle, and not allowing the task to run if the computer is running on batteries. Task security protects against modifications to the task by unauthorized personnel.

Task management involves reviewing tasks that the Task Scheduler service has attempted to start. The Scheduled Tasks window provides summary results of task operation. Detailed results are contained in the Task log. The log is stored in *%systemroot%* and is named SCHEDLGU.TXT. Viewing the log file is an important troubleshooting measure to determine exactly why a task has failed to run. View the log file by clicking the View Log command on the Advanced menu in the Scheduled Tasks window. Other important management tasks completed from the Advanced menu include configuring the user context for all AT scheduled tasks, configuring notification of missed tasks, and controlling the state of the Task Scheduler service.

All tasks scheduled from the Scheduled Task Wizard can run using any valid user account. Tasks scheduled using the AT utility appear in the Scheduled Tasks window but run in the user context of the AT service account. Modifying the properties of an AT scheduled task in the Scheduled Tasks window converts the AT task to a scheduled task. Scheduling or modifying a task requires that the Task Scheduler service is either running or paused. The task will run only if the Task Scheduler service is running.

Windows Backup (NTBACKUP.EXE) uses the Task Scheduler service when backups are scheduled. Use the View Log option in Task Scheduler to verify that the backup started. For details on the backup process, view the Backup log in the Backup Reports dialog box in Windows Backup.

Objective 4.2 Questions

70-210.04.02.001

Your Pentium computer runs Windows 2000 Professional and has an internal Seagate STT8000 tape backup device. You successfully performed a full system backup using the tape device. You use Task Scheduler to create a scheduled job to run Windows Backup. The backup operation fails. What is the most likely cause of this failure?

A. The backup tape has failed.

B. The correct tape is not mounted in the tape drive.

C. The correct device driver for the tape drive is not loaded.

D. Windows 2000 does not support the tape device.

70-210.04.02.002

Which two methods can you use to create a scheduled task in Windows 2000 Professional? (Choose two.)

A. Open Control Panel and double-click the Scheduled Tasks program.

B. Open Control Panel and double-click the Administrative Tools folder.

C. On the Start menu, point to Programs, point to Administrative Tools, and click Scheduled Tasks.

D. On the Start menu, point to Programs, point to Accessories, point to System Tools, and click Scheduled Tasks.

70-210.04.02.003

You are the administrator of APM-compliant and ACPI-compliant computers running Windows 2000 Professional. Each computer is accessed by multiple users.

You want to achieve these results: schedule disk defragmentation to occur during nonworking hours; ensure that computers in Sleep mode are also defragmented; set up the same disk defragmentation maintenance task on other computers in the workgroup running Windows 2000 Professional; and prevent users from manually running a scheduled task that you create.

The proposed solution is as follows: use the Scheduled Task Wizard to create a task to defragment the disk during nonworking hours; use the Security tab in the Scheduled Task Wizard Advanced Options dialog box to set the appropriate permissions; and copy the scheduled task to all other Windows 2000 Professional computers in the workgroup.

Which results does the proposed solution provide? (Choose all that apply.)

A. Disk defragmentation is scheduled to occur during nonworking hours.

B. Computers in Sleep mode are also defragmented.

C. The same disk defragmentation maintenance task occurs on other Windows 2000 Professional computers in the workgroup.

D. Users are prevented from manually running the scheduled task.

70-210.04.02.004

You are the administrator of ACPI-compliant Pentium III computers running Windows 2000 Professional.

You want to achieve these results: schedule disk defragmentation to occur during nonworking hours; ensure that computers in Sleep mode are also defragmented; set up the same disk defragmentation maintenance task on other Windows 2000 Professional computers in the workgroup; and prevent users from manually running a scheduled task that you create.

The proposed solution is as follows: use the Scheduled Task Wizard to create a task to defragment the disk during nonworking hours; select the Wake The Computer To Run This Task check box; copy the scheduled task to all other Windows 2000 Professional computers in the workgroup; and use the Security tab in the Scheduled Task Wizard Advanced Options dialog box to set the appropriate permissions for the task on each computer in the workgroup.

Which results does the proposed solution provide? (Choose all that apply.)

A. Disk defragmentation is scheduled to occur during nonworking hours.

B. Computers in Sleep mode are also defragmented.

C. The same disk defragmentation maintenance task occurs on other Windows 2000 Professional computers in the workgroup.

D. Users are prevented from manually running the scheduled task.

Objective 4.2 Answers

70-210.04.02.001

▶ **Correct Answers: B**

A. **Incorrect:** A tape failure is possible but is not the most likely cause of a failed backup job. A hardware failure might appear in the System or Application event logs. Viewing the backup report generated from backup logging in Windows Backup will show when and if the backup started and completed. The default backup summary logging level is sufficient to indicate a failed backup procedure.

B. **Correct:** When the tape media mounted in the drive is different than the media name specified in Windows Backup and a changer containing the correct media is not in use, the backup operation fails. Review the Backup log to identify this failure.

C. **Incorrect:** The question states that a successful backup has been performed using this hardware. Therefore, it is likely that the correct device driver is installed and running. To verify that the device driver is operational, review the properties of the device in Device Manager.

D. **Incorrect:** The question states that a successful backup has been performed using this hardware, so it is unlikely that Windows 2000 does not support the device. If an incompatibility is suspected, check the Hardware Compatibility List (HCL).

70-210.04.02.002

▶ **Correct Answers: A and D**

A. **Correct:** Double-clicking the Scheduled Tasks program in Control Panel opens the Scheduled Tasks window. In this window, you can schedule a new task or modify or delete an existing task.

B. **Incorrect:** The Administrative Tools folder in Control Panel points to the \Documents and Settings\All Users\Start Menu\Programs\Administrative Tools folder. Even if the Administrative Tools program group is configured not to appear on the Programs menu, the Administrative Tools folder still appears in Control Panel. This folder does not contain a shortcut to the Scheduled Tasks window.

C. **Incorrect:** The Administrative Tools program group points to the same set of shortcuts contained in Control Panel's Administrative Tools folder.

D. **Correct:** The Scheduled Tasks program appears in the System Tools program group.

70-210.04.02.003

▶ **Correct Answers: A**

A. **Correct:** The first sentence in the proposed solution states that the task is scheduled to occur during nonworking hours. A task is scheduled when you create it using the Scheduled Task Wizard. You adjust an existing task's schedule by accessing the properties of the task and then clicking the Schedule tab to modify the settings on this tab.

B. **Incorrect:** Nothing in the proposed solution suggests that the task was modified to wake up a computer to run the task. The Wake The Computer To Run This Task check box appears on the Settings tab of the task's properties on computers that support this feature. ACPI-compliant computers include this feature; non-ACPI-compliant computers do not.

C. **Incorrect:** The last part of the proposed solution states that the task is copied to all other computers in the workgroup. Tasks are sent and received as files. Thus, you can send tasks in a number of ways. For example, within Windows Explorer, double-click the My Network Places icon and double-click a computer icon. Then double-click the Scheduled Tasks program for each Windows 2000 computer to view its Scheduled Tasks folder. Task files have an extension of .job and are stored in the *%systemroot%*\Tasks folder. For efficiency, create a batch file that copies the scheduled task to each computer on the network that should run it.

The problem with attempting to run a task copied to other computers in the workgroup is that the user account specified to run the task will be invalid. User accounts in a workgroup are computer specific. Therefore, a user logged on locally to a computer in a workgroup must configure the task with a valid user account before it will run. Moving to a domain model solves this administrative problem.

Another option is to use the AT command-line utility to create a scheduled task to run on all computers in the workgroup. The first AT parameter is the Universal Naming Convention (UNC) name of the computer. Make sure to configure the AT Service Account on each computer in the workgroup. To configure the AT Service Account, in the Scheduled Tasks window, click Advanced and then select the AT Service Account option. When the AT Service Account Configuration dialog box appears, specify an account capable of running the scheduled tasks. Next create a batch file containing the AT command targeted at each computer in the workgroup.

D. **Incorrect:** The proposed solution explains that you set security on the task before copying it to members of the workgroup. It is possible to restrict the task so only specific personnel are allowed to manually run the task. However, copying the task to other computers in the workgroup causes the permissions to be reset to the default settings of the Scheduled Task folder on the target computer. The default settings include Read & Execute, Read, and Write assigned to the Everyone special group. As a result of the Write permission, members of this group are able to manually run the task. One way to solve this problem is to create a Windows 2000 domain and move all members of the workgroup to the domain. Then follow the procedures as outlined in the proposed solution.

70-210.04.02.004

▶ **Correct Answers: A, B, and D**

A. **Correct:** The first sentence in the proposed solution states that the task is scheduled to occur during nonworking hours. A task is scheduled when it is created using the Scheduled Task Wizard. You adjust an existing task's schedule by accessing the properties of the task and then clicking the Schedule tab to modify the settings on this tab. You can also use the AT command-line utility to schedule a task for the computer. The task you schedule using the AT command appears in the Scheduled Tasks window on each computer in the workgroup.

B. **Correct:** The proposed solution explains that the task was modified to wake up a computer to run the task. The Wake The Computer To Run This Task check box appears on the Settings tab of the task's properties on computers that support this feature. As explained in the question, all computers in the workgroup are ACPI compliant, so this feature will be available.

C. **Incorrect:** As outlined in the previous question, the problem with attempting to run a task copied to other computers in the workgroup is that the user account specified to run the task will be invalid. User accounts in a workgroup are computer specific. Therefore, a user logged on locally to a computer in a workgroup must configure the task with a valid user account before it will run. Moving to a domain model solves this administrative problem.

D. **Correct:** The question states that privileges are reassigned *after* the task is copied to target computers in the workgroup. This approach will take significant administrative effort if more than a dozen or so computers are in the workgroup. Moving a workgroup of computers to a domain model will reduce administrative overhead by centralizing user account administration.

OBJECTIVE 4.3

Manage and troubleshoot the use and synchronization of Offline Files.

Traditionally, files accessed over a network connection were unavailable when the network connection was lost. The **Offline Files** feature in Windows 2000 Professional is a facility to **synchronize** files from a network to a local disk so if the network is disconnected, files are available off line. Offline files are made available on a network resource through folder sharing. The computer that hosts the share runs the Server service and is considered the server; the computer that accesses the share runs the client redirector and is considered the client. The Microsoft Network Server service and client redirector use the Server Message Block (SMB) protocol and a transport protocol for network communication. This is the only network software combination that supports Offline Files.

After sharing a network-accessible resource, the Offline Files feature is enabled and configured centrally using group policies, or it is configured independently on each computer on the Offline Files tab of the Folder Options dialog box. To locate the Offline Files tab, access the network share using Windows Explorer and then locate a folder below the share that will be synchronized. On the Tools pull-down menu, click Folder Options to open the Folder Options dialog box and then click the Offline Files tab. You also use this tab to access the Offline Files folder, and you can create a shortcut to this folder on the desktop from the Offline Files tab.

Enabling and configuring Offline Files initiates an update of the *%systemroot%*\Csc hidden database cache folder with offline file configuration information. The Client Side Cache (CSC) is the database for the cache.

Tip If the boot partition has limited disk space, use the Offline Files Cache Mover utility (CACHEMOV.EXE) in the Windows 2000 Professional or Server Resource Kit to move the CSC database to a partition on a fixed disk with more space.

Files are not automatically synchronized as a result of enabling and configuring Offline Files. Instead, files are made available off line through either **automatic file caching** or **manual file caching**. Automatic file caching copies any files selected or opened on the client computer to the cache. Interestingly, selecting a file without opening it stores it in the cache. Automatic file caching is configured from the server (the computer containing the shared resource) at the share level so that any files or folders below the share are configured for automatic file caching. The default caching setting on the share is Manual Caching For Documents, so this must be changed to support automatic file caching. The cache size on the client is adjustable and is set by default to 10 percent of the total disk capacity available on the partition containing the CSC folder. Files cached automatically are not guaranteed to be available in the cache. As the cache approaches the maximum configured cache size, files are deleted on a first in, first out (FIFO) basis.

Files are made permanently available off line on a client through manual file caching, which is configured on the client using the Offline Files Wizard. To start the Offline Files Wizard, open Windows Explorer and then select a share or any of its contents. On the File menu, click Make Available Offline. The share must be located on a remote computer and it must be configured for caching, or the Make Available Offline command will not appear. A folder's contents or a specific file selected and configured for manual file caching is considered *pinned* because it is always available off line.

Certain file types cannot be cached, such as .pst (Microsoft Outlook personal store files) and .mdb (Microsoft Access database files). You can modify this exclusion list through the Files Not Cached Group Policy setting.

Files are synchronized between the online and offline cache either manually or automatically based on one of the following events: logon, logoff, idle time, or a fixed schedule. To accomplish manual synchronization, click Synchronize on the Tools menu in Windows Explorer to open the Items To Synchronize dialog box. Then click the Synchronize button. To configure synchronization settings, click the Setup button in the Items To Synchronize dialog box.

Objective 4.3 Questions

70-210.04.03.001

You are an administrator for a local area network (LAN) supporting computers running Windows 2000. Every day, you store your data on a computer running Windows 2000 Server. You want to use the Offline Files feature on your laptop computer running Windows 2000 Professional while you are away from the office on business. Which computer or computers must you configure?

A. None

B. The server

C. Your laptop

D. Both the server and your laptop

70-210.04.03.002

Your company operates a LAN supporting computers running Windows 2000 Professional. Other users on the network need to edit offline documents in one folder on your computer running Windows 2000 Professional. You want opened files to be automatically downloaded and made available when working off line. After you have configured the server for automatic download, users will enable and configure Offline Files on the Offline Files tab in the Folder Options dialog box. How should you configure the share to support automatic download?

A. Share the appropriate folder on your computer.

B. Share the appropriate folder on your computer. On the Sharing tab in the *folder_name* Properties dialog box, click the Caching button and select the Automatic Caching For Documents setting.

C. Share the appropriate folder on your computer. On the Sharing tab in the *folder_name* Properties dialog box, click the Caching button and select the Automatic Caching For Programs setting.

D. Share the appropriate folder on your computer. On the Sharing tab in the *folder_name* Properties dialog box, click the Caching button and select the Manual Caching For Documents setting.

70-210.04.03.003

Your company operates a LAN supporting computers running Windows 2000 Professional. Other users on the network need to edit offline documents in one folder on your computer running Windows 2000 Professional. If users edit both the cached offline copy of a file and the network version of a file, which two choices exist when you want to save all changes without renaming one version of the file? (Choose two.)

A. Use the Indexing Service to merge the changes.

B. Use the Synchronization Merge Wizard to merge the changes.

C. Overwrite the cached version with the version on the network.

D. Retain the cached version and do not update the network copy.

70-210.04.03.004

You are an administrator for a LAN supporting computers running Windows 2000. Every day, you store your data on a computer running Windows 2000 Server. You want to use the Offline Files feature on your laptop computer running Windows 2000 Professional while you are away from the office on business. This feature is enabled on the laptop, and the Offline Files Wizard has been run previously for another share on the network. The Offline Files Wizard defaults were specified when it was run previously. The laptop is connected to the network. Before you leave, you want to accomplish these results:

- Synchronize the appropriate files.

- Automatically synchronize files after your laptop has been idle for 15 minutes.

- Automatically repeat synchronization every 60 minutes that your laptop remains idle.

- Prevent synchronization when your laptop is running on battery power.

The proposed solution is to share the folder located on the computer running Windows 2000 Server that contains the files. On the client, open Windows Explorer, select the share containing the files, and on the File menu, click Make Available Offline. In the Confirm Offline Subfolders dialog box, choose whether just the folder share content or the folder share content and all subfolders and their content should be available off line. After synchronization completes, click Synchronize on the Tools menu. In the Items To Synchronize dialog box, click the Setup button. On the Logon/Logoff tab in the Synchronization Settings dialog box, select the offline files to synchronize.

Which result or results does the proposed solution provide? (Choose all that apply.)

A. The appropriate files are automatically synchronized when you log on or log off the laptop computer.

B. Files are automatically synchronized after your laptop has been idle for 15 minutes.

C. Synchronization runs automatically every weekday at 11:45 AM.

D. Synchronization is prevented when your laptop is idle and running on battery power.

Objective 4.3 Answers

70-210.04.03.001

▶ **Correct Answers: D**

A. **Incorrect:** Offline file caching must be configured before the client computer—the laptop in this question—will store cached files.

B. **Incorrect:** The computer that hosts the share is always considered the server, whether the share is hosted on a computer running Windows 2000 Server or Windows 2000 Professional. Setting up a share is the first step in configuring the Offline Files feature. After the share is created, use the Windows interface (Windows Explorer or My Computer) to access the properties of the share. On the Sharing tab, click Caching to open the Caching Settings dialog box and configure how data will be cached. In this dialog box, you enable or disable caching and you configure how data will be cached. The default cache setting is Manual Caching For Documents. This setting supports only manual file caching. The other two settings, Automatic Caching For Programs and Automatic Caching For Documents, support both automatic and manual file caching. Use the former if the share hosts read-only data or applications that run from the network; use the latter if the share hosts data that users modified.

C. **Incorrect:** The computer that accesses the share and maintains a local cache of offline files is the client computer. The client computer maintains the caching database, whose default location is the *%systemroot%\Csc* folder. If a share is configured for caching, the client computer is able to pin a folder's contents or files for manual file caching using the Offline Files Wizard. When the Offline Files Wizard is run once, any additional files pinned are automatically synchronized without launching the wizard. If the share is configured for automatic file caching, the client computer will automatically cache selected or opened files. Files that are automatically cached are not guaranteed to be available. When the cache reaches its maximum size, automatically cached files are removed from the local cache on a FIFO basis. Files that are manually cached are not limited by the specified cache size. Manually cached files can occupy up to 2 GB of disk space if it's available on the client computer.

D. **Correct:** As described in answer explanation B, a share must be configured on the server. Caching is automatically enabled and set to Manual Caching For Documents. As described in answer explanation C, the client computer accesses the share and files are either manually or automatically cached. To guarantee that files are available off line, pin the files below the share using the Make Available Offline command on the File menu in the Windows interface.

70-210.04.03.002

▶ **Correct Answers: B**

A. **Incorrect:** Sharing the folder is an important first step. Simply sharing the folder enables caching with a setting of Manual Caching For Documents. When a user selects or opens a file located below a cached share configured for manual caching, the file is not automatically downloaded.

B. **Correct:** After a disk or folder is shared, caching is enabled and set only for manual caching. Clicking the Caching button opens the Caching Settings dialog box. In the Setting drop-down list box, select Automatic Caching For Documents. After a client computer is configured for offline file access to this share or its contents, selecting or opening any file or folder automatically downloads the file. The Automatic Caching For Documents setting will download programs to the cache only when the program is opened.

C. **Incorrect:** Selecting the Automatic Caching For Programs setting in the Cache Settings dialog box downloads programs and their components automatically when the program is selected or opened. This behavior is important so that any components of the program run inside the program are automatically downloaded to the cache as well. This setting is not recommended for program access on computers that are frequently disconnected from the network, such as portable computers. Instead, install programs that must be available off line directly onto the portable computer. Automatic caching for programs works best for programs that are regularly run over a network where share access is intermittent.

D. **Incorrect:** This is the default setting when a share is created. When a user selects or opens a file located below a cached share configured for manual caching, the file is not automatically downloaded.

70-210.04.03.003

▶ **Correct Answers: C and D**

A. **Incorrect:** The Indexing Service runs in the background and creates indexes of the contents and properties of documents on the local computer, on network-accessible shares, and on local Web content if Microsoft Internet Information Services (IIS) is installed. This service does not play a direct role in managing Offline Files or the synchronization process.

B. **Incorrect:** There is no such wizard included with the operating system.

C. **Correct:** If both the cached copy and the network copy of a file are changed, during synchronization, a Resolve File Conflicts dialog box opens. This dialog box contains three radio buttons. The first radio button allows you to save both files with different names. The locally cached copy of the file is renamed by appending the username and a version number to the prefix of the file, and then it is copied to the network. The cached version of the original file is replaced with the network copy of the file. The second radio button allows you to overwrite the network version with the cached version of the file. The third radio button overwrites the cached version with the network version of the file.

D. **Correct:** This is equivalent to the first radio button in the Resolve File Conflicts dialog box. The cached version is renamed and copied to the network. The network copy of the file is not updated but during the synchronization process, it will replace the locally cached version of the file. The Resolve File Conflicts dialog box also includes file version information, the ability to view both versions of the file, and a check box for configuring how all synchronization conflicts will be addressed.

70-210.04.03.004

▶ **Correct Answers: A and D**

A. **Correct:** The default setting for the Offline Files Wizard is to automatically synchronize files on logon and logoff. These settings are initially configured in the wizard. After the wizard completes, clicking Synchronize on the Tools menu opens the Items To Synchronize dialog box. Clicking the Setup button in this dialog box opens the Synchronization Settings dialog box. On the Logon/Logoff tab, both the When I Log On To My Computer and the When I Log Off Of My Computer check boxes are enabled. Automatic synchronization on logon and logoff is *not* the same as automatic file caching. The Offline Files Wizard specifically configures files for manual file caching. Therefore, the files are permanently available on the client computer.

B. **Incorrect:** Configuring synchronization based on how long a computer has been idle is completed in the Synchronization Settings dialog box on the On Idle tab. Select the Offline Files path from the Synchronize The Following Checked Items box, select the Synchronize The Selected Items While My Computer Is Idle check box, and then click Advanced. Clicking the Advanced button opens the Idle Settings dialog box. The default settings are to automatically synchronize the selected items after the computer is idle for 15 minutes. This synchronization is completed every 60 minutes if the computer remains idle. The proposed solution does not include enabling the Synchronize The Selected Items While My Computer Is Idle check box.

C. **Incorrect:** You schedule a synchronization task in the Synchronization Settings dialog box on the Scheduled tab. Clicking the Add button on the Scheduled tab starts the Scheduled Synchronization Wizard. This wizard provides a scheduled task interface. If the client is off line when scheduled synchronization is to occur, a computer appears on the taskbar. Double-clicking the computer shows the Offline Files Status dialog box, which informs you of a failed scheduled synchronization. The synchronization task can be canceled, or, when the computer is reconnected to the network, this synchronization task can be completed. In the proposed solution, no task was scheduled for this synchronization.

D. **Correct:** Another setting in the Idle Settings dialog box is the Prevent Synchronization When My Computer Is Running On Battery Power check box. This check box is enabled by default. However, in the proposed solution, the Synchronize The Selected Items While My Computer Is Idle check box is not selected. Therefore, synchronization will *never* occur when the computer is idle. The fact that the computer is running on battery power when the computer is idle is irrelevant. Synchronization will occur on logon and logoff only. The computer is not idle during these events.

OBJECTIVE 4.4

Optimize and troubleshoot performance of the Windows 2000 Professional desktop.

Determining system performance is accomplished by monitoring how the operating system and applications use hardware resources. Performance is measured in terms of *system throughput*, the amount of work done in a unit of time. A user perceives performance as *response time*, the amount of time required to complete a task. As system throughput degrades in an overused system, the queue length for hardware service such as disk I/O or processor time increases. The user perceives this condition as poor response time. The feedback provided by monitoring throughput and queue length is then used to optimize response time. The system is monitored for an extended period of time when response time is satisfactory. The data collected during this period serves as the baseline for measuring future performance.

How Windows 2000 and applications are using hardware resources is best viewed using the **Performance console**. The Performance console contains the System Monitor ActiveX control (SYSMON.OCX) and the Performance Logs and Alerts snap-in. A summary view of activity is available from Windows **Task Manager**.

Task Manager displays information on applications and their processes currently running on the computer and how the processes are using a processor or processors and memory. You can start Task Manager in a number of ways. One way is to press Ctrl+Shift+Esc. Task Manager contains three tabs: Applications, Processes, and Performance. One important feature available in Task Manager but not available in the Performance console is the ability to forcibly end an application or its processes.

The Performance console (PERFMON.MSC) collects data from *instances*, unique copies of performance objects. *Performance objects* are symbolic representations of hardware resources, applications, protocols, and services. To tie the concept of objects to instances, consider the following example. If Windows 2000 is using two paging files, the Paging File object will show an instance of each paging file and a Total instance representing both paging files. Attributes of performance objects are called *counters* in the Performance console. To continue with the paging file example, the counters of the Paging File object are %Usage and %Usage Peak.

When you open the Performance console, performance counters query the registry for system resource data. Typing **perfmon /wmi** instructs the console to query the Windows Management Instrumentation (WMI) repository instead of the registry to obtain system resource data. The repository is to WMI as the registry is to the operating system.

Data is displayed immediately using the System Monitor node in the Performance console. Data is collected for later viewing by configuring the Counter logs and Trace logs in the Performance Logs and Alerts snap-in. Data is *sampled* using Counter logs and *traced* using, you guessed it, Trace logs. Sampling collects data at fixed intervals, such as every 15 seconds, whereas tracing collects data based on system events, such as processes created or deleted.

Counter logs can be configured to output binary (.blg), comma-delimited (.csv), or tab-delimited (.tsv) file data. All Counter log file types are viewable using System Monitor. Comma-delimited and tab-delimited text files are also viewable using applications that can read them, such as Excel. Two types of binary log files exist: circular and linear. Circular log files create log files until they reach a user-defined size and then a new log file is generated. Linear log files can be limited to a user-defined size or be set to grow to 1 GB or all remaining disk space, whichever comes first.

Trace logs generate binary (.etl) files. System Monitor cannot read these files. A utility such as TRACEDMP.EXE must be used to extract data from Trace logs for viewing in other applications. TRACEDMP.EXE is a utility contained in the Windows 2000 Server and Professional Resource Kits. This utility reads the .etl file and creates a SUMMARY.TXT file and a DUMPFILE.CSV file for review.

The Performance Logs and Alerts snap-in also contains an Alerts node that is used to configure thresholds for system events, such as a disk partition reaching capacity. The thresholds fire triggers. The triggers are configured to perform any function that can run in Windows 2000, such as sending a network message or running a program.

Because System Monitor is an ActiveX control, it is easily displayed in applications that support this object type. For example, System Monitor can be displayed in Internet Explorer or in a Microsoft Office application, such as Microsoft Word. The simplest way to export the OLE Custom eXtension (OCX) is to select a Counter log and on the Action menu, click Save Settings As. The file is then saved as a standard .html file and viewed in Internet Explorer. System Monitor is fully functional whether it is running as part of the Performance console or in another application.

You view data in System Monitor in one of three views: chart, histogram, or report. The chart and histogram views are typically used for analyzing real-time data. The report view is ideal for viewing a summary of data collected in counter logs. You can use all views to see real-time and logged data.

Through logging, obtain a baseline and then continue to monitor the counters that are part of your baseline settings. At minimum, track utilization and throughput counters and those counters that might indicate a resource bottleneck. For instance, to monitor utilization, collect data on Logical Disk\%Free Space, Processor\%Processor Time, Memory\Available Bytes, and Network Segment\%Net Utilization. To monitor throughput, collect data on Network Interface\Packets/sec and PhysicalDisk\Disk Bytes/sec. To monitor bottlenecks, collect data on System\Processor Queue Length, Processor\Interrupts/sec, and LogicalDisk\Avg. Disk Queue Length.

Note Logical disk counters are not enabled by default. At the command line, type **diskperf /yv** and restart the computer.

Hardware, operating system, and application troubleshooting is often necessary to solve performance problems. For example, a network adapter that is failing might overburden the processor with unnecessary interrupt request (IRQ) calls. This activity might manifest itself through unusually high processor use. Task Manager, the System Monitor node, and the Performance Logs and Alerts snap-in are important tools for monitoring and troubleshooting operating system and application performance problems.

This objective covers a lot of ground. Most of the overview provided here explores the utilities used to monitor performance. The questions included with this objective explore configuration changes that help you optimize and troubleshoot a computer running Windows 2000 Professional. The "Further Readings" section for this objective includes Chapters 27–30 in the Windows 2000 Professional Resource Kit, which you should review to supplement your studies of this objective.

Objective 4.4 Questions

70-210.04.04.001

You want to move the paging file to another hard disk on your computer running Windows 2000 Professional. What should you do?

A. In the System Properties dialog box, click the General tab and then click the Change button.

B. In the System Properties dialog box, click the Performance tab and then click the Change button.

C. In the System Properties dialog box, click the Environment tab and then click the Change button.

D. In the System Properties dialog box, click the Advanced tab and then click the Performance Options button.

E. In the System Properties dialog box, click the Advanced tab and then click the Environment Variables button.

F. In the System Properties dialog box, click the Advanced tab and then click the Startup And Recovery button.

70-210.04.04.002

You suspect that the processor is causing a performance bottleneck on your computer running Windows 2000 Professional. What should you do to validate this assumption?

A. Use System Monitor to collect data on Processor\% Processor Time and Processor\Interrupts/sec. Analyze when and for how long these values are low.

B. Use System Monitor to collect data on Processor\% Processor Time and Processor\Interrupts/sec. Analyze when and for how long these values are high.

C. Use System Monitor to collect data on Processor\% Processor Time and System\Processor Queue Length. Analyze when and for how long these values are low.

D. Use System Monitor to collect data on Processor\% Processor Time and System\Processor Queue Length. Analyze when and for how long these values are high.

70-210.04.04.003

You want to improve the performance of the New Technology File System (NTFS) fixed disks on your computer running Windows 2000 Professional. Which options might you consider to improve NTFS performance? (Choose three.)

A. Disable the last access update.

B. Disable creation of long names.

C. Disable creation of short names.

D. Reserve appropriate space for the master file table (MFT).

Objective 4.4 Answers

70-210.04.04.001

► **Correct Answers: D**

A. **Incorrect:** The General tab in the System Properties dialog box contains summary information about the operating system; to whom the product is registered, including the registration ID; and the processor type or types, system compatibility, and amount of installed RAM.

B. **Incorrect:** There is no Performance tab in the System Properties dialog box. The Performance tab is part of Task Manager and provides summary information on processor and memory utilization.

C. **Incorrect:** There is no Environment tab in the System Properties dialog box.

D. **Correct:** Clicking the Advanced tab's Performance Options button opens the Performance Options dialog box. You use this dialog box to optimize response time for foreground (applications) or background (service) operations.

In the Performance Options dialog box, click the Change button and the Virtual Memory dialog box opens. Select a new drive that will host the paging file, and then use the options in the Paging File Size For Selected Drive section to set the paging file's initial size and maximum size. Next select the drive that is currently hosting the paging file and set its initial size and maximum size to 0. After you restart the computer, PAGEFILE.SYS will be created in the new location. You also use the Virtual Memory dialog box to view total paging file size and to set the maximum allowable registry size.

One reason to consider moving the paging file is if monitoring the system suggests that the disk hosting the paging file is overused. Continue to monitor the original disk and the new disk to verify that moving the paging file remedied the problem. If not, excessive disk use on the drive hosting the paging file might suggest that the bottleneck is because of insufficient RAM. Consider increasing the amount of installed RAM. Additionally, check the running processes to verify that there isn't a memory leak or an application that is overusing RAM.

E. **Incorrect:** Clicking the Advanced tab's Environment Variables button opens the Environment Variables dialog box. User and system-level environment variables are added, modified, or deleted from here.

F. **Incorrect:** Clicking the Advanced tab's Startup And Recovery button opens the Startup And Recovery dialog box. You configure system startup and system failure behavior in this dialog box.

Unlike Windows NT, the system failure dump directory can be located anywhere, not just on the boot partition. However, a paging file must be available on the boot partition to initially hold the dump information. Windows 2000 provides three types of system dumps: Small Memory Dump (64 KB), Kernel Memory Dump, and Complete Memory Dump. The Small Memory Dump (64 KB) option requires a paging file on the boot partition that is only 2 MB in size. On the other end of the spectrum, the Complete Memory Dump option requires a paging file equal to the size of physical RAM to hold the entire contents of RAM if a system failure occurs.

70-210.04.04.002

▶ **Correct Answers: D**

A. **Incorrect:** The Processor\%Processor Time value measures the percentage of time that the processor was busy running nonidle threads during the specified time interval. This counter is a primary indicator of processor activity because it measures all process activity except for the System Idle Process. Measuring this counter for its lowest value will not identify a busy processor.

A processor is always running at full speed; however, on a processor that is not overused, most of the processor time is spent running the System Idle Process, which has no base priority, so all other processes run at a higher priority. On a system whose processor is not the bottleneck, open Task Manager and review the CPU and CPU Time columns for this process. You should see that this is the busiest process in the system.

The Processor\Interrupts/sec value measures the average rate at which a processor handles interrupts from attached hardware devices. This counter is an indirect indicator of interrupt-driven device activity, such as disk controllers and network adapters. A failing device might raise an excessive number of interrupts, so monitoring the system for an excessive number of Processor\Interrupts/sec values could indicate a failing device. Measuring this counter for its lowest value will not identify a busy processor.

B. **Incorrect:** Processor\% Processor Time is an important indicator of processor activity, but an excessively high value for Processor\Interrupts/sec might indicate failing hardware. See answer explanation A for details on both of these counters.

C. **Incorrect:** As outlined in answer explanation A, Processor\% Processor Time is an important indicator of processor use. However, analyzing when the value for this counter is low doesn't help to determine when the processor is overused.

System\Processor Queue Length measures the number of threads ready for processing but not running. The Processor Queue Length counter is part of the System object instead of the Processor object because there is a single queue for processor time even on multiprocessor computers. A sustained processor queue of greater than two threads might be an indication of a processor bottleneck. Measuring this counter when it's at its lowest is likely to return a result of 0 unless the processor is always running at 100 percent utilization. This counter displays only the last observed value; it is not an average.

D. **Correct:** As summarized in answer explanation A, Processor\% Processor Time is a useful indicator of an overused processor if the value sustains a high value, perhaps 80 percent or greater. This, combined with a System\Processor Queue Length greater than 2, suggests that the processor is a bottleneck.

70-210.04.04.003

▶ **Correct Answers: A, C, and D**

A. **Correct:** NTFS tags each folder with the last access date and time in an NTFS partition whenever the folder structure is traversed. Traversing large disks with large folder structures is slowed by this date-and-time stamping process. To disable the last access update on NTFS partitions, add the NtfsDisableLastAccessUpdate value name with a REG_DWORD data type and a value of 1 to the HKEY_LOCAL_MACHINE\SYSTEM\CurrentControlSet\Control\FileSystem key.

B. **Incorrect:** Creation of long filenames (LFNs) is automatic and cannot be disabled in NTFS. The file allocation table (FAT) file system can be prevented from creating LFNs by setting the value of the Win31FileSystem registry entry to 1. This entry is located in the HKEY_LOCAL_MACHINE\SYSTEM\CurrentControlSet\Control\FileSystem key. Preventing LFN creation on the FAT file system might be necessary if the computer multiboots a legacy operating system and if disk tools unaware of LFNs are used to manage the FAT partitions. Files that already have both long and short filenames are unaffected by this change. Therefore, legacy disk tools might destroy LFNs on existing files.

C. **Correct:** For compatibility with MS-DOS or Windows 3.*x* applications that are unaware of LFNs, FAT, FAT32, and NTFS generate short filenames in 8.3 format when a file is created. Generating short filenames contributes to file system overhead. To disable the generation of 8.3 filenames on NTFS partitions, change the value of the NtfsDisable8dot3NameCreation registry entry from 0 to 1. This entry is located in the HKEY_LOCAL_MACHINE\SYSTEM\CurrentControlSet\Control\FileSystem key. Files that already have both long and short filenames are unaffected by this change.

D. **Correct:** NTFS uses the MFT as a file index. File properties including location information and entire files, if the files are small, are stored in the MFT. The MFT stores at least one entry for every file on an NTFS partition. As files are added to a partition, the MFT grows. Because the MFT is a file itself, it is susceptible to fragmentation. Excessive fragmentation in files impacts performance. The standard disk defragmenter included with Windows 2000 does not defragment the MFT. Therefore, to avoid fragmentation in the MFT, NTFS reserves space for it. The default space reservation is adequate for relatively small partitions that will not contain many files. To increase contiguous space allocation for larger partitions that will contain many files, add the NtfsMftZoneReservation value name with a REG_DWORD data type and a value of 2, 3, or 4 to the HKEY_LOCAL_MACHINE\SYSTEM\CurrentControlSet\Control\FileSystem key. The larger the value of this registry entry, the more space that is allocated to the MFT.

OBJECTIVE 4.5

Manage hardware profiles.

A **hardware profile** contains configuration information that Windows 2000 Professional checks during the startup process to determine which drivers to load and which services to start. Hardware profiles are particularly important to support portable computers that are used in and out of a docking station.

Hardware profiles are created automatically or manually. Windows 2000 automatically creates two profiles—the Docked Profile and the Undocked Profile—when an operating system basic input/output system (BIOS) query detects a hardware manufacturer's dock ID and serial number. Through Plug and Play enumeration, the operating system automatically selects the correct hardware profile based on whether the portable computer is docked or undocked. Portable computers that are not fully Plug and Play compliant might require manual hardware profile creation.

You create hardware profiles by opening the System Properties dialog box and clicking the Hardware tab. On this tab, click the Hardware Profiles button, and in the Hardware Profiles dialog box, copy the default profile. You also configure how a hardware profile is selected on startup in this dialog box. A copied profile contains the same device and service startup configuration as the original profile. So the next step is to configure the copied profile.

You configure a hardware profile by first starting the computer and selecting the profile to be configured. After Windows 2000 has started, use Device Manager and the Services window to modify the profile's configuration. In Device Manager, access the properties of a device. On the General tab of the device's properties, select the Device Usage drop-down list box to specify whether the device is enabled for all profiles, disabled for the current profile, or disabled for all profiles. In the Services window, access the properties of a service. On the Log On tab, select the hardware profile appearing in the You Can Enable Or Disable This Service For The Hardware Profiles Listed Below check box. Then click Enable or Disable to change the state of the service for the selected profile.

Objective 4.5 Questions

70-210.04.05.001

Your laptop computer running Windows 2000 Professional is not fully Plug and Play compliant, and you want to create new hardware profiles for docked and undocked states. How do you navigate to the dialog box used to create a new profile?

A. Open the Computer Management console, expand the System Tools node, and click the Hardware Profiles node.

B. Open the Computer Management console, expand the Services and Applications node, and click the Hardware Profiles node.

C. Open the System program in Control Panel, click the Hardware tab in the System Properties dialog box, and click the Hardware Profiles button.

D. Open the System program in Control Panel, click the Advanced tab in the System Properties dialog box, and then click the Hardware Profiles button.

70-210.04.05.002

You have a laptop computer that is not fully Plug and Play compliant running Windows 2000 Professional, and you want to modify the hardware profile. What should you do before modifying the hardware profile?

A. No preparation is recommended.

B. Back up the system partition and the registry, and then restart the computer.

C. Make a copy of the default profile, restart the computer, and then select and modify the copied profile.

D. Make a copy of the default profile, restart the computer, and then select and modify the default profile.

70-210.04.05.003

You purchase a new laptop computer running Windows 2000 Professional. You plan to use it in a docking station to connect to a network at your office. All devices and device drivers support Plug and Play, and the computer is ACPI compliant. You want to use two hardware profiles corresponding to docked and undocked states. What should you do?

A. No action is required.

B. Create a new hardware profile for the docked state.

C. Create two new hardware profiles, one for the docked state and one for the undocked state.

D. In the *profile_name* Properties dialog box, select the This Is A Portable Computer option.

Objective 4.5 Answers

70-210.04.05.001

▶ **Correct Answers: C**

A. **Incorrect:** The System Tools node of the Computer Management console does not contain a Hardware Profiles node for creating hardware profiles. Hardware profiles can be modified in the Computer Management console by selecting the Device Manager snap-in located below the System Tools node and accessing the properties of devices appearing in the details pane.

B. **Incorrect:** The Services and Applications node of the Computer Management console does not contain a Hardware Profiles node. Note that Hardware Profiles is not a snap-in, a snap-in extension, or an ActiveX control.

C. **Correct:** The Hardware Profiles button is located on the Hardware tab in the System Properties dialog box. One way to open the System Properties dialog box is from Control Panel's System program. Another way to open the System Properties dialog box is by accessing the properties of the My Computer icon.

D. **Incorrect:** The Advanced tab in the System Properties dialog box contains three buttons: Performance Options, Environment Variables, and Startup And Recovery. If you are not familiar with these buttons, review the answer explanations to the first question in the previous objective.

70-210.04.05.002

▶ **Correct Answers: C**

A. **Incorrect:** Improper profile modification could cause the computer to fail when it is restarted; for example, stopping a critical service or disabling a necessary device driver. If the computer is not fully Plug and Play compliant, it might not be able to recover from this failure. One possible solution is to select Last Known Good Configuration on the Advanced Options menu when the computer is restarted.

B. **Incorrect:** Completing a backup of the system partition and the registry is a good disaster recovery measure. However, this is not an efficient way to prepare for modifying a hardware profile.

C. **Correct:** After copying the existing profile, you must restart the computer before you can modify the new (copied) profile by using Device Manager. If your goal is to modify only services that are enabled or disabled for a particular hardware profile, a restart is not necessary. If the modifications made to the new hardware profile leave the operating system in an unstable state, restart the computer and select the original hardware profile. After Windows 2000 has started using the default profile, navigate to the copied profile and delete it.

D. **Incorrect:** You should not alter the default profile created during the Windows 2000 Professional installation process.

70-210.04.05.003

▶ **Correct Answers: A**

A. **Correct:** Windows 2000 Professional creates a Docked Profile and an Undocked Profile if a portable computer is docking capable, is fully ACPI compliant, and runs only Plug and Play devices and device drivers. You should never manually alter the two hardware profiles on a computer meeting all of these conditions.

B. **Incorrect:** Copying the existing hardware profile and configuring it to load device drivers for the docked state and the devices contained in the docking station is not necessary for the computer described in the question. If the computer is not fully ACPI compliant or it runs legacy non-Plug and Play devices, then creating a separate docked hardware profile might be necessary.

C. **Incorrect:** Both hardware profiles are created on the computer described in the question. Windows 2000 Professional queries the BIOS to find a dock ID and serial number. If it finds this identifier, it automatically creates the docked and undocked hardware profiles.

D. **Incorrect:** The Hardware Profiles dialog box contains a Properties button. Clicking this button displays the *profile_name* Properties dialog box where *profile_name* is the name of the selected profile. This dialog box shows dock ID and serial number information if any is found by querying the BIOS. If the computer does not meet the hardware specifications outlined in the question, you can manually configure the hardware profile to indicate that it is used on a portable computer and to specify the computer's docking state. In addition, the *profile_name* Properties dialog box is used to control whether the profile appears when Windows starts. You should not alter these configuration settings for the computer described in the question.

O B J E C T I V E   4 . 6

Recover systems and user data.

Windows 2000 Professional includes a powerful set of tools and utilities that, in combination, can help you recover a failed system and the user data contained on it. The tools summarized here include **Windows Backup (NTBACKUP.EXE)**, the **Advanced Options menu** (**Safe Mode** and other advanced startup options), and the **Recovery Console**.

Windows Backup backs up data to tape or to disk. The tape can be housed in a single tape drive or be part of a media changer. The Removable Storage Service manages tape backups for Windows Backup. File backups to fixed or removable disks are managed directly by Windows Backup. The target of a compressed file backup can be a local disk or a network-accessible share. Windows Backup supports a number of backup types: Normal (full backup), Incremental, Differential, Copy, and Daily. Normal, Incremental, and Differential backup types are part of a scheduled backup routine. Copy and Daily backup types work independently of a backup schedule. Users with Administrator or Backup Operator-level privileges can back up and restore files.

Windows Backup also provides a **System State** backup option. This option appears in Windows Backup on the Backup tab. A System State backup backs up the Windows 2000 boot files, system files on the boot partition (both in the Program Files folder and the System32 folder), performance counter configuration files, the COM+ Class Registration database, and the registry. Boot files include the system files. By using backup advanced options, it is possible to include all files under Windows File Protection (WFP) control with the System State backup. System State data is typically restored locally. Except for the COM+ Class Registration database, a restore of system state can be redirected to an alternate location. A user with local administrative privileges is necessary to restore system state data.

Note Windows Backup also includes the command on the Tools menu to create an **Emergency Repair Disk (ERD)**.

When a backup runs, files locked by the operating system are backed up. Files locked by other processes and remote registry files are not backed up. Therefore, you must close all applications before a backup runs. Windows Backup also does not back up files when the proper privilege is not granted or when the file is listed on the Exclude Files tab in the Windows Backup Options dialog box. System State data on remote computers cannot be backed up. Instead, create a local backup of System State data and then use a remote backup procedure to back up the System State data located in a share on the remote computer.

The encrypted file attribute is maintained when files are backed up. Therefore, you should also back up the certificates corresponding to the encrypted files. Create a custom console, and add the Certificates snap-in to the console. Select a certificate to save to disk, and click Export on the All Tasks menu. The export procedure starts the Certificate Export Wizard. After the certificate is exported, use Windows Backup to store it on the backup media.

In the event of a system failure, you can use Windows Backup to perform restore procedures. Before deciding to run a restore procedure, you can try other, more efficient ways to recover from system failures. Use the Advanced Options menu to solve startup delays or failures. Some common failures include system instability from a recently installed device driver or application, or an incompatible video display setting.

You open the Advanced Options menu by pressing F8 during startup. Menu commands valid for Windows 2000 Professional include various Safe Modes (with and without networking, and command prompt only). Use the Safe Mode startup commands to resolve device driver, system service, or autostarting application failures. When the computer is started in any Safe Mode, boot logging is automatic. You enable boot logging for a normal startup by clicking Enable Boot Logging on the menu. The Boot log is stored in *%systemroot%* and is named NTBTLOG.TXT. If the file already exists, the next logging procedure appends to the existing file. You resolve incompatible display settings by selecting the Enable VGA Mode command. You can solve system configuration changes that cause the system to fail by selecting the Last Known Good Configuration command. Troubleshooting a system with a kernel debugger starts by choosing Debugging Mode on the menu.

If the procedures available from the Advanced Options menu do not resolve a system error, the Recovery Console might do the trick. The Recovery Console runs a Windows 2000 command interpreter to provide access to the local disk. You start the Recovery Console in one of two ways: either from the Windows 2000 Setup routine or from the local disk. To start it from the setup routine, press R when prompted by the installation routine; this displays the Repair Options screen. From the Repair Options screen, press C to start the Recovery Console.

To install the Recovery Console to the local disk, locate the \i386 folder on the Windows 2000 Professional installation CD-ROM and then type **winnt32 /cmdcons**. Installing the utility to the local disk is a convenient method of starting the Recovery

Console, but if the disk is failing, starting the Recovery Console from the Windows 2000 Setup routine might be the only viable option. When the Recovery Console is started, you are prompted to select the Windows 2000 installation you want to start and to type the administrator password of that installation. The Recovery Console provides limited access to specific folders on the system. Removing the prompt for an Administrator password and gaining unrestricted access to all drives and folders can be accomplished through two policy settings:

- Recovery Console: Allow Administrative Logon

- Recovery Console: Allow Floppy Copy and Access to All Drives and All Folders

After setting the second listed policy, type **set allowallpaths = true** in the Recovery Console to enable full access to all drives and folders, and type **set allowsremovablemedia = true** to allow copying files to removable media, such as disks. The spaces separating the equal sign from the value names and values are required.

Note You modify policy settings using the Local Security Settings console or through the Group Policy snap-in. Creating a custom console with the Group Policy snap-in configured for the local computer appears as the Local Computer Policy node in the console.

All file systems that Windows 2000 supports are accessible by using the Recovery Console. The console includes a number of disk utilities, such as Chkdsk, Diskpart, Fixboot, and Fixmbr; file system utilities like Expand, Md, Rd, and Ren; and miscellaneous utilities like Systemroot, Map, Set, and Listsvc. When at the Recovery Console command prompt, typing **Help** displays a list of all available commands. To learn more about a specific command, type the command's name followed by **/?** or **/help**.

If the *%systemroot%*\Repair\Regback folder is current, use the Recovery Console to recover the registry. After the Recovery Console is started, copy the registry files from the *%systemroot%*\Repair\Regback folder to the *%systemroot%*\System32\Config folder.

Using the Recovery Console is a better way to restore a damaged registry than running an Emergency Repair. This is because the registry files in the *%systemroot%*\Repair folder are from the original installation of Windows 2000 Professional, so any changes to the system after the original installation are lost when you run an Emergency Repair. In contrast, the registry data from the *%systemroot%*\Repair\Regback folder is current if one of two procedures are followed: if a backup of System State data is run, or if the creation of an ERD in Windows Backup included enabling the Also Backup The Registry To The Repair Directory check box. Interestingly, running the ERD creation process with this check box enabled doesn't update the *%systemroot%*\Repair folder as you might expect from its name; instead, it updates the *%systemroot%*\Repair\Regback folder.

Objective 4.6 Questions

70-210.04.06.001

You need to plan a backup strategy for your computer running Windows 2000 Professional. You need to back up data every night. Using Windows Backup, which backup plan should you choose to both minimize the time needed to back up data and restore data?

A. Normal

B. Copy

C. Incremental

D. Differential

E. Normal and Differential

F. Normal and Incremental

70-210.04.06.002

You receive a new computer running Windows 2000 Professional, and you want to have the ability to use the Windows 2000 Recovery Console. What should you do to enable the Recovery Console to be started?

A. No action is required because it is installed by default.

B. Open the System program in Control Panel, click the Advanced tab, click the Startup And Recovery button, and install the Recovery Console.

C. Insert the Windows 2000 Professional installation CD-ROM, and close the Setup dialog box if it appears. At a command prompt, switch to the root folder on the CD-ROM, run SETUP /CMDCONS, and install the Recovery Console.

D. Insert the Windows 2000 Professional installation CD-ROM, and close the Setup dialog box if it appears. At a command prompt, switch to the \i386 folder on the CD-ROM, run WINNT32 /CMDCONS, and install the Recovery Console.

70-210.04.06.003

Which methods can you use to repair a Windows 2000 Professional installation? (Choose two.)

A. Use the Local System Restore mode.

B. Use the Recovery Console.

C. Use the Emergency Repair process.

D. Use the Directory Services Restore mode.

70-210.04.06.004

Your Windows 2000 Professional system fails to start, and you want to try starting in Safe Mode. After restarting the computer, what should you do to start in Safe Mode?

A. Use the Recovery Console.

B. Use the Emergency Repair process.

C. Press F8 during startup when prompted.

D. No action is required because Windows 2000 automatically initiates Safe Mode after system startup has failed.

Objective 4.6 Answers

70-210.04.06.001

▶ **Correct Answers: E**

   A. **Incorrect:** A Normal backup type, typically known as a Full backup, backs up every file regardless of whether it was backed up previously. The archive attribute is cleared from the files using this backup type. It is the operating system's job to place an archive attribute on any new or modified file. A Normal backup takes the most time of any backup type that is part of a schedule and the least time to perform a restore procedure. A restore procedure using this backup type alone requires the most recent Normal backup. Because it is the most time-intensive backup type for performing nightly backups, running this backup type for all scheduled backups does not provide the most efficient backup plan.

   B. **Incorrect:** A Copy backup type is used outside of a regularly scheduled backup routine and backs up all targeted files. This backup type ignores the archive attribute and does not alter it on any targeted files containing the attribute. A restore procedure requires the most recent Copy backup type. The Copy backup type is not part of a backup plan.

   C. **Incorrect:** The Incremental backup type backs up all targeted files containing the archive attribute. This backup type clears the archive attribute on files it backs up. So every time it is run, only new and modified files targeted for backup are backed up. This is the fastest backup type for backing up data and the slowest to restore data. An Incremental backup type is usually combined with a Normal backup type to form a backup plan.

   D. **Incorrect:** The Differential backup type backs up all targeted files containing the archive attribute. This backup type does *not* clear the archive attribute on files it backs up. So every time it is run, all targeted files with the archive attribute are backed up. This is a moderately fast backup type for backing up and restoring data. An Incremental backup type is usually combined with a Normal backup type to form a backup plan.

   E. **Correct:** A daily backup plan that includes a weekly Normal backup type and on all other days, a Differential backup type is the most efficient backup plan for both backup and recovery. The Normal backup type clears the archive attribute when it runs, while the Differential backup type does not. Therefore, if a Normal backup runs on Monday morning, then a Differential backup runs on Tuesday morning. The Differential backup contains only the files that changed between Monday morning and Tuesday morning. The contents of a Differential backup run on Tuesday morning are identical to an Incremental backup, but the next Differential backup will be different. The Differential backup run on Wednesday morning will contain all new and modified files since the last Normal backup on Monday morning. This is because a Differential backup backs up all targeted files containing the archive attribute but does not clear the archive attribute. A full restore procedure requires the most recent Normal backup (Monday morning), followed by the most recent Differential backup (Wednesday morning).

F. **Incorrect:** A daily backup plan that includes a weekly Normal backup type and on all other days, an Incremental backup type, is the most efficient backup plan for backup but not for recovery. Both backup types clear the archive attribute when they run. Therefore, if a Normal backup runs on Monday morning, then an Incremental backup runs on Tuesday morning. The Incremental backup contains only the files that changed between Monday morning and Tuesday morning. The contents of an Incremental backup run on Tuesday morning are identical to a Differential backup, but the next Incremental backup will be different. The Incremental backup run on Wednesday morning will contain all new and modified files since the last Incremental backup on Tuesday morning. This is because each Incremental backup clears the archive attribute during the backup process. This restore process is less efficient than the Normal and Differential backup plan outlined in answer explanation E because a full restore procedure requires the most recent Normal backup (Monday morning), followed by each Incremental backup in sequence (Tuesday morning and then Wednesday morning).

70-210.04.06.002

▶ **Correct Answers: D**

A. **Incorrect:** The Recovery Console is not installed by default. If the Recovery Console is not installed locally, it can still be run from the Windows 2000 Setup routine.

B. **Incorrect:** Clicking the Advanced tab's Startup And Recovery button opens the Startup And Recovery dialog box. System startup and system failure behavior is configured in this dialog box. The Recovery Console is not installed in this dialog box.

C. **Incorrect:** SETUP.EXE located on the root of the Windows 2000 Professional installation CD-ROM opens the Windows Setup dialog box. The program does not contain any switches.

D. **Correct:** Typing **Winnt32 /cmdcons** starts the Setup routine and installs approximately 7 MB of files, primarily drivers. Some of these files are used to start the Windows 2000 command interpreter from the local disk. The files are installed to the system partition (usually C) into a folder named \Cmdcons. The Cmdcons folder is marked with the System, Hidden, and Read Only attributes (SHR). An option to start the Recovery Console is added to BOOT.INI. The Recovery Console path in BOOT.INI points to the BOOTSECT.DAT file contained in the Cmdcons folder.

70-210.04.06.003

▶ **Correct Answers: B and C**

A. **Incorrect:** This is not a valid recovery option.

B. **Correct:** The Recovery Console provides access to the local disk so that recovery commands can be run, such as Fixmbr to repair the Master Boot Record or Disable *servicename*, where *servicename* is the name of a service to disable. The Recovery Console is the preferred method of restoring a damaged registry given that the *%systemroot%*\Repair\Regback folder contains current registry information.

C. **Correct:** You start Emergency Repair by entering the Repair Options console in Text mode of the Windows 2000 Setup routine and pressing R. There are two ways to run Emergency Repair: use Manual Repair or Fast Repair. A Manual Repair allows you to choose which repair procedures should occur; Fast Repair runs all repair procedures. The Emergency Repair process returns the computer to its state when Windows 2000 was first installed. All system changes and updates are lost. System files are replaced with the files on the Windows 2000 Professional installation CD-ROM, and the registry is restored from the Repair folder. In Windows 2000, the registry files are not copied to the ERD as they were in Windows NT. Therefore, the *%systemroot%*\Repair folder is critical to a registry restore when the Emergency Repair is run.

D. **Incorrect:** This command does appear on the Advanced Options menu, but it is valid only for computers running Server editions of Windows 2000 and Microsoft Active Directory directory services.

70-210.04.06.004

▶ **Correct Answers: C**

A. **Incorrect:** The Recovery Console runs the Windows 2000 command interpreter. The console does not run any installation of Windows 2000 on the local computer; it simply makes an installation accessible from the command line.

B. **Incorrect:** You start the Emergency Repair process from the Repair Options screen of the Windows 2000 Setup routine. Safe Mode is not started from the Windows 2000 Setup routine.

C. **Correct:** Pressing F8 when prompted during Windows 2000 startup opens the Advanced Options menu. There are three versions of Safe Mode available on the menu: Safe Mode, Safe Mode With Networking, and Safe Mode With Command Prompt. Safe Mode starts the operating system but loads only critical device drivers and services. Safe Mode With Networking starts the operating system and loads critical device drivers and network services. If network-based group policies are running, they will be applied if you select this version of Safe Mode. Safe Mode With Command Prompt is similar to Safe Mode except that a command prompt serves as the shell instead of the Windows Explorer interface. The Video Graphics Adapter (VGA) driver is loaded so graphical utilities are available from the command-line interface.

D. **Incorrect:** Unlike Windows 95 and Windows 98, Safe Mode is *not* automatically started by Windows 2000 after a failed startup.

Configuring and Troubleshooting the Desktop Environment

Objective Domain 3 examined troubleshooting hardware and the Microsoft Windows 2000 device drivers that support such troubleshooting. Objective Domain 4 examined how to configure Windows 2000 for optimal performance and reliability. This objective explores how to *configure* a Microsoft Windows 2000 Professional desktop to support the user experience and how to *troubleshoot* problems with the desktop environment.

Like hardware profiles, **user profiles** are created to distinguish between different computing environments. They are specifically designed to personalize a user's desktop settings based on a user's account name. Unlike hardware profiles, user profiles can be configured to move between computers on the network. This feature is called *roaming*, and a profile configured in this way is aptly called a **roaming user profile**. You customize a profile by adjusting desktop settings, such as adding a shortcut to the desktop. If a roaming user profile should not be customized by users, it can be converted to a **mandatory user profile**. A mandatory user profile is ideal for sharing among multiple users who use the same desktop settings.

Localization is an important language feature of a personalized desktop environment. Localization includes supporting one or multiple languages in the Windows interface, configuring local settings appropriate to a user, and configuring Windows 2000 Professional to operate in multiple locations.

User-specific requirements extend beyond user profiles and localization. Another critical feature of a personalized desktop is user-specific application availability. For example, a computer user in the Accounting department will need access to accounting software, while a user in the Marketing department will need access to contact management software. Both staff members will need access to standard desktop applications such as Microsoft Office. Working together, network-based **Group Policy** and the Microsoft **Windows Installer Service** make custom application delivery possible. Objective 5.3 focuses specifically on managing applications using the Windows Installer Service and Windows Installer packages.

You personalize Windows 2000 Professional desktops by configuring desktop settings, such as enabling the **Active Desktop**, configuring a screen saver, and redirecting the My Documents folder to the network. These settings are centrally managed through Group Policy. You configure Group Policy locally by using the Local Computer Policy object of the Group Policy snap-in. This snap-in is not part of a default console in Windows 2000 Professional, but it can be made part of a custom console by typing **gpedit.msc** in the Run dialog box. The Group Policy snap-in appears as the Local Computer Policy node in the console. You accomplish central network management of Group Policy by using Active Directory services and a console containing the Group Policy snap-in. From server editions of Windows 2000 configured as domain controllers, Group Policy can be applied at the domain, domain controller, organizational unit (OU), site, or computer level.

Accessibility services are an important part of personalizing a desktop for computer users with special needs, such as high-contrast display settings for users who have difficulty seeing the display and translation of sounds into visual captions for users who have difficulty hearing computer sounds. You configure these settings and many other accessibility options locally from the Accessibility Options program in Control Panel or from the icons contained in the Accessibility program group.

Another important user-configurable service in Windows 2000 Professional is the desktop fax facility. This feature allows you to send and receive fax transmissions on the computer rather than through a fax machine.

Desktop settings, accessibility services, and fax services may require troubleshooting steps to maintain proper operation. A number of important troubleshooting tools are contained in the Windows 2000 Professional Resource Kit. Some of these tools are mentioned in the objective overviews accompanying each objective in this chapter.

Tested Skills and Suggested Practices

The skills you need to successfully master the Configuring and Troubleshooting the Desktop Environment Objective Domain on Exam 70-210: Installing, Configuring, and Administering Microsoft Windows 2000 Professional include the following:

- **Manage user profiles.**

    - Practice 1: Go to the command line, and type **set** to see a list of configured environment variables. First identify the environment variable that points to *%systemdrive%*\Documents and Settings\All Users. Next identify the path defined by the *%userprofiles%* environment variable.

    - Practice 2: Access the contents of the All Users profile and the Local User profile folders.

- Practice 3: Delete a local user account, and then re-create a user account using the same name as the deleted user account. Log on with the new user account. Go to the command line, and determine the profile folder name assigned to the new user. Repeat this procedure at least twice.

- Practice 4: Configure a roaming user profile on a workgroup computer. Then configure a fully functional roaming user profile on Microsoft Windows 2000 Server. Copy a local user profile to the network location designated for the roaming user profile. Configure a domain user account for the roaming user profile, and log on as the domain user.

- Practice 5: Configure both types of mandatory user profiles (NTUSER.MAN) and *profile_folder*.MAN. Log on to domain user accounts configured for each of these mandatory user profiles. Disconnect the workstation from the network, and then attempt to log on again as the domain users configured for the two types of mandatory user profiles. Identify which mandatory user profile allows you to log on with the cached version of the profile.

- Practice 6: Deploy and support language features in Windows 2000 Professional.

- Practice 7: Install an additional language group to provide multilingual viewing and editing. Visit a Web site written in a language supported by the newly installed language group. Print a page of the Web site to verify that printing in the language appearing in your Web browser is possible.

- Practice 8: Using the Microsoft Windows 2000 MultiLanguage Version CD-ROM, install menu and dialog box support for a language contained in the language group you installed in the previous practice. Configure the Menus And Dialogs drop-down list box in the Regional Options dialog box for the newly installed language.

- Practice 9: After installing the Windows 2000 MultiLanguage Version, verify that *%systemroot %*\Muisetup.log was created. If any errors were generated during MultiLanguage Version setup, review the log.

- Practice 10: Verify that installing and running the MultiLanguage Version of Windows 2000 do not change applications that are not part of the operating system installation.

- Practice 11: Configure the various settings available in the Regional Options program in Control Panel, such as adding an input locale and switching between the installed input locales from the status area of the taskbar.

- Practice 12: Create an automated installation of Windows 2000 Professional that installs several language groups. To lessen the effort of creating the answer file, use the Setup Manager Wizard.

- **Automate the process of software installation using the Windows Installer Service.**

  - Practice 1: Run a Windows Installer package (.msi) installation routine. Use the Add/Remove Programs program to modify the installation and to remove it.

  - Practice 2: Customize a Windows Installer package installation routine using a transform (.mst) file. Run the customized installation routine by calling the .mst file in the Windows Installer command line.

  - Practice 3: Use the Software Installation extension (part of the Windows 2000 Server Group Policy snap-in) to assign an .msi file under the User Configuration node, and then log on as a domain user targeted for this assignment. Open the shortcut created by the assignment to install the application. Complete the same procedure with a different .msi package, but this time, assign the .msi package to a Computer Configuration node and verify that after restarting the targeted computer, the application is installed. Finally publish a third .msi package, and verify that it appears in the Add/Remove Programs dialog box by clicking the Add New Programs icon.

  - Practice 4: Configure the Apply Group Policy permission so that the Authenticated Users group does not get an assigned package and another group that you designate does get the package.

- **Customize desktop settings.**

  - Practice 1: Enable Web content on the Active Desktop. Configure the Active Desktop to display an HTML document as a background. Visit the Microsoft Windows Technologies Active Desktop Gallery to add Active Desktop items. To access the gallery, click the Visit Gallery button in the New Active Desktop Item dialog box.

  - Practice 2: Run the Local Computer Policy object of the Group Policy snap-in to view local policy settings. Experiment with the settings contained in the Administrative Templates folder of the User Configuration node. Concentrate on the following folders: Desktop, Desktop\Active Desktop, Start Menu & Task Bar, and Control Panel\Display.

  - Practice 3: Experiment with the Start menu and taskbar configuration by modifying the settings contained in the Taskbar And Start Menu Properties dialog box.

  - Practice 4: Right-click the Start menu to open its context menu, and then click Explore All Users. Repeat this procedure, but this time, click Explore. Compare the contents of the two Windows Explorer windows that appear.

- **Install and use the Windows 2000 Fax Service.**

    - Practice 1: On a computer containing a fax-capable device, verify that the Fax Service and a fax printer are installed.

    - Practice 2: Use the Fax Service Management console to enable both inbound and outbound fax support. Configure the fax device so that received faxes are automatically printed, saved in a folder, and sent to an e-mail profile on the computer.

    - Practice 3: Use the Fax Service Management console to enable the archiving of sent faxes.

    - Practice 4: Open the Fax program, and complete the fields on the User Information tab. Create a new cover page using the Cover Page Editor, available by clicking New on the Cover Page tab.

    - Practice 5: Delete the Fax printer appearing in the Printers window. Then, on the Advanced Options tab in the Fax Properties dialog box, click Add A Fax Printer.

    - Practice 6: After sending and receiving faxes, view the Application log to verify fax activity. Reconfigure logging levels using the Fax Service Management console, and then revisit the Application log to view the changes to fax logging activity.

- **Configure accessibility services.**

    - Practice 1: Log on as a user with Administrative privileges, and then use the Accessibility Wizard to configure accessibility-related administrative options available to a user with Administrative privileges. Complete the same procedure, but log on as a user with User privileges to note the difference in the available settings.

    - Practice 2: Log on as a user with Administrative privileges, and then start Utility Manager to configure startup options for the accessibility tools appearing in Utility Manager.

    - Practice 3: Configure the Magnifier, Narrator, and On-Screen Keyboard.

    - Practice 4: Use the Accessibility Options program to configure the various accessibility features appearing in this interface. Use the General tab of the Accessibility Options dialog box to set administrative options. Compare the administrative options appearing on the General tab to the options you examined by running the Accessibility Wizard as a user with Administrative privileges.

Further Reading

This "Further Reading" section provides lists of important readings to supplement your current understanding of the skills tested within this Objective Domain. The lists are delineated into pertinent readings for each objective within this Objective Domain. If you feel that you need additional preparation prior to taking the exam, study these sources thoroughly.

Objective 5.1

Microsoft Corporation. *Microsoft Windows 2000 Professional Resource Kit*. Redmond, Washington: Microsoft Press, 2000. Read pp. 286–288 in Chapter 7, "Introduction to Configuration Management," and pp. 446–447 in Chapter 10, "Mobile Computing."

Microsoft Corporation. *MCSE Training Kit—Microsoft Windows 2000 Professional*. Redmond, Washington: Microsoft Press, 2000. Read and complete the practices in Lesson 4, Chapter 10, "Setting Up and Managing User Accounts."

Microsoft Corporation. "*Users and Computers*" in *Windows 2000 Server Help*. Redmond, Washington: Microsoft Corporation, 2000. Read the How To section of "User Profiles."

Microsoft Corporation. The *Windows 2000 Server Deployment Planning Guide* volume of the *Microsoft Windows 2000 Server Resource Kit*. Redmond, Washington: Microsoft Press, 2000. Read Chapter 24, "Applying Change and Configuration Management." Visit the Microsoft TechNet site at *http://www.microsoft.com/TechNet/win2000/dguide/chapt-24.asp* to read this chapter. This resource ties together the technologies involved in user configuration management.

Objective 5.2

The Global Software Development Web site. Visit this site at *http://www.microsoft.com/globaldev*. If the site has been moved, search on the Web site title. Review the FAQs and articles about globalization.

Microsoft Corporation. *Microsoft Windows 2000 Professional Resource Kit*. Redmond, Washington: Microsoft Press, 2000. Read pp. 179–181 in Chapter 5, "Customizing and Automating Installation," and pp. 316–322 in Chapter 7, "Introduction to Configuration Management."

Windows 2000 MUI SetupHelp. Review the three topics contained in this online help file. This file (MUISETUP.HLP) is at the root of the Windows 2000 MultiLanguage Version CD-ROM.

Objective 5.3

Microsoft Corporation. *Microsoft Windows 2000 Professional Resource Kit*. Redmond, Washington: Microsoft Press, 2000. Read pp. 188–189 in Chapter 5, "Customizing and Automating Installations," and pp. 446–447 in Chapter 10, "Mobile Computing."

Microsoft Corporation. *The Distributed Systems Guide* volume of the *Microsoft Windows 2000 Server Resource Kit*. Redmond, Washington: Microsoft Press, 2000. Read the "Windows Installer Technology" section.

Microsoft Corporation. "Step-by-Step Guide to Software Installation and Maintenance." You can download this article by searching on its title at *http://www.microsoft.com/windows2000*.

Microsoft Corporation. "Windows Installer." You can download this article by searching on its title at *http://www.microsoft.com/windows2000*.

Objective 5.4

Microsoft Corporation. *Microsoft Windows 2000 Professional Resource Kit*. Redmond, Washington: Microsoft Press, 2000. Read pp. 289–301 in Chapter 7, "Introduction to Configuration and Management," and Chapter 8, "Customizing the Desktop."

Microsoft Corporation. *MCSE Training Kit—Microsoft Windows 2000 Professional*. Redmond, Washington: Microsoft Press, 2000. Read and complete the practices in Lesson 2, Chapter 17, "Configuring Group Policy and Local Security Policy."

Objective 5.5

Microsoft Corporation. *MCSE Training Kit—Microsoft Windows 2000 Professional*. Redmond, Washington: Microsoft Press, 2000. Read and complete the practices in Lesson 4, Chapter 25, "Implementing, Managing, and Troubleshooting Hardware Devices and Drivers."

Microsoft Corporation. *Control Panel in Windows 2000 Help*. Redmond, Washington: Microsoft Corporation, 2000. Read the "Fax" section.

Objective 5.6

The Microsoft Accessibility Web site. Visit this site at *www.microsoft.com/enable*. If the site has been moved, search on the Web site title. Read the introductory sections on "Accessibility" and "Microsoft," and review the step-by-step guides.

Microsoft Corporation. *Microsoft Windows 2000 Professional Resource Kit*. Redmond, Washington: Microsoft Press, 2000. Read Appendix A, "Accessibility for People with Disabilities."

OBJECTIVE 5.1

Configure and manage user profiles.

User profiles make it possible to personalize desktop settings based on the user's account name. Individual desktop settings, such as network connections, the location of the My Documents folder, and the contents of the Quick Launch toolbar are contained in a user profile. There are two types of user profiles: local and roaming. **Local user profiles** are generated in one of two ways: when Windows 2000 Professional is installed and when a user logs on for the first time. The two local user profiles automatically created when Windows 2000 Professional is installed are the **All Users profile** and the **Default User profile.** Each profile is stored below the *%systemdrive%*\Documents and Settings folder with these folder names: All Users and Default User, respectively.

When a user with no user profile below the Documents and Settings folder logs on, a profile folder is automatically generated for the user account by copying the contents of the Default User folder to a folder uniquely named after the user account name. Naming conflicts are resolved by appending the profile's folder name with *.computername* for a workgroup-based logon or *.domainname* for a domain-based logon. If appending the workgroup name or domain name does not resolve to a unique folder name, a three-digit number, such as .000 or .001, is appended to the *.computername* or *.domainname* extension. The environment variable pointing to the folder containing the user's profile is *%userprofile%*. The user's profile and the All Users profile remain in distinct folders, but their settings are merged in the user's desktop environment. The environment variable that points to the All Users folder is *%allusersprofile%*.

You can copy local user profiles to other users of the local computer. Copying and permitting another user to use a profile is configured on the User Profiles tab in the System Properties dialog box. Local user profiles and **roaming user profiles** stored on the local computer also appear on the User Profiles tab. Local user profiles are specific to the computer where they are created.

Roaming user profiles allow a user to move from one computer to another in a network and retain his or her unique desktop settings. To change a local user profile into a domain-based roaming user profile, copy the local user profile to a network location. Then, from the properties of a domain user account, click the Profile tab and set the

Profile Path text box to the network location containing the copied profile. Be sure you share the roaming user profile parent folder and give users the ability to read and write to it. When the user logs on to another computer using his or her domain account name, the profile is accessed from the server and a local copy of the roaming user profile is cached to the local computer. When the user logs off from the computer, any desktop updates are copied to the roaming user profile assigned to the user account. If updates to a roaming user profile are not allowed, the roaming user profile can be configured as a **mandatory user profile**. Mandatory user profiles are ideal when many users share the same profile, such as computers used in a public kiosk or computers in a highly secure environment where custom settings are not allowed.

You can make a profile mandatory in two ways: either rename the NTUSER.DAT file (located in the user's Roaming User Profile folder) to NTUSER.MAN, or rename the profile folder by appending a .man extension to it—for example, setting a user's profile path to a folder named \Restricted.man. The important difference between these two methods of creating a mandatory user profile is that the first method, renaming the file, permits the user to log on with a locally cached version of the profile if the roaming user profile folder is unavailable. In contrast, adding a .man extension to the profile folder does *not* allow the user to log on unless the roaming user profile folder is available. Users of a mandatory user profile can customize their desktops, but the changes are not saved, so the desktop environment is reset for the next time they log on to the network.

Note Contrary to much of the documentation on roaming user profiles, it *is* possible to create a roaming user profile in a workgroup. However, the other features of user configuration management, such as centralized Group Policy and, in particular, folder redirection, are not available in a workgroup-based network.

Two important profile and Group Policy troubleshooting tools contained in the Windows 2000 Professional and Server Resource Kits are the Group Policy Results (GPRESULT.EXE) utility and the Delete Profile (DELPROF.EXE) utility. Typing **gpresult** at the command line displays important information such as which group policies were applied to the computer at logon, where the roaming and local user profiles are contained, and security group membership for the currently logged on user. You use the Delete Profile command-line utility to delete unwanted or unused profiles. Removing unused profiles can be important if available disk space is at a premium.

Objective 5.1 Questions

70-210.05.01.001

You are the administrator of your company's network supporting computers running Windows 2000 Professional and Windows 2000 Server. You want users of Windows 2000 Professional on your network to be able to log on to any computer on the network and have their user settings follow them. What should you do?

A. Configure the Windows 2000 Professional computers to join the domain, and create a local user profile for each user.

B. Configure the Windows 2000 Professional computers to join the domain, and configure a roaming user profile for each user.

C. Configure the Windows 2000 Professional computers to join the workgroup, and create a local user profile for each user.

D. Configure the Windows 2000 Professional computers to join the workgroup, and create a roaming user profile for each user.

70-210.05.01.002

You are the administrator of a local area network (LAN) supporting Windows 2000 Professional computers. You are not currently supporting Certificate Services. Which items can you include in a client's roaming user profile? (Choose two.)

A. Documents

B. Network drives

C. Encrypted files

D. Encrypted folders

70-210.05.01.003

You are the administrator of your company's network supporting computers running Windows 2000 Professional and Windows 2000 Server. You want users of Windows 2000 Professional on your network to be able to log on to any computer on the network and have their user settings follow them. You also want to prevent users from saving changes to their profiles. What should you do?

A. Configure the computers running Windows 2000 Professional to join the workgroup, and create a mandatory user profile for each user.

B. Configure the computers running Windows 2000 Professional to join the workgroup, and create a roaming user profile for each user.

C. Configure the computers running Windows 2000 Professional to join the domain, and create a roaming user profile for each user.

D. Configure the computers running Windows 2000 Professional to join the domain, and configure a mandatory user profile for each user.

70-210.05.01.004

You are the administrator of a small network supporting five client computers running Windows 2000 Professional. Which type of user profile can you use if you want to keep profile administration to a minimum, you want to let users manage their own desktop settings, and you don't want to install an additional computer on the network?

A. Local

B. Mandatory

C. Roaming

D. Roving

Objective 5.1 Answers

70-210.05.01.001

▶ **Correct Answers: B**

A. **Incorrect:** Joining the domain is an important configuration step in a Windows 2000–based network to support user logon from any workstation. However, this is not enough to support the requirement that user settings follow the user from workstation to workstation. The first time a user logs on to a domain, a local user profile is created automatically by copying the contents of the default user profile to a folder named after the user account name. If the folder name isn't unique, it is appended with the domain name in which the computer is a member. If this doesn't resolve to a unique name, then a three-digit number is appended to the folder name as well. For example, the first time the Administrator account from the MICROSOFT domain is used to log on to a workstation, a profile is generated in a folder named Administrator.Microsoft because a local user profile named Administrator already exists. The operating system knows that these two user accounts are different because the security ID (SID) of the local Administrator account and the SID of the Administrator account in the domain are different. The resulting profile is a combination of the folders whose values are contained in the *%userprofile%* and *%allusersprofile%* environment variables. A local user profile applies only to the computer where it is created.

B. **Correct:** After joining the computers to the domain, you configure roaming user profiles for each user through the properties of the user account. Locate the Profile tab in the user's Properties dialog box, and in the Profile Path text box, type in the path to a network share where the user profile will be stored. The path you specify must be a network location to which the user has read and write privileges. Include the environment variable *%username%* at the end of the network path so that a unique folder for the user is created below the network share. For example, create a network share named \\server01\profiles. Then access the user account properties of a user account named MaxN, and in the Profile Path text box, type **\\server01\profiles\%username%**. A folder named MaxN will be created below the network share. The user MaxN will be granted Full Control permission to this folder, and all other user rights, including access by the Administrators group, are removed. If this is undesirable, a member of the Administrators group can take ownership of the folder and reassign privileges, or an easier method is to create the folder manually and assign local permissions to the folder before pointing the user account profile path to the folder. To retain a local user account's desktop settings, copy the local user profile to the network location for the roaming user profile. After the profile is configured, each time MaxN moves from computer to computer, the profile is cached from the server location to the local computer. At logoff, the server profile is updated.

C. **Incorrect:** The first time a user logs on to a workgroup computer, a local user profile is created automatically by copying the contents of the default user profile to a folder named after the user account name. If the folder name isn't unique, it is appended with the computer name. If this doesn't resolve to a unique name, then a three-digit number is appended to the folder name as well. This naming conflict might occur if a local account is deleted and then an account of the same name is re-created. Even though the account names are identical, the SID of each account is different. The resulting profile is a combination of the folders whose values are contained in the *%userprofile%* and *%allusersprofile%* environment variables. A local user profile applies only to the computer where it is created. Furthermore, a user account on a workgroup computer is stored locally and applies only to the computer that contains it.

D. **Incorrect:** A workgroup computer *does* support roaming user profiles. Accessing the properties of a local user account shows the Profile tab and the Profile Path text box for configuring a roaming user profile. The profile path can be a local folder or a network share. A local user profile configured using the Profile Path text box appears as a roaming user profile in the System Properties dialog box on the User Profiles tab. The profile is cached locally in a folder assigned to the *%userprofile%* environment variable. When the user logs off the computer, the locally cached profile is copied to the location designated in the Profile Path text box. A roaming user profile configured on a workgroup computer is not as functional as a domain-based user account and roaming user profile combination because the user account is local to the workgroup computer where it is created. It is possible to set up a user account with the same name and password on another computer in the workgroup and designate the same network share profile path. However, this is not the ideal method of supporting roaming user profiles because of the administrative overhead associated with implementing this solution.

70-210.05.01.002

► **Correct Answers: A and B**

A. **Correct:** The contents of the My Documents folder are stored locally in a user's cached profile unless the target path of My Documents is changed to an alternate location. Applications such as Microsoft Word will use the target path designated by My Documents as the location to open and store files. When the user logs off a computer, the contents of My Documents in the local cache update the contents of My Documents in the network share containing the roaming user profile. The Folder Redirection Group Policy setting for domain user accounts allows for the separation of user data from the roaming user profile.

B. **Correct:** Any network connections made by a user of a computer configured for a roaming user profile are saved to the network share containing the roaming user profile unless the user is configured to use a mandatory user profile.

C. **Incorrect:** By default, encrypted files and folders cannot be included in a roaming user profile. To store encrypted files in a roaming user profile, you must use Certificate Services to store the keys necessary to decrypt the files or directories in the profile. After the keys are available in the profile, it is possible to store the encrypted files and folders. Alternatively, you can redirect encrypted files using Group Policy.

D. **Incorrect:** Like encrypted files, encrypted folders cannot be included in a roaming user profile without additional configuration. To store encrypted files in a roaming user profile, you must use Certificate Services to store the keys necessary to decrypt the files or directories in the profile. After the keys are available in the profile, it is possible to store the encrypted files and folders. Alternatively, you can redirect encrypted files using Group Policy.

70-210.05.01.003

► **Correct Answers: D**

A. **Incorrect:** The user accounts on a computer in a workgroup are local to the computer. Therefore, roaming user profiles, mandatory or otherwise, are difficult to support because an account on each computer in the workgroup that a user can log on to would need to be created to support the profile. In addition, each user account would need to be able to access the network share containing the mandatory roaming profile.

B. **Incorrect:** The user accounts on a computer in a workgroup are local to the computer. Local computer accounts are an administrative burden for profile management because an account on each computer in the workgroup that a user can log on to would need to be created to support the profile. In addition, each user account would need to be able to access the network share containing the roaming profile. Additionally, using roaming user profiles that are not mandatory does not prevent users from saving desktop settings to their profile when they log off.

C. **Incorrect:** Domain user accounts are required to ease administration of roaming user profiles. In the properties of the domain user account, specify a profile path using the following syntax: *computer_name**share_name*\%*username*%, where *computer_name**share_name* specifies the Universal Naming Convention (UNC) path to the parent folder for user profiles. The %*username*% variable resolves to the user's logon name. If a subfolder named after the user does not exist below the profile parent folder, the folder is created and the user account is assigned the Full Control permission to the folder. Using roaming user profiles that are not mandatory does not prevent users from saving desktop settings to their profiles when they log off.

D. **Correct:** After following the steps just outlined, there are two methods to configure a profile to be mandatory. The first method is to rename the NTUSER.DAT file to NTUSER.MAN. NTUSER.DAT is automatically created in the parent profile folder. For example, if you create a profile folder named Restricted, rename the NTUSER.DAT in that folder to NTUSER.MAN. The next time a user whose profile path points to this folder logs off, his or her locally cached version of the profile will be labeled Mandatory. You can confirm this by opening the My Computer Properties dialog box and then clicking the User Profiles tab. The locally cached profile will display Mandatory in the Type column.

70-210.05.01.004

▶ **Correct Answers: A**

A. **Correct:** When a user logs on for the first time, the default user profile is copied to a profile folder named after the user. Folder naming conflicts are resolved as explained in the objective overview. The desktop settings that appear are a combination of the Local User profile and the All Users profile. This is ideal for a small network where roaming user profiles are not necessary. This keeps profile administration to a minimum because profiles are created automatically.

B. **Incorrect:** A mandatory user profile is a roaming user profile set to mandatory by renaming NTUSER.DAT to NTUSER.MAN or by appending a roaming user profile folder below a profile share with a .man extension. Pointing the user's profile path to a mandatory user profile on one of the computers in the workgroup will work, but as a result, the users will not be able to customize their desktops.

C. **Incorrect:** It is possible to configure roaming user profiles in a workgroup, but this does not reduce administrative overhead. In addition, the question states that you do not want to install an additional computer on the network. Therefore, setting up domain-based roaming user profiles is not an option.

D. **Incorrect:** The word *roving* is sometimes used to describe a user's movement from computer to computer in a routed network. Roving is not used to describe profiles.

OBJECTIVE 5.2

Configure support for multiple languages or multiple locations.

Three different versions of Windows 2000 Professional exist: the **English Version**, the **Translated Version**, and the **MultiLanguage Version**. Each version provides varying levels of **multilanguage support**. The English Version allows the user to edit, view, and print information in more than 60 languages. This feature is called **Multilingual Editing and Viewing**. The Translated Version provides the same support as the English Version, and it includes a language-specific user interface for menus, help files, dialog boxes, and file system components. The MultiLanguage Version provides the same language support as the other two versions, and it allows the user to switch the user interface language, hence the name *multilanguage*. Selecting the appropriate version depends on the level of required language support. The English Version is sufficient for infrequent electronic communication in a non-English language. The Translated Version is appropriate when full language support is needed for a small number of languages throughout an organization. Each edition of the Translated Version user interface is language specific. The MultiLanguage Version is ideal when full language support is needed for many languages throughout an organization. Using the MultiLanguage Version eases administration because a single version of Windows 2000 Professional is deployed throughout the network using the Multilanguage Pack, and users or administrators are able to switch the user interface language as necessary.

Multilingual editing, viewing, and printing settings for all versions of Windows 2000 are configured in the Regional Options dialog box, which you open by double-clicking the Regional Options program in Control Panel. In this dialog box, you can do the following:

- Configure locale information using predefined language schemes, such as English (United States) or Dutch (Belgium). You can also define custom settings for the defined language schemes.

  This applies to the current user and affects date, time, and currency formatting.

- Set up system language settings to support viewing and editing documents in other languages.

This applies to the computer. Any check box enabled in the Language Settings For The System box requires the corresponding language groups to be installed. For example, if the computer will read documents in Korean, Spanish, and English, the Korean check box and the Western Europe And United States check box must be enabled. The Western Europe And United States language group includes support for Spanish, English, and other languages, such as German.

- Modify input locales to change keyboard layouts, such as Dvorak right-handed or left-handed keyboard layouts.

If the MultiLanguage Version of Windows 2000 is installed, a Menus And Dialogs drop-down list box appears on the General tab in the Regional Options dialog box. Use this drop-down list box to select any installed language. The language can apply to all users logging on to the computer or just to the user installing the language version files. After restarting the computer, the majority of Windows 2000 menu, dialog box, and help file text appears in the selected language. This does not change the language appearing in applications and help files not bundled with the operating system, some icons on the desktop, and folder names. For example, the English Version Windows 2000 Resource Kit help files appear in English.

Objective 5.2 Questions

70-210.05.02.001

Users in your company need multiple-language support. A user wants to create documents in Windows Notepad: some in English and some in Greek. What should you do at the user's computer running Windows 2000 Professional?

A. In Notepad, select the Greek version.

B. Install the Greek localized version of Windows 2000 Professional.

C. Close Notepad. Use the Regional Options program in Control Panel to enable support for Greek language system settings. After the language support files are installed, restart Notepad.

D. Use the Regional Options program in Control Panel to enable support for Greek language system settings. After the language support files are installed, restart the computer and then restart Notepad.

70-210.05.02.002

You want to perform an unattended upgrade of Microsoft Windows NT 4 Workstation to the English Version of Windows 2000 Professional. You use the Windows 2000 Setup Manager Wizard to create an answer file named UNATTEND.TXT at the root of the C drive. You also use the wizard to configure the [RegionalSettings] section of your answer file to specify the locale settings as English and include the Korean language group and the Japanese language group. In the [Unattended] section of the answer file, you specify NTUpgrade=yes and set UnattendMode=Fullunattended. In the [UserData] section, you have included the ProductID if one was supplied with your copy of the Windows 2000 Professional installation CD-ROM. All other installation settings necessary to automate the installation, such as OemSkipEula=Yes, are specified in the appropriate sections of the answer file. When you run the Windows 2000 setup routine, you include the /unattend switch and the path to the answer file. Which other command-line settings must be specified to make sure that the proper files are copied and that the installation does not pause for user input? (Choose two.)

A. Specify /rx:lang\kor in your WINNT32.EXE command.

B. Specify /copysource:lang\kor /copysource:lang\jpn in your WINNT32.EXE command.

C. Set OEMSkipRegional = 1 in the [GuiUnattended] section of the answer file.

D. Specify /s:*install_source*, where *install_source* is the location of the Windows 2000 Professional distribution files.

70-210.05.02.003

You are preparing to install the Windows 2000 Professional MultiLanguage Version on a new Pentium III computer. You want to specify the language applied to all new user accounts created on the computer. Which tool should you use?

A. CACHEMOV.EXE

B. GPRESULT.EXE

C. MUISETUP.EXE

D. SECEDIT.EXE

Objective 5.2 Answers

70-210.05.02.001

▶ **Correct Answers: D**

A. **Incorrect:** You use Windows applications, including Notepad, to view, edit, and print documents in multiple languages provided the proper language groups are installed on the system. Toggling between languages is not an available setting in Notepad.

B. **Incorrect:** Localized versions of the operating system are available, but this is an inefficient and expensive way to gain multilanguage support for viewing, editing, and printing documents in other languages. The localized version provides multilingual editing, viewing, and printing capability and additional support for interface-specific language changes.

If your goal is to provide a *fully* localized version of Windows 2000, you should use the localized version of Windows 2000 rather then the MultiLanguage Version. When the MultiLanguage Version is configured for a language, it will look and behave similarly to the localized version, with some exceptions. All 16-bit code, bitmaps, registry keys, values, folders, and filenames are not localized.

C. **Incorrect:** All versions of Windows 2000 provide multilingual editing, viewing, and printing capability, but the proper language group must be installed to support this capability. The Western Europe and United States language group, installed by default in the English language version of Windows 2000, supports English and other languages, such as Spanish. The Greek language group must be installed to support Greek language system settings. The language group installation requires files from the Windows 2000 Professional installation CD-ROM unless you installed the distribution files elsewhere. After the installation of a new language group, you are prompted to restart the computer.

D. **Correct:** After the installation of a new language group, you are prompted to restart the computer. After the language group is installed, you can view, edit, and print the document in its native language.

70-210.05.02.002

▶ **Correct Answers: B and D**

A. **Incorrect:** The /rx switch is valid for 16-bit Windows 2000 Professional Setup (WINNT.EXE). Typing **winnt /rx:lang\kor** from the Windows 2000 Professional installation CD-ROM on a computer running a 16-bit operating system will copy the Korean language group files that are located in the \I386\Lang\Kor folder. This is not a valid 32-bit Windows 2000 Professional Setup switch.

B. **Correct:** The /copysource switch is valid for 32-bit Windows 2000 Professional Setup (WINNT32.EXE). The Korean language group files will be copied from the \Lang\Kor folder, and the Japanese language group files will be copied from the \Lang\Jpn folder.

C. **Incorrect:** This answer file setting allows unattended Setup to skip the Regional Settings page in GUI mode Setup and Mini-Setup. The question states that regional settings were specified using the Setup Manager Wizard and that all settings necessary to fully automate the installation were included in the answer file.

D. **Correct:** The /s:*install_source* source switch and parameter is required so that the Windows 2000 Professional setup routine does not prompt you for the location of the installation files. If the installation is run from the Windows 2000 Professional installation CD-ROM and the drive containing the CD-ROM appears as D in Windows NT Workstation, the switch is /s:d:\i386.

Combined with the information provided in the question, in this answer explanation, and in the previous answer explanation, the command you would type to fully automate the installation is **d:\i386\winnt32 /s:d:\i386 /unattend:c:\unattend.txt /copysource:lang\jpn /copysource:lang\kor**.

70-210.05.02.003

▶ **Correct Answers: C**

A. **Incorrect:** The Cache Move utility (CACHEMOV.EXE) allows for the relocation of the Offline Files cache to a different volume. By default, the cache is created on the boot partition (*%systemdrive%*). If disk capacity is at a premium on the boot partition, use Cache Move to relocate the cache to a different volume, thus providing additional capacity for the Offline Files cache.

B. **Incorrect:** The application of Group Policy and other settings, such as group membership, are displayed by the Group Policy Results tool (GPRESULT.EXE). This tool is included in the Windows 2000 Professional and Server Resource Kits. Typing **gpresult** at the command line displays information relevant to troubleshooting the application of Group Policy, such as which group policies were applied to the computer at logon, where the roaming and local user profiles are contained, and security group membership for the currently logged on user. This tool is not used to specify language settings.

C. **Correct:** The Windows 2000 MultiLanguage Version Setup utility (MUISETUP.EXE) installs language setting files onto versions of Windows 2000 supporting a MultiLanguage Version upgrade. The MultiLanguage Version Setup utility runs in the user interface or at the command line. Running the utility in the user interface displays the Multilanguage File Installation dialog box. In the main area of this dialog box, you enable or disable language settings for menus and dialogs. From the drop-down list box also appearing in this dialog box, you select the default language settings for menus and dialogs to be used for all existing users and any new users added to the system. If the language group necessary to support a language setting is not installed, MultiLanguage Version Setup will attempt to install the required language group. If Windows 2000 Professional was installed from CD-ROM, MUISETUP.EXE will prompt you to insert the Windows 2000 Professional installation CD-ROM to install the language group. After the language group is installed, MultiLanguage Version Setup continues to install the files necessary to support language settings. If a required language group was not installed prior to running MUISETUP.EXE, a reboot will be necessary to complete the language group installation.

MultiLanguage Version Setup runs from the command line to support automated installation. For example, assuming that MUISETUP.EXE is located at the root of the D drive, typing the following command, **d:\muisetup.exe /i 040c 0413 /d 0413 /r /s**, will install two language settings, set a default language, and complete the command without user involvement. The /i switch installs the languages corresponding to the specified language IDs, /d sets the default language, /r suppresses the reboot message, and /s suppresses the installation complete message. In the example, 040c corresponds to French and 0413 corresponds to Dutch. The languages and their corresponding language IDs are listed in the help file accompanying MUISETUP.EXE. The installation process and any errors encountered during MultiLanguage Version Setup are recorded in *%systemroot%*\Muisetup.log.

D. **Incorrect:** The SECEDIT.EXE command-line utility creates and applies security templates and analyzes system security. It is typically used on a network where security must be analyzed, applied automatically, or both. It is useful for deploying a consistent security policy to all computers on a network.

OBJECTIVE 5.3

Manage applications by using Windows Installer packages.

To improve the reliability and availability of applications and their installation routines, Windows 2000 Professional includes the **Windows Installer Service**. This service provides a framework within the operating system for installing and maintaining applications. Features and components of an application managed by the Windows Installer Service can be installed when the installation routine is run or when a feature or component not installed is called by the user. Windows Installer features and components can also be configured to run from the CD-ROM or to never be installed with the application. Damaged applications are automatically repaired by the Windows Installer Service, and application removal is standardized through the Add/Remove Programs dialog box. To use the Windows Installer Service, an application installation must be *packaged* into an .msi file.

Note Windows Installer packages are created by software manufacturers such as Microsoft. Custom applications are packaged using third-party installation packaging tools. The Windows 2000 Server and Professional installation CD-ROMs include the .msi packaging console by Veritas Software, WinInstall LE. The installation routine for this console is contained in the \Valueadd\3rdparty\Mgmt\Winstle folder.

Each Windows Installer .msi file is a self-contained database called a *package* that is read by the Windows Installer Service to install entire applications, application features, and application components. A *feature* is part of an application; for example, Microsoft Excel for Windows is part of the Microsoft Office suite. A *component* is part of a feature; for example, EXCEL.EXE is a component of Microsoft Excel for Windows. The application's product files are compressed into cabinet (.cab) files and stored in the same folder with the .msi or in subfolders below the package. Instructions in a Windows Installer package include the features or components to install or remove. Installation includes everything required for proper operation, such as adding registry entries, configuring shortcuts, adding program groups, and installing .dll and .exe files. Some Windows Installer packages, such as Microsoft Office 2000, can be customized using transform (.mst) files and Setup settings (.ini) files. There might be a number of additional command-line parameters included with the package. Read the documentation accompanying an .msi package to determine which command-line parameters the package supports.

Objective 5.3 Questions

70-210.05.03.001

You want to use Windows Installer to deploy software applications on computers running Windows 2000. The software should appear as though it has been installed, but it should not actually be installed until users attempt to run the application. You also want to ensure that only authorized users can run the application. How should you configure the package? (Choose two.)

A. Assign the application to the users.

B. Publish the application to the users.

C. Set the Deny check box on the Apply Group Policy permission for the Authenticated Users group. Next add a group containing members and grant the group Allow for the Apply Group Policy permission.

D. Clear the Allow check box on the Assign Group Policy permission for the Authenticated Users group. Next add a group containing members, and grant the group Allow for the Apply Group Policy permission.

70-210.05.03.002

You are the administrator for a network supporting Windows 2000 Active Directory services. You want to use Windows Installer to deploy a software application on computers running Windows 2000 Professional while achieving these desired results:

- The software should appear as though it has been installed, but it should not actually be installed until users attempt to run the application.

- The application should always be available to roaming users who log on to several different computers in a typical workday.

- If the software is deleted for any reason, it should be reinstalled at logon.

- Only authorized users should be allowed to run the application.

Your proposed solution is to assign the software package to the users in the appropriate OU.

Which results does the proposed solution provide? (Choose three.)

A. The software appears to be installed, but it is not actually installed until users attempt to run the application.

B. The application is always available to roaming users who log on to several different computers in a typical workday.

C. If the software is deleted on a user's computer, it will be reinstalled at logon.

D. Only authorized users can run the application.

70-210.05.03.003

You are the administrator for a network supporting Windows 2000 Active Directory services. You want to use the Windows Installer Service to deploy software applications on computers running Windows 2000 Professional. You do not want the applications to be advertised. What should you do?

A. Assign applications to users.

B. Assign applications to computers.

C. Publish applications to users.

D. Publish applications to computers.

Objective 5.3 Answers

70-210.05.03.001

▶ **Correct Answers: A and D**

A. **Correct:** Using the Software Installation extension (part of the Windows 2000 Server Group Policy snap-in), Windows Installer (.msi) files are assigned or published to a user or assigned to a computer. Assigning an application using the extension under the User Configuration Group Policy node advertises the application to all applicable users at their next logon to a computer running Windows 2000. The assignment is available from any Windows 2000 Professional computer where the users can log on. The assigned application is installed the first time the user attempts to run it by either selecting the application on the Start menu or activating a document associated with the application.

Alternatively, assigning an application using the Software Installation extension under the Computer Configuration Group Policy node causes the installation to be performed automatically, and it usually occurs soon after the computer finishes its startup process. If installation begins after startup, the logon process is delayed until the installation completes.

B. **Incorrect:** Publishing an application using the Software Installation extension under the User Configuration Group Policy node makes the application available for installation. To install a published application, targeted users can click the published application in the Add/Remove Programs program or attempt to open a file associated with the application. Published applications appear in the Add/Remove Programs dialog box by clicking the Add New Programs icon. Publishing an application to users does not install the application or create a desktop shortcut on computers where the targeted users log on.

C. **Incorrect:** The Apply Group Policy permission is an access control entry (ACE) placed on the Group Policy object (GPO). For example, a GPO created for an organizational unit (OU) contains the Apply Group Policy permission. By default, the Authenticated Users special group is assigned Allow for the Apply Group Policy permission. The result of this setting is that all group policies set on a container, such as an OU, pertain to all user objects within the container. User objects are made members of the Authenticated Users group when they successfully log on to the Microsoft Active Directory domain. Setting Deny on the Apply Group Policy permission explicitly disables the application of the container's Group Policy settings. Group members or individual users authorized to run the assigned application won't be able to run the application because of the explicit denial.

D. **Correct:** Clearing the Allow check box does not explicitly grant or deny members of the Authenticated Users group the ability to apply Group Policy settings; therefore, membership in the Authenticated Users group will have no effect on allowing or denying Group Policy settings. Group members or individual users assigned Allow for the Apply Group Policy permission will be authorized to run the assigned application.

70-210.05.03.002

▶ **Correct Answers: A, B, and C**

A. **Correct:** Assigning an application package (.msi) file using the Software Installation extension under the User Configuration Group Policy node advertises the application to all applicable users at their next logon to a computer running Windows 2000. The assigned application is installed the first time the user attempts to run it either by selecting the application on the Start menu or by activating a document associated with the application.

B. **Correct:** The assignment is available from any Windows 2000 Professional computer where the users can log on. By default, a GPO created or linked to an OU applies to all applicable objects within the OU.

C. **Correct:** This is a feature of the Windows Installer Service. This service automatically repairs a damaged or deleted application in much the same way that an assigned application is installed. When an assigned application that is not installed calls the Windows Installer Service to resolve a path, the service installs the package's components. A component is a collection of files, registry keys, and other resources that are all installed or uninstalled together. If the component was previously installed, the Windows Installer Service determines whether it is damaged by verifying the existence of the component's *keypath*. A keypath is a resource within a component, such as a program file or registry value. If a keypath is missing, a repair is performed automatically. Therefore, if a user deletes an application that is assigned, it will be automatically reinstalled at logon.

D. **Incorrect:** Because the Apply Group Policy permission is granted to all authenticated users, the assigned application is available to all users within the OU. To restrict the application to authorized users, clear the Allow check box on the Assign Group Policy permission for the Authenticated Users group. Next add a group containing members who are authorized to run the application, and grant the group Allow for the Apply Group Policy permission. Group members must also be assigned the Read permission to the distribution point containing the package files.

70-210.05.03.003

▶ **Correct Answers: C**

A. **Incorrect:** Assigning an application to users advertises the Windows Installer package to them at their next logon to a computer running Windows 2000.

B. **Incorrect:** Assigning an application to a computer causes the installation to be performed automatically and usually soon after the computer finishes its startup process. If installation begins after startup, the logon process is delayed until the installation completes.

C. **Correct:** Publishing an application to users makes the Windows Installer package available for installation. To install a published application, targeted users can click the published application in the Add/Remove Programs program or attempt to open a file associated with the application. Published applications appear in the Add/Remove Programs dialog box by clicking the Add New Programs icon. Publishing an application to users does not advertise the Windows Installer package because the application is not installed and a shortcut is not created on computers where the targeted users log on.

D. **Incorrect:** Applications cannot be published to computers, only assigned. Assigning an application to a computer causes the installation to be performed automatically.

O B J E C T I V E   5 . 4

Configure and troubleshoot desktop settings.

Configuring desktop settings allows you to customize most user interface elements, such as the Start menu, taskbar, toolbars, desktop shortcuts, the desktop background, and Active Desktop items. Earlier objectives explored some desktop and feature customizations, such as adding printers to the Printers window, creating scheduled tasks, configuring Offline Files, and adjusting display settings. This objective focuses on less essential desktop customizations that help increase productivity.

Two common methods exist for configuring desktop settings: through the various user interface components supporting the desktop or through Group Policy. For example, the Active Desktop is enabled or disabled in the General tab in the Folder Options dialog box or in the Group Policy snap-in from the \User Configuration\Administrative Templates\Desktop\Active Desktop container. Group Policy serves largely to enforce desktop settings. The Group Policy snap-in categorizes configuration options on a per-user or per-computer basis. All desktop settings specific to a user are written below the HKEY_CURRENT_USER registry key; all desktop settings specific to a computer are written below the HKEY_LOCAL_MACHINE key. In the Group Policy snap-in, the majority of desktop policy settings are located under the \User Configuration\Administrative Templates folder, specifically the Start Menu & Taskbar, Desktop, Desktop\Active Desktop, and Control Panel\Display Group Policy folders. For example, use the Control Panel\Display Group Policy folder to disable the Display program in Control Panel or set password protection on the screen saver.

Tip To use a custom shell instead of EXPLORER.EXE, copy the new shell to an accessible location. Then, from the \User Configuration\Administrative Templates\System Group Policy folder, specify the shell filename in the Custom User Interface Group Policy setting.

The desktop settings of a computer *not* on a Windows 2000 network running Active Directory services are enforced using the Local Computer Policy node of the Group Policy snap-in, or using the System Policy Editor (POLEDIT.EXE). The System Policy Editor is included with Windows 2000 Server, primarily for Windows NT 4, Windows 95, and Windows 98–style policy configuration. Desktop settings of Windows 2000 computers on a Windows 2000 network running Active Directory services are centrally controlled by network-based Group Policy. To avoid policy conflicts, it is best *not* to enable Windows NT 4 System Policy and use only Windows 2000 Group Policy specifically for computers running Windows 2000.

The Windows 2000 Active Desktop is an important part of desktop customization. This feature displays Web components, such as Web pages or Microsoft ActiveX controls, on the desktop. Active Desktop is enabled in a number of ways. One way is to open the Folder Options dialog box and select the Enable Web Content On My Desktop option button. Standard Hypertext Markup Language (HTML) is displayed as the Active Desktop *background* from the Display Properties dialog box in the Background tab. Active Desktop *items*, such as a .jpeg image file or a Uniform Resource Locator (URL), are added to the desktop in the Display Properties dialog box in the Web tab. When a local file is added as a desktop item, such as a Web page or a .gif file, it is static content. When a URL is added as an item to the Active Desktop, the Offline Files feature is used to provide dynamic content from the URL. Offline File synchronization settings allow for offline content update on demand or on a schedule. Web content is made available off line, updated, browsed, and locked down in the Display Properties dialog box in the Web tab or directly from the Active Desktop context menu. Active Desktop settings are enforced using the settings contained in the Desktop\Active Desktop Group Policy container.

The \User Configuration\Administrative Templates\Desktop Group Policy folder contains settings to remove, hide, or show some of the default icons that appear on the desktop and on the Start menu, such as My Computer, My Network Places, and Microsoft Internet Explorer. Prohibiting modifications to some critical desktop settings are configured from the Desktop Group Policy folder, such as prohibiting users from changing the My Documents path. This is an especially important setting if the target folder location for My Documents is redirected to a network share. Another important setting available from this Group Policy folder is the ability to prevent saving taskbar and window repositioning when a user logs off. This is useful in maintaining a consistent desktop for multiple users who share the same logon ID.

The Start and Programs menus are important launching points for modifying system and desktop settings and running applications. Properties of the menu are configured from the Taskbar And Start Menu Properties dialog box. This dialog box is available from the Taskbar And Menu item on the Settings menu. Some of the Start menu properties configured from here include enabling or disabling the Personalized Menus feature, adding or removing shortcuts from the Start menu, viewing the contents of the Start menu from Windows Explorer, re-sorting the menu's contents, and choosing menu settings, such as displaying the Administrative Tools group under the Start menu's Programs group. Some taskbar-specific settings include enabling and disabling the appearance of the clock in the status area and autohiding the taskbar.

The Programs menu, which you access from the Start menu, contains menu groups and icons created from two user profiles, the All Users profile and the currently logged on user's profile. Either profile's menu is conveniently opened for editing from the context menu of the Programs group.

The taskbar consists of toolbars, running tasks, and the status area. Windows 2000 Professional includes the Quick Launch, Address, Desktop, and Links toolbars. These default toolbars are selected for viewing from the Toolbars option located on the taskbar's context menu. You can also create new toolbars from the New Toolbar option. A new toolbar consists of a folder's contents or a URL. A toolbar can float on the desktop or be part of the taskbar. Start menu and taskbar settings are enforced using policy settings in the Start Menu & Taskbar Group Policy container.

When you *troubleshoot* desktop settings, start by checking which Group Policy objects (GPOs) are being applied to the user's desktop. Group Policy registry application and other settings, such as group membership, are displayed by the Group Policy Results tool (GPRESULT.EXE). This tool is included in the Windows 2000 Professional and Server Resource Kits. Both Resource Kits include the Group Policy reference. This reference and the explanations of each Group Policy included in the Group Policy snap-in will help you understand the implications of specific Group Policy settings. Common desktop errors are often related to new features, such as personalized menus and Active Desktop settings. Enable or disable these features as necessary to resolve errors associated with them.

Objective 5.4 Questions

70-210.05.04.001

You are the administrator of a local area network (LAN) supporting computers running Windows 2000. A user calls and reports that he selected a .bmp file for the background wallpaper on his Windows 2000 Professional computer before choosing to use Active Desktop wallpaper. The Active Desktop runs in the foreground, covering up the system wallpaper. When he presses Ctrl+Alt+Delete, Active Desktop is disabled and his .bmp file appears.

What is the most likely cause of this behavior?

A. The registry is corrupt.

B. This behavior is normal.

C. A conflicting user profile exists.

D. A conflicting GPO exists.

70-210.05.04.002

You are the administrator of a LAN supporting computers running Windows 2000 Professional. You want to configure the network so users retain their desktop settings when they log on to other Windows 2000 computers on the network, and you want them to access their documents from a network location. This must be accomplished without compromising mobile user network and data access over a slow-bandwidth connection. What should you do? (Choose two.)

A. Configure local user profiles.

B. Configure roaming user profiles.

C. Use Group Policy to redirect personal folders to a network server.

D. Use the Indexing Service to redirect personal folders to a network server.

70-210.05.04.003

You are the administrator for a LAN supporting new computers running Windows 2000 Professional. You want to prevent users from seeing local drives in My Computer. What should you do?

A. Disable the local drives in the basic input/output system (BIOS).

B. In CONFIG.SYS, specify LASTDRIVE=A.

C. Use Windows Explorer to hide all local drives.

D. Configure the appropriate Group Policy settings.

70-210.05.04.004

You are the administrator of a LAN supporting computers running Windows 2000 Professional. You have almost completed your Group Policy settings, and all users have access to Windows Help. You want to achieve these results:

- Prevent common users from using the Administrative Tools folder in Control Panel.

- Prevent common users from using the Display program in Control Panel.

- Prevent common users from using the Internet Options program in Control Panel.

- Prevent common users from using the Network And Dial-Up Connections program in Control Panel.

Your proposed solution is to configure the Hide Specified Control Panel Applets Group Policy setting to hide the icons for Administrative Tools, Display, Internet Options, and Network And Dial-Up Connections.

Which result does the proposed solution provide?

A. Users are prevented from using the Administrative Tools folder in Control Panel.

B. Users are prevented from using the Display program in Control Panel.

C. Users are prevented from using the Internet Options program in Control Panel.

D. Users are not prevented from accessing any of the specified Control Panel programs or folders.

E. Users are prevented from using the Network And Dial-Up Connections program in Control Panel.

Objective 5.4 Answers

70-210.05.04.001

▶ **Correct Answers: B**

A. **Incorrect:** Active Desktop configuration information is stored in the registry under the HKEY_CURRENT_USER\Software\Microsoft\InternetExplorer\Desktop registry key. Below this registry key, the Components key contains information on all added Active Desktop items. There are other important subkeys, such as the Safe Mode key, which is loaded when starting the computer in Safe Mode. If the Desktop area of the registry were corrupted, Active Desktop would fail to load on startup.

B. **Correct:** Active Desktop is part of Internet Explorer and is overlaid on the Windows Explorer shell. If you choose a .bmp file for the desktop wallpaper and then use an Active Desktop element for the desktop wallpaper, the Active Desktop element is displayed on top of the .bmp. When you log off or when you are logged in and you press Ctrl+Alt+Delete, Active Desktop is not running, so the .bmp file appears.

C. **Incorrect:** User profiles are connected to the user logging on to the system. A single user profile is merged with the All Users profile when a user logs on to the system.

D. **Incorrect:** Local Group Policy settings are stored on each computer running Windows 2000. This GPO contains a subset of the settings available in Windows 2000 Server–based GPOs. Any Local Group Policy settings in conflict with Windows 2000 Server–based Group Policy settings are overwritten by default when the equivalent server-based Group Policy settings are enabled. Group Policy conflicts are handled in a predictable way. The question describes configuration procedures undertaken by the user, so the behavior exhibited by the computer is unlikely to be related to Group Policy settings.

70-210.05.04.002

► **Correct Answers: B and C**

A. **Incorrect:** A local user profile does not move from computer to computer. For users to retain their desktop settings from computer to computer, configure roaming user profiles.

B. **Correct:** After a user account is configured to use a roaming user profile and the user logs on to the network, the user's profile located on the network is cached to the local computer. Updates to desktop settings are written to the cached profile. When the user logs off the network, the cached profile updates the network profile. As long as the roaming user profile is not mandatory, when a user logs on to a computer that is disconnected from the network, the locally cached profile is loaded transparently.

C. **Correct:** By default, a roaming user profile contains a number of personal folders, including the My Documents and My Pictures folders. By redirecting these folders to an alternate network location, users work on the data contained in these folders as if the folders were local to the computer. Additionally, when a user logs off the network, My Documents and My Pictures are not synchronized with the roaming user profile. To complete the process of decoupling My Documents and My Pictures, configure Offline Files for these folders. In combining folder redirection with Offline Files, mobile users transparently synchronize the network-based My Documents folder contents with a locally cached copy of the files. If My Pictures is not specifically redirected through Group Policy, it will be redirected with My Documents because it is contained within My Documents. When users are no longer connected to the network, they can continue to work on the locally cached copy of their data files.

D. **Incorrect:** The Indexing Service runs in the background and creates indexes of the contents and properties of documents on the local computer, on network-accessible shares, and on local Web content if Microsoft Internet Information Services (IIS) is installed. This service does not play a direct role in managing roaming user profiles or folder redirection.

70-210.05.04.003

▶ **Correct Answers: D**

A. **Incorrect:** Drives are not disabled in the BIOS. It is possible to disable a disk device in the BIOS, but either this will cause a system startup failure if the disk containing the active partition is disabled, or the disabled disk will not be detected by the operating system. If the operating system successfully starts, disabled disks will be unavailable to both the computer user and the operating system.

B. **Incorrect:** Windows 2000 does not read the legacy startup file CONFIG.SYS. If a shortcut is created for an MS-DOS application, you can specify the startup files for the Windows 2000 command interpreter for MS-DOS. The default startup files for the command interpreter are CONFIG.NT and AUTOEXEC.NT, and they are contained in the *%systemroot%*\System32 folder.

The LASTDRIVE command is used by operating systems other than Windows NT or Windows 2000, such as MS-DOS and Windows 98, to make driver letters accessible to the operating system.

C. **Incorrect:** Windows Explorer does not contain a setting for hiding local drives.

D. **Correct:** The Hide These Specified Drives In My Computer Group Policy setting allows you to hide all drives or a combination of drives from A through D. This Group Policy setting is applied through local computer policy or in a network running Windows 2000 Server, through network Group Policy. The specified drives are hidden in My Computer, My Network Places, and Windows Explorer. This policy is located under Administrative Templates in the Windows Components\Windows Explorer container.

The Prevent Access To Drives From My Computer Group Policy setting, also in the Windows Explorer container, prevents access to viewing content on drives appearing in My Computer, Windows Explorer, and in My Network Places. If this policy is configured, the drives will appear in the interface (unless Hide These Specified Drives In My Computer is enabled), but double-clicking them will open a Group Policy restriction message box. This setting also disables the Run command, the Map Network Drive dialog box, and running a directory command (DIR) at the command line.

70-210.05.04.004

▶ **Correct Answers: D**

A. **Incorrect:** The Hide Specified Control Panel Applets Group Policy setting allows you to disallow Control Panel programs (.cpl) files or folders from appearing in Control Panel. This *does not* restrict the program from being started by other means. Control Panel programs are associated with CONTROL.EXE so that when a .cpl file such as ACCESS.CPL is run, CONTROL.EXE opens the Accessibility Options dialog box. Control Panel folders, such as the Administrative Tools folder, are opened by EXPLORER.EXE. Therefore, just hiding the program or folder does not restrict the user from accessing the feature in some other way. Many of these programs are also available from Windows 2000 Help.

The Hide Specified Control Panel Applets Group Policy setting is applied through local computer policy or, in a network running Windows 2000 Server, through network Group Policy. The specified .cpl or folder name added to this policy setting will not appear in Control Panel. This policy is located under the User Configuration node in the Administrative Templates\Control Panel container.

To limit access to the Administrative Tools folder, verify that the Display Administrative Tools check box is cleared in the Advanced tab of the Taskbar And Start Menu Properties dialog box. Then enable the Disable Changes To Taskbar And Start Menu Settings Group Policy setting. This setting is located under the User Configuration node in the Administrative Templates\Start Menu & Taskbar container.

B. **Incorrect:** As described already, the program or folder can be accessed in other ways even if it does not appear in Control Panel. You can open the Display Properties dialog box by opening DESK.CPL. Opening this .cpl file is equivalent to accessing the Display program in Control Panel.

To disable access to the Display Properties dialog box, enable the Disable Display In Control Panel Group Policy setting. Configure this setting under the User Configuration node in the Administrative Templates\Control Panel\Display container.

C. **Incorrect:** As described already, the program or folder can be accessed in other ways, even if it does not appear in Control Panel. You can open the Internet Properties dialog box by opening INETCPL.CPL. Opening this .cpl file is equivalent to accessing the Internet Options program in Control Panel.

To disable access to the Internet Properties dialog box, enable the Group Policy settings located under the User Configuration node in the Administrative Templates\Windows Components\Internet Explorer\Internet Control Panel container.

D. **Correct:** As described already, a number of other ways exist to start programs or open folders that are typically available in Control Panel. To disable a user from accessing all .cpl files, enable the Disable Control Panel Group Policy setting. This setting is located under the User Configuration node in the Administrative Templates\Control Panel container.

E. **Incorrect:** As described already, the program or folder can be accessed in other ways even if it does not appear in Control Panel. You can open the Network And Dial-Up Connections dialog box by opening NCPA.CPL. Opening this .cpl file is equivalent to accessing the Network And Dial-Up Connections program in Control Panel.

To disable access to the Network And Dial-Up Connections dialog box, configure the Group Policy settings located under the User Configuration node in the Administrative Templates\Network\Network And Dial-Up Connections container.

O B J E C T I V E   5 . 5

Configure and troubleshoot fax support.

Windows 2000 Professional includes the necessary software to send and receive faxes through a fax-capable device, such as a fax modem. If Windows 2000 detects the presence of a fax device, it installs the Fax Service and the Windows NT Fax Driver. The Fax Service appears in the Services window, and the Windows NT Fax Driver appears in the Printers window as a printer named Fax. Faxes are sent from an application as a print job whose destination is the Fax printer. Sending a print job to the Fax printer starts the Send Fax Wizard to gather information about how, when, and where the fax is to be sent. The Fax printer driver receives the job details and sends it to the Fax Service. The Fax Service queues the fax job for sending through the fax-capable device. The fax-capable device uses the instructions provided by the Fax Service to transmit the fax. The Fax printer cannot be shared. Thus, other users on the network are unable to send faxes through a fax printer on another computer.

Faxes are received through the fax device. The Windows 2000 Fax Monitor watches for incoming faxes and receives the fax as a .tif image file. When the image file is received, it can be saved to a folder, sent via e-mail to a configured e-mail profile, or sent to a printing device. Any combination of these three options is available, but routing the image file to the Received Faxes folder is the default setting. The image files are viewed through the Imaging For Windows Preview utility or any installed image viewer capable of reading .tif files. To route faxes to a network printer or to an e-mail profile, the Fax Service *must* be configured with a logon account with the necessary rights to read the user's e-mail profile or profiles, to access a network printer, or both. By default, the Fax Service is configured to use the Local System account, which does not support network printing or local e-mail profile access.

Two common paths exist to configure fax support: from the Fax program in Control Panel and from icons in the Fax program group. To access the Fax program group, go to the Start menu, point to Programs, point to Accessories, and then click Communications.

You complete the following tasks from the Fax program:

- Configuring user information that will be inserted on a cover page

- Creating, opening for editing, and deleting cover pages and adding them to the list of available cover pages

You create and edit cover pages by using the Cover Page Editor. This editor starts automatically when a new cover page is created or when an existing cover page is opened for editing. This utility reads and saves files with a .cov extension.

- Configuring Status Monitor options, such as displaying the status monitor on the status bar portion of the taskbar and enabling Manual Answer for the first fax-capable device in the computer

  Selecting Manual Answer for the first fax-capable device sets to 99 the number of rings necessary to answer an incoming fax request. When the Fax Service detects an incoming call, a message box appears asking you whether the fax device should answer the call.

- Running the Fax Service Management console to configure incoming and outgoing fax service using a fax-capable device and to configure fax logging

  Logging information is stored in the Windows 2000 Application log and viewed using Event Viewer. Fax logging events are categorized as Inbound, Outbound, Initialization/Termination, and Unknown.

- Opening Fax Service Management help

- Adding a fax printer to the Printers window

  Use this feature if a user has deleted the Fax printer from the Printers window.

The following tasks are completed from the Fax program group:

- Viewing and managing the outgoing fax queue

- Starting the Fax Service Management console

- Sending a cover page as a fax

- Viewing the fax Help file

  This is not the same help file that is started from the Fax program.

- Opening and managing the contents of the My Faxes folder

  This folder can contain subfolders for both incoming and outgoing faxes, depending on how incoming and outgoing faxes are configured.

To fax a document through Microsoft Outlook, you must install the Fax Mail Transport service to an e-mail profile. Create a new profile containing your personal store, your address book, and the Fax Mail Transport service. Any address book entries containing a fax number as a transport option will be able to receive e-mails as a faxed document sent through the Fax Mail Transport service. Incoming faxes can also be received as e-mail, but this feature does *not* require the Fax Mail Transport service. Instead, incoming faxes are routed to an e-mail profile by the Fax Service.

Objective 5.5 Questions

70-210.05.05.001

TonyV, a user on the network, attempts to configure his computer running Windows 2000 Professional to use the Fax Service. TonyV is able to send outgoing faxes using Windows 2000 Professional but is unable to receive incoming faxes. What should you do to allow Windows 2000 Professional to receive incoming fax documents?

A. Open the Fax program in Device Manager, open the Advanced Options tab, and open the Fax Service Management console to configure the Fax Service on the local computer.

B. Open the Fax program in Control Panel, open the Advanced Options tab, and open the Fax Service Management console to configure the Fax Service on the local computer.

C. Open the Fax program in Control Panel, access the Advanced Options tab, and open Fax Service Management Help to configure the Fax Service on the local computer.

D. Open the Fax program in Control Panel, access the Advanced Options tab, and add and configure a Fax printer on the local computer.

70-210.05.05.002

A new user on your network calls you to ask for help with using the Windows 2000 Professional Fax Service. The user reports that no Fax program appears in Control Panel. You know that the user's computer is new, and all hardware is on the Windows 2000 Hardware Compatibility List (HCL). What is the most likely cause of this behavior?

A. The computer has a defective fax device installed.

B. The computer has no fax device logically installed.

C. The computer has no fax device physically installed.

D. The Windows 2000 Professional registry files are corrupt.

70-210.05.05.003

A new user on your network calls you to ask for help with using the Windows 2000 Professional Fax Service. The user needs to set up the Fax Service to store sent faxes on a network drive. How should you advise the user?

A. Open the Fax program in Control Panel, open the User Information tab, and open the Fax Service Management console to configure the Fax Service on the local computer.

B. Open the Fax program in Control Panel, open the Advanced Options tab, and open the Fax Service Management console to configure the Fax Service on the local computer.

C. Open the Fax program in Control Panel, open the Advanced Options tab, and open Fax Service Management Help to configure the Fax Service on the local computer.

D. Open the Fax program in Control Panel, open the Advanced Options tab, and add and configure a Fax printer on the local computer.

Objective 5.5 Answers

70-210.05.05.001

▶ **Correct Answers: B**

A. **Incorrect:** Fax hardware and the device driver installed to support the hardware appear in Device Manager. The Fax Service Management console is not available from Device Manager.

B. **Correct:** In the Fax Service Management console, select the Devices node in the console tree. Next, in the details pane, click the fax device to be used for receiving faxes and then, on the Action menu, click Properties. In the *device name* Properties dialog box, select the Enable Receive check box.

The Fax Service Management console is also accessible by clicking the Fax Service Management program located on the Start menu in the Programs\Accessories\Communications\Fax program group.

C. **Incorrect:** The Open Fax Service Management Help icon in the Advanced Options tab provides an overview of Fax Service Management and instructions on using and configuring Fax Service Management options. This help file is also available by clicking the Help toolbar button in the Fax Service Management console. Another important help file for using fax services is available by clicking Help in the Fax program group.

D. **Incorrect:** The Add A Fax Printer button in the Advanced Options tab is used to add a Fax printer to the Printers window. If Windows 2000 Professional detects the presence of a fax-capable device, it automatically creates a Fax printer in the Printers folder. Applications can then print to the Fax printer. When the job is spooled to the Fax printer, the Fax Service intercepts the job and launches the fax-sending interface so that you can specify additional fax information and send the fax to a fax destination. If the Fax printer is accidentally deleted from the Printers folder, Add A Fax Printer is an important feature for reinstalling the Fax printer.

70-210.05.05.002

▶ **Correct Answers: C**

A. **Incorrect:** If the Windows 2000 installation routine detects a fax-capable device, it installs the Fax Service, the Fax program in Control Panel, the Fax program group, and the Fax printer to the Printers window. It is unlikely that a defective fax device will cause Windows 2000 to fail fax device detection.

B. **Incorrect:** When the Windows 2000 installation routine detects a fax-capable device, it installs the necessary driver and interface software to show a logical fax device in Control Panel, a Fax program group, and a Fax printer. It is unlikely that the user deleted the FAX.CPL file from the *%system-root%*\System32 folder. It is possible that a Group Policy setting restricts the Fax program from appearing in Control Panel, but nothing in the question suggests that Group Policy settings have been customized.

C. **Correct:** If the Windows 2000 installation routine does not detect a fax-capable device, it will not install the Windows 2000 fax components. Therefore, this is the most likely reason for the absence of the Fax program in Control Panel.

D. **Incorrect:** It is unlikely that a registry corruption would cause the disappearance of the Fax program in Control Panel.

70-210.05.05.003

▶ **Correct Answers: B**

A. **Incorrect:** The User Information tab contains data that is used by the Fax Service to complete fields in a fax cover page. The Fax Service Management console is not opened from this tab.

B. **Correct:** In the Fax Service Management console, select Fax Service On Local Computer, the root of the console tree. On the Action menu, click Properties. In the Fax Service On Local Computer Properties dialog box, select the Archive Outgoing Faxes In check box. In the text box that appears, specify the network location where sent faxes should be stored.

The Fax Service Management console is also accessible by clicking Fax Service Management, located on the Start menu in the Programs\Accessories\Communications\Fax program group.

C. **Incorrect:** The Open Fax Service Management Help icon in the Advanced Options tab provides an overview of Fax Service Management and instructions on using and configuring Fax Service Management options. This help file is also available by clicking the Help toolbar button in the Fax Service Management console. Another important help file for using fax features is available by clicking Help in the Fax program group.

D. **Incorrect:** The Add A Fax Printer button in the Advanced Options tab is used to add a Fax printer to the Printers window. If Windows 2000 Professional detects the presence of a fax-capable device, it automatically creates a Fax printer in the Printers folder. Applications can then print to the Fax printer. When the job is spooled to the Fax printer, the Fax Service intercepts the job and launches the fax-sending interface so that you can specify additional fax information and send the fax to a fax destination. If the Fax printer is accidentally deleted from the Printers folder, clicking the Add A Fax Printer button is a simple way to reinstall the Fax printer.

O B J E C T I V E   5 . 6

Configure and troubleshoot accessibility services.

Accessibility services in Windows 2000 Professional provide a set of features to make the computer more manageable to people with various disabilities. Three tools are available for *configuring* accessibility services: the **Accessibility Options program** in Control Panel and two tools in the **Accessibility program group**, **Utility Manager** and the **Accessibility Wizard**. To show the contents of the Accessibility program group, go to the Start menu, point to Programs, point to Accessories, and then point to Accessibility.

Use the Accessibility Options program to configure keyboard, sound, display, and mouse settings to assist people with special mobility, visual, or hearing needs. Use the General tab in the Accessibility Options dialog box to control how the computer's accessibility options react to idle time and to control how notifications are delivered when an accessibility feature is enabled or disabled. Additionally, use this tab to configure **SerialKey** devices, to determine whether accessibility options apply to only the logged on user or all users, and to determine whether new users will receive the accessibility service configuration. A **SerialKey device** is alternative keyboard and mouse input hardware that connects to a computer's serial port.

The Accessibility Wizard aggregates accessibility features that are related. For example, you can use this wizard to select the text size that is most appropriate to the user. This setting can range from the default text size to text enlarged using the Magnifier utility. Other wizard options allow you to choose statements that describe the disability. Based on your selection or selections, wizard screens appear to configure the computer for the disability. Accessibility-related administrative options are also available from the wizard.

Running Utility Manager shows a screen that consolidates three important accessibility utilities: the Magnifier, the Narrator, and the On-Screen Keyboard. Any of these utilities can be configured by a user with Administrative privileges to start automatically when Utility Manager starts or when Windows starts. The Narrator utility starts automatically to aid a visually impaired user in configuring Utility Manager settings.

The Narrator is a text-to-speech utility that reads text displayed on the desktop, including the contents of an active window and text you select or type. The Narrator is not guaranteed to work with all applications. It has been tested with utilities such as Notepad, Microsoft Wordpad, the Windows Explorer shell, and the Windows 2000 setup routine. The Magnifier utility makes anything appearing on the desktop more readable by creating a separate window that displays a magnified view of the desktop, a high-contrast view of the desktop, or both. The Narrator and Magnifier are designed to assist users with visual disabilities. The On-Screen Keyboard utility displays a keyboard on the desktop to enable users with mobility impairments to type data using a pointing device or a joystick.

The Magnifier, Narrator, and On-Screen Keyboard can be started independently of Utility Manager by clicking their corresponding icons in the Accessibility program group. These three utilities provide minimum levels of functionality. Most computer users with visual or mobility impairments will need utilities with greater capability. The Microsoft Accessibility Web site at *http://www.microsoft.com/enable* contains a comprehensive list of hardware and software designed to assist computer users with visual, auditory, or mobility impairments.

Note The SoundSentry and ShowSounds features for the hearing impaired are part of the Accessibility Options program and do not appear as icons in the Accessibility program group.

Objective 5.6 Questions

70-210.05.06.001

Kathy has difficulty using a standard PC keyboard and mouse. You log on to her computer as Administrator and enable the StickyKeys and FilterKeys options. When Kathy logs on to her computer, the accessibility options you set are not loaded. What should you do?

A. Log on as Kathy, and use Utility Manager to configure the settings.

B. Log on as Administrator, and use Utility Manager to configure the settings.

C. Log on as Kathy, and use the Accessibility Wizard or the Accessibility Options program to enable the appropriate options.

D. Log on as Administrator, and use the Accessibility Options program in Control Panel to enable the Apply All Settings To Defaults For New Users option.

70-210.05.06.002

David has difficulty seeing a computer monitor. You want to configure David's computer to run the Magnifier each time he logs on to his computer, but you don't want the Magnifier to start when other users log on to the computer. What should you do?

A. Log on as David, and use Utility Manager to enable the appropriate option.

B. Log on as Administrator, and use Utility Manager to enable the appropriate option.

C. Log on as David, and use the Accessibility Wizard to enable the appropriate option.

D. Log on as Administrator, and use the Accessibility Options program in Control Panel to enable the High Contrast setting.

70-210.05.06.003

Randy has difficulty hearing computer sounds, and you want to configure his Windows 2000 Professional computer to generate visual warnings when the computer makes a sound. Which accessibility option should you enable?

A. FilterKeys

B. ShowSounds

C. SoundSentry

D. StickyKeys

Objective 5.6 Answers

70-210.05.06.001

▶ **Correct Answers: C**

A. **Incorrect:** Utility Manager consolidates three important accessibility utilities: the Magnifier, the Narrator, and the On-Screen Keyboard. All of these utilities are configured to start automatically when Utility Manager starts or when Windows starts. The Narrator utility starts automatically to aid a visually impaired user in configuring the Utility Manager settings. Regardless of how you log on to the computer, Utility Manager is not used to configure a computer to use the StickyKeys and Filter-Keys options.

B. **Incorrect:** As described already, Utility Manager is not used to configure a computer to use the StickyKeys and FilterKeys options.

C. **Correct:** The Accessibility Wizard is located on the Start menu in the Programs\Accessories\Accessibility program group. After starting this wizard, navigate to the Set Wizard Options screen and then select the I Have Difficulty Using The Keyboard Or Mouse check box. After clicking Next, the StickyKeys screen appears where you can enable the StickyKeys feature. Clicking Next again displays the BounceKeys screen. Enabling this feature is equivalent to enabling FilterKeys in the Accessibility Options program. Advanced configuration settings for FilterKeys are available from the Accessibility Options program, not through the wizard.

If you were logged on with Administrative privileges and you selected the I Want To Set Administrative Options check box, the third to last screen in the Accessibility Wizard would be the Default Accessibility Settings screen. From this screen, you can make the accessibility settings apply to the currently logged on user and all new user accounts or just the currently logged on user. Because you are logged on as Kathy, accessibility settings apply only to her user profile.

The second to last screen in the wizard allows you to save the settings to an Accessibility Wizard Settings (.acw) file so that the settings can be imported to another computer. To import the settings to another computer, simply open the .acw file on the new computer.

Using the Accessibility Options program, you enable StickyKeys and FilterKeys in the Keyboard tab in the Accessibility Options dialog box. After you enable and configure these features, click the General tab and select the Apply All Settings To Logon Desktop check box so that the settings apply only when the Kathy user account is used to log on to the computer.

D. **Incorrect:** This setting is available in the General tab in the Accessibility Options dialog box. Setting this Administrative option means that all new users will receive whatever accessibility settings were enabled in the Accessibility Options program or through the Accessibility Wizard.

70-210.05.06.002

► **Correct Answers: C**

A. **Incorrect:** Unless David is granted Administrative privileges to the computer, he will not be able to configure Utility Manager so that the Magnifier starts automatically when Windows starts.

B. **Incorrect:** A user account with Administrative privileges to the computer is able to configure Utility Manager. To start the Magnifier when Windows starts, click the Magnifier in the top box and then select the Start Automatically When Windows Starts check box. This sets the Start With Windows registry entry to 1 in the HKEY_LOCAL_MACHINE\SOFTWARE\Microsoft\Windows NT\Current-Version\Accessibility\Utility Manager\Magnifier registry key. Then, when Windows 2000 is started, the Magnifier will start automatically. The Magnifier will appear each time *any* user logs on to the system, not just David.

C. **Correct:** After logging on as David and starting the Accessibility Wizard, navigate to the Display Settings screen and then select the Use Microsoft Magnifier check box. The Microsoft Magnifier dialog box appears, and a portion of the screen is magnified. After you click OK, the Magnifier Settings dialog box appears. After configuring the Magnifier, continue to move through the Accessibility Wizard to complete additional accessibility options. Because you are logged on as David, this accessibility configuration applies only to his user profile.

D. **Incorrect:** The Use High Contrast setting is enabled in the Display tab in the Accessibility Options dialog box or using the Accessibility Wizard. This setting may help David see the computer, but it does not enable the Magnifier.

70-210.05.06.003

► **Correct Answers: C**

A. **Incorrect:** The FilterKeys feature is designed to assist users with mobility impairments by configuring the keyboard to ignore brief or repeated keystrokes and to adjust the keyboard repeat rate.

B. **Incorrect:** The ShowSounds feature is designed to assist users with auditory impairments by configuring programs that usually convey information only by sound to provide all information visually, such as by displaying text captions or informative icons.

C. **Correct:** The SoundSentry feature is designed to assist users with auditory impairments by flashing part of the desktop screen every time the system's built-in speaker plays a sound. You can specify which part of the screen flashes by clicking Settings. The settings include flashing the active caption bar, the active window, or the entire desktop.

D. **Incorrect:** The StickyKeys feature is designed to assist users who have difficulty pressing two keys simultaneously by configuring the keyboard so that when the Ctrl, Alt, Shift, or Windows logo keys are pressed, they remain active until the next time the user presses a key other than one of these four keys.

Implementing, Managing, and Troubleshooting Network Protocols and Services

The **Transmission Control Protocol/Internet Protocol (TCP/IP)** is a mature and feature-rich transport protocol used for Internet and most intranet data communications throughout the world. The services provided by TCP/IP have evolved with the explosive growth of computer networks. Understanding how to install, configure, and troubleshoot the protocol and the services it provides is critical to uninterrupted data communications, and it is an important part of most Microsoft Windows 2000 networks. Specifically, you must be proficient with installing, maintaining, and troubleshooting TCP/IP and its related services in Windows 2000.

Network protocols and services extend beyond local area network (LAN) communication. An important extension to the LAN is the wide area network (WAN). Many types of WAN technologies provide varying levels of services to expand the reach of the network. This Objective Domain is primarily concerned with **dial-up** and **virtual private network (VPN)** WAN connections. Windows 2000 provides these connection services through the remote access client. You must be proficient with installing, configuring, and troubleshooting the remote access client features.

The physical LAN or WAN medium and the transport protocol are only part of establishing a connection with a Microsoft network. A common task after connecting to a Microsoft network is accessing shared network resources. The two types of shared resources common to Microsoft networks are folders and printers. You must be able to create and configure these shared resources and troubleshoot them if resource sharing is not operating properly.

Note This Objective Domain specifically focuses on folder shares. See Objective Domain 2, "Implementing and Conducting Administration of Resources," for information on printer shares.

Tested Skills and Suggested Practices

The skills you need to successfully master the Implementing, Managing, and Troubleshooting Network Protocols and Services Objective Domain on Exam 70-210: Installing, Configuring, and Administering Microsoft Windows 2000 Professional include the following:

- **Install, configure, and maintain the proper operation of TCP/IP and core services of this protocol suite.**

  - Practice 1: Install TCP/IP on two computers and configure them for static IP addressing. Then verify that the two computers can communicate using TCP/IP.

  - Practice 2: Configure TCP/IP to use APIPA. Verify that two computers configured for APIPA are able to communicate with each other.

  - Practice 3: Install the DHCP Server service on a computer running Microsoft Windows 2000 Server. Activate a scope so that an IP address and a subnet mask are dynamically allocated to DHCP clients. Verify that the two computers previously configured for APIPA now receive their dynamic addressing from the DHCP Server service.

  - Practice 4: Install the DNS server and the WINS server on a computer running Windows 2000 Server.

  - Practice 5: Configure the DHCP Server service to supply DHCP clients with DNS, WINS, node type, and default gateway information.

- Practice 6: Configure advanced TCP/IP settings in the properties of a LAN. For example, add a connection-specific DNS suffix, create and import an LMHOSTS file, and add a WINS server address.

- Practice 7: Manually configure routes using the Route command. Next, if there is a router on the network that uses RIP to send route updates, install the RIP Listener networking service.

- **Install, configure, and maintain the proper operation of remote access client connections: dial-up, VPN, and incoming connection types.**

  - Practice 1: Using the Network Connection Wizard, create and configure a dial-up, VPN, and incoming connection. Use the dial-up and VPN connections to connect to remote resources. Use the dial-up connection again to connect to the incoming connection.

  - Practice 2: After connecting to a remote resource, review the authentication protocol data encryption and other settings from the status details of an active connection. Disconnect from the external resource, and then reconfigure the security settings of the connections. Attempt to reconnect to an external resource, and review the status details of the connection again.

  - Practice 3: Share a connection and review the IP addressing settings allocated to the ICS computer and computers on the network that will connect to external resources through this connection. Use the ICS connection by configuring and running a Web browser on another computer on the same network. Verify that demand dialing is enabled, and review the advanced settings of an ICS connection.

  - Practice 4: Create and configure a Multilink connection. Use the connection to access external resources. Use the status details of an active Multilink connection to suspend or resume a physical connection.

  - Practice 5: Use the Netsh dial-up scripting utility to enable PPP logging. Also, run the utility to review some of the advanced remote access scripting capabilities it provides. After logging a PPP session, review the log and disable PPP logging using Netsh.

- **Create and configure shared resources in a Windows 2000 network so that Windows clients can use the shares.**

    - Practice 1: At the command line, type **net use /?** and **net share /?** to review the switches available for connecting to a share and for sharing a local resource.

    - Practice 2: Configure share permissions and access shared resources using accounts that are granted different share permissions.

    - Practice 3: Configure local permissions for a share on an NTFS partition. Test access to the contents of the share, and resolve any conflicts between share permissions and local permissions.

    - Practice 4: Create user accounts and assign each user account to one of the following groups: Administrators, Backup Operators, Power Users, and Users. Log on as each user, and test the privileges granted to each user through the group membership.

    - Practice 5: Use the Shared Folders snap-in to perform share management tasks on the local computer and on a remote computer running either Windows 2000 or Microsoft Windows NT 4.

Further Reading

This "Further Reading" section provides lists of important readings to supplement your current understanding of the skills tested within this Objective Domain. The lists are delineated into pertinent readings for each objective within this Objective Domain. If you feel that you need additional preparation prior to taking the exam, study these sources thoroughly.

Objective 6.1

Daily, Sean. "Navigating Name Resolution," Part 1, June 2000 and Part 2, July 2000, *Windows 2000 Magazine*. Duke Communications International, Denver, Colorado. Sean Daily discusses name resolution and how to troubleshoot problems with the name resolution mechanism in Windows 2000.

Microsoft Corporation. *Microsoft TechNet*. Redmond, Washington: Microsoft Corporation, 2000. Read "MS Windows 2000 TCP/IP Implementation Details" located under Microsoft Windows 2000 Server—Technical Notes.

Microsoft Corporation. *Microsoft Windows 2000 Professional Resource Kit*. Redmond, Washington: Microsoft Press, 2000. Read about and run the troubleshooting tools listed on pp. 1452–1465, Chapter 31, "Troubleshooting Tools and Strategies"; read pp. 900–905, Chapter 21, "Local and Remote Network Connections"; and read Chapter 22, "TCP/IP in Windows 2000 Professional."

Microsoft Corporation. *Microsoft Windows 2000 Server Resource Kit—Windows 2000 Server TCP/IP Core Networking Guide*. Redmond, Washington: Microsoft Press, 2000. For an excellent introduction to TCP/IP and troubleshooting TCP/IP in Windows 2000, read Chapter 1, "Introduction to TCP/IP," Chapter 2, "Windows 2000 TCP/IP," and Chapter 3, "TCP/IP Troubleshooting."

Microsoft Corporation. *MCSE Training Kit—Microsoft Windows 2000 Professional*. Redmond, Washington: Microsoft Press, 2000. Read and complete the practices in Lesson 1, Chapter 7, "Installing and Configuring Network Protocols," and Chapter 8, "Using the DNS Service"; Read Appendix C, "Understanding the DHCP Service."

Objective 6.2

Microsoft Corporation. *Microsoft Windows 2000 Server Resource Kit Internetworking Guide*. Redmond, Washington: Microsoft Press, 2000. Read Chapter 2, "Routing and Remote Access."

Microsoft Corporation. *Microsoft Windows 2000 Professional Resource Kit*. Redmond, Washington: Microsoft Press, 2000. Read pp. 575–587, Chapter 13, "Security," and Chapter 21, "Local and Remote Network Connections."

Microsoft Corporation. *Windows 2000 Professional Help—Networking and Dial-up Connections*. Read this entire online help file.

Microsoft Corporation. *MCSE Training Kit—Microsoft Windows 2000 Professional*. Redmond, Washington: Microsoft Press, 2000. Read and complete the practices in Chapter 21, "Configuring Remote Access."

Microsoft Corporation. "Privacy Protected Network Access: Virtual Private Networking and Intranet Security." You can download this article from *http://www.microsoft.com/windows2000* by searching on the article title.

Microsoft Corporation. "Windows 2000-Based Virtual Private Networking: Supporting VPN Operability." You can download this article from *http://www.microsoft.com/windows2000* by searching on the article title.

Microsoft Corporation. "Virtual Private Networking: An Overview." You can download this article from *http://www.microsoft.com/windows2000* by searching on the article title.

Objective 6.3

Microsoft Corporation. *MCSE Training Kit—Microsoft Windows 2000 Professional.* Redmond, Washington: Microsoft Press, 2000. Read and complete the practices in Chapter 15, "Administering Shared Folders."

Microsoft Corporation. *Microsoft Windows 2000 Professional Resource Kit.* Redmond, Washington: Microsoft Press, 2000. Read pp. 545–559, Chapter 13, "Security."

OBJECTIVE 6.1

Configure and troubleshoot the TCP/IP protocol.

After you install and *bind* Transmission Control Protocol/Internet Protocol (TCP/IP) to a local area network (LAN) or a wide area network (WAN) adapter, including **IP over ATM** in Windows 2000, the core tasks for configuring TCP/IP on a network include the following: configuring **dynamic** or **static** IP addressing, configuring **name resolution**, and configuring **TCP/IP security**. Addressing information, such as IP address, subnet mask, and default gateway, is either manually assigned (static) or automatically assigned (dynamic). Dynamic Host Configuration Protocol (DHCP) is used to automatically assign such addressing information. You can also dynamically assign a default gateway using **Internet Control Message Protocol (ICMP) Router Discovery** and discover network routes through **Routing Information Protocol (RIP) listening**. RIP listening is especially useful for automatic route configuration on computers with multiple LAN adapters, called **multihomed** computers. On small networks, you can use **Automatic Private IP Addressing (APIPA)** to dynamically assign an IP address and a subnet mask to client computers. APIPA is disabled if the DHCP Server service is detected and operational for the subnet containing the client computer.

Note Like APIPA, **Internet Connection Sharing (ICS)** dynamically assigns IP addressing information. ICS is explored in Objective 6.2.

You accomplish **name resolution**, the method used to translate friendly names into IP addresses, by using files—HOSTS and LMHOSTS; or you use services—Domain Name System (DNS) and Microsoft Windows Internet Naming Service (WINS) servers. The primary function of the HOSTS file and DNS service is to translate IP host names into IP addresses. The primary function of the LMHOSTS file and WINS is to translate NetBIOS names into IP addresses. You accomplish TCP/IP security in Windows 2000 by configuring filtering, authentication, and encryption services. **TCP/IP filters**, **IP Security (IPSec)**, and **virtual private networks (VPN)** are some of the resources available in Windows 2000 used to secure data transmission.

Protocol performance is an important consideration, particularly in larger networks and networks requiring specific services. The Windows 2000 implementation of TCP/IP supports a number of performance enhancements, including a larger default **TCP receive window** size than previous implementations of TCP/IP for Windows. This feature allows TCP/IP hosts to send more data at once before requiring an acknowledgment from the receiver. The Windows 2000 TCP/IP protocol is capable of negotiating an even larger window size with the sending host. This ability to increase window size is provided by the **Window Scale** option. This feature is especially important for maintaining performance levels in high-bandwidth, high-latency networks. A number of other performance enhancements exist such as TCP/IP **Selective Acknowledgement (SACK)** and **Quality of Service (QoS)** support.

TCP/IP is a complex and mature protocol suite. With this complexity and maturity comes a robust toolset for troubleshooting TCP/IP-based networks. To diagnose whether the TCP/IP stack is loaded and configured properly, use tools such as Ipconfig, Ping, Pathping, Tracert, and Route. Also, check that the DHCP Server service is available and that the DHCP Client service is running. The DHCP Client service is important for dynamic address allocation from DHCP or from the APIPA DHCP allocator component and for dynamic DNS (DDNS) registration.

To troubleshoot name resolution problems, determine whether the problem is related to NetBIOS name resolution or host name resolution. If it is a NetBIOS name resolution issue, review the LMHOSTS file, check that WINS is functioning properly, and run Nbtstat to display NetBIOS over TCP/IP activity. If it is a host resolution problem, review the HOSTS file and verify proper DNS operation using utilities such as Nslookup. To get a summary status report of network activity, run the Network Diagnostics (NETDIAG.EXE) utility.

A useful troubleshooting utility used for capturing and analyzing network traffic is Network Monitor. Network Monitor is one of the Management and Monitoring Tool installation options in Windows 2000 Server. The Windows 2000 Server version of Network Monitor is not available for installation in Windows 2000 Professional. A Windows 2000 Professional computer can install the Network Monitor driver from the Windows 2000 Professional installation CD-ROM to capture network packets on behalf of Network Monitor. The Network Monitor driver is remotely configured and controlled from a computer running the version of Network Monitor included with Systems Management Server (SMS) 2.0. The version of Network Monitor included with SMS 2.0 can be installed on any version of Windows 2000.

Objective 6.1 Questions

70-210.06.01.001

You are the administrator of a LAN supporting computers running Windows 2000 Professional. Because of the small size of the network, a DHCP server has not yet been installed and you and an assistant assign IP addresses manually.

A TCP/IP error is detected on a computer running Windows 2000 Professional. You investigate by running the Ipconfig command-line utility, which reports an IP address and subnet mask of 0.0.0.0. What is the most likely cause of this problem?

A. The network adapter card has failed.

B. A duplicate IP address exists on the network.

C. A duplicate default gateway exists on the network.

70-210.06.01.002

You are the administrator of a LAN supporting computers running Windows 2000 Professional. One DHCP server is used to configure TCP/IP on client computers. APIPA is disabled.

A TCP/IP error is detected on a computer running Windows 2000 Professional. The computer is configured to obtain an IP address automatically. You investigate by running the Ipconfig command-line utility, which reports an IP address of 0.0.0.0. What is the most likely cause of this problem?

A. A duplicate IP address exists on the network.

B. A duplicate subnet mask exists on the network.

C. A duplicate default gateway exists on the network.

D. The client was unable to obtain an IP address from a DHCP server.

70-210.06.01.003

The user of computer Student1 is unable to connect to resources on server FilePrint1 using the computer name, but a connection is possible using an IP address.

Review the diagram below to see the TCP/IP configuration of Student1.

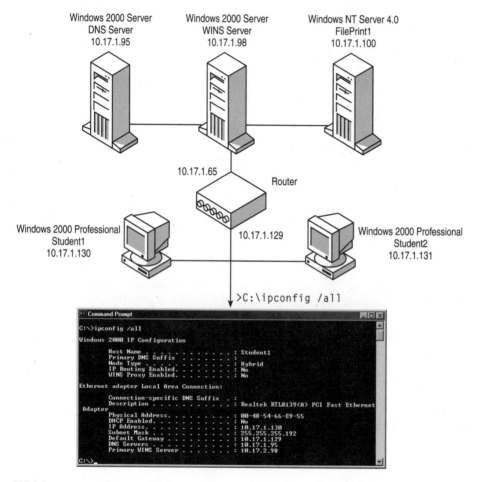

Which parameter is most likely preventing a connection using the computer name?

A. The IP address

B. The subnet mask

C. The default gateway

D. The primary WINS server

70-210.06.01.004

The user of Student2 is unable to connect to a shared resource on FilePrint1.

Review the diagram of the TCP/IP configuration of Student2 below.

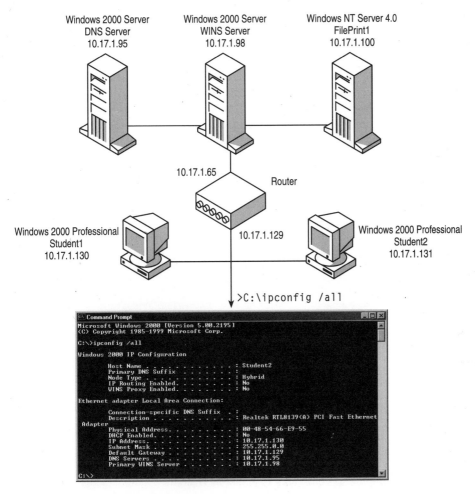

Which parameter is most likely preventing a connection?

A. The IP address

B. The subnet mask

C. The default gateway

D. The primary WINS server

Objective 6.1 Answers

70-210.06.01.001

▶ **Correct Answers: B**

A. **Incorrect:** If the network adapter card fails, the local area connection information shown by running Ipconfig would not appear for the failed adapter.

B. **Correct:** Two hosts on the same network cannot use the same IP address. In some types of client operating systems, it is possible to configure an identical IP address on two computers located on the same network. However, network communications for the two computers sharing the same IP address are unreliable and will ultimately fail. The Windows 2000 TCP/IP protocol stack checks the network to verify that the same IP address isn't already running. If it is and both computers are connected to the network and running Windows 2000, a Microsoft TCP/IP message box appears on the computer where the identical address is configured (computer B). This message box explains that the IP address is already in use. On the computer already using this address (computer A), a Windows – System Error message box appears. This message box explains that an IP address conflict has been detected and directs the user to consult the System log for details. The System log on computer A shows the Media Access Control (MAC) address of computer B. Typing ipconfig shows IP addressing information so that you can extract the subnet ID from the portion of an IP address that is the host ID.

If a host with an IP address of 10.17.1.130 has a subnet mask of 255.255.255.192, the network ID is 10.17.1.128, the subnet ID is 0.0.0.128, and the host ID is 0.0.0.2.

C. **Incorrect:** The default gateway is the IP address of a network interface in a router. Routers contain two or more network interfaces so that packets from one network can be sent to another network through the router. Each client computer needing to send packets through the router is configured with one or more default gateways. Each default gateway is located on the same network as the client computer. When a router receives a packet that is destined for another network, it is the router's job to direct the traffic to the correct network or forward the packet to another router.

70-210.06.01.002

▶ **Correct Answers: D**

A. **Incorrect:** Because the computer is configured to obtain an IP address automatically, it is unlikely that an address running on the network is also assigned (leased) to the client computer. It is possible for an IP address to be manually assigned to a device on the network that is within an address scope activated in the DHCP server. However, the DHCP Client service running on a Microsoft Windows 98 or Windows 2000 client will recognize the conflict and decline the lease offer from the server. The DHCP Server service then tags the address with a BAD_ADDRESS attribute so that it will no longer be offered to clients. To avoid the client's involvement in this conflict detection, you can configure the DHCP Server service to detect IP address conflicts before an address is assigned to a client. By default, conflict detection is disabled on the DHCP Server service because server-based conflict detection will slow the assignment of IP addresses; therefore, you should enable this feature only for troubleshooting purposes.

B. **Incorrect:** All computers located on the same network segment share the same subnet mask. The subnet mask is a 32-bit value that distinguishes the portion of an IP address that is the network ID and subnet ID from the portion of an IP address that is the host ID.

C. **Incorrect:** The default gateway is the IP address of a network interface in a router. Routers contain two or more network interfaces so that packets from one network can be sent to another network through the router. Each client computer needing to send packets through the router is configured with one or more default gateways. Each default gateway is located on the same network as the client computer. When a router receives a packet that is destined for another network, it is the router's job to direct the traffic to the correct network or forward the packet to another router.

D. **Correct:** If the DHCP server is unavailable or if there is a problem with the client computer's network adapter configuration, the client will not be able to obtain an IP address lease from the DHCP Server service. If other client computers on the same network are able to lease an address from the DHCP Server service, check the client's network configuration. If client computers on the network are unable to lease an address from the DHCP Server service, check the server's configuration.

70-210.06.01.003

▶ **Correct Answers: D**

A. **Incorrect:** The question states that Student1 is able to connect to FilePrint1 using the IP address of 10.17.1.100. If a connection is possible with an IP address but a connection is not possible using a host name, then the problem is likely related to an improper entry in a name resolution file, such as the HOSTS file, or an improperly configured name resolution service, such as the DNS service.

B. **Incorrect:** Because Student1 is able to connect to FilePrint1 using the IP address of FilePrint1, it appears that network addressing is configured correctly.

You can verify a legal network configuration using the information provided in the diagram. The subnet mask for the network containing Student1 is 255.255.255.192. The range of IP addresses for this network is 10.17.1.129–10.17.1.190. The IP address of 10.17.1.130 assigned to Student1 falls within this range. Assuming that the subnet mask for FilePrint1 is also 255.255.255.192, the address range for computers on this network is 10.17.1.64–10.17.1.127. The IP address of 10.17.1.100 assigned to FilePrint1 falls within this range.

C. **Incorrect:** Because the Student1 computer is able to connect to FilePrint1 using the IP address of FilePrint1, it is able to send and receive packets through the router shown in the diagram or Exhibit.

According to the diagram, Student1 should use the router interface of 10.17.1.129 as its default gateway. The default gateway always specifies the IP address of a router interface on the same network segment as the client. The diagram verifies that Student1 is configured for the 10.17.1.129 default gateway address.

D. **Correct:** The only WINS server appearing in the diagram is located on the network containing FilePrint1. Student1 is capable of using this WINS server to resolve NetBIOS names to IP addresses. However, notice that in the diagram, the WINS server address is 10.17.1.98, but in the diagram, the client is configured for a primary WINS server address of 10.17.2.98. According to the diagram, there is no WINS server with this IP address on the network.

70-210.06.01.004

▶ **Correct Answers: B**

A. **Incorrect:** Nothing in the diagram suggests that the IP address assigned to Student2 of 10.17.1.131 is incorrect. The other client, Student1, uses an address of 10.17.1.130, which is only 1 bit different in the fourth octet and thus appears to be a legal address for this network.

B. **Correct:** Three classes of addresses are used for typical TCP/IP communications: class A, class B, and class C. Each class allows a specific number of networks and hosts per subnet, as defined by the subnet mask. The subnet mask for a class A address is 255.0.0.0, for a class B address is 255.255.0.0, and for a class C address is 255.255.255.0. The class specification also defines the value of the first octet in the IP address. The first octet decimal value for a class A address ranges from 1–126, for a class B address from 128–191, and for a class C address from 192–223. Therefore, an IP address with a value of 10 in the first octet suggests a class A address type. A class A address supports up to 16,777,214 hosts per network.

   Notice that in the diagram, Student2 is using a subnet mask of 255.255.0.0, which is typically used for class B addressing. Windows 2000 doesn't prevent this configuration even though it doesn't comply with the class A addressing specification. Most routers will comply with the class addressing specification so the router will not forward the packets from Student2 to FilePrint1. Therefore, Student2 will not be able to connect to shared resources on FilePrint1 using TCP/IP.

   It is worth pointing out that if Student1 is configured with a subnet mask such as 255.255.255.192 and Student 2 is configured with a subnet mask of 255.255.0.0, the two computers will be able to communicate with each other using their IP addresses. Ideally, though, they should both be configured with the subnet mask of 255.255.255.192.

C. **Incorrect:** According to the diagram, Student2 should use the router interface of 10.17.1.129 as its default gateway. The default gateway always specifies the IP address of a router interface on the same network segment as the client. The diagram verifies that Student2 is configured for the 10.17.1.129 default gateway address.

D. **Incorrect:** The only WINS server appearing in the diagram is located on the network containing FilePrint1. Student2 is capable of using this WINS server to resolve NetBIOS names to IP addresses. Notice that in the diagram, the WINS server address is 10.17.1.98 and in the diagram, the client is configured for a primary WINS server address of 10.17.1.98.

O B J E C T I V E   6 . 2

Connect to computers by using dial-up networking.

The purpose of dial-up networking is to allow you to connect to and access remote network resources, such as an Internet service provider (ISP) or a corporate intranet. You accomplish this in Windows 2000 Professional by creating a **connection** in the Network And Dial-Up Connections window. Each connection appearing in this window contains settings that are unique to the connection. All network adapters detected by Windows 2000 are automatically displayed in this window. Any other connection types, such as **dial-up**, **virtual private network (VPN)**, or **incoming**, are created by running the Network Connection Wizard. You start this wizard by opening the Make New Connection icon in the Network And Dial-Up Connections window.

Dial-up interface hardware specified using the Network Connection Wizard includes modems, Integrated Services Digital Network (ISDN) and Asymmetric Digital Subscriber Line (ADSL) adapters, or an X.25 device. Dial-up connections (incoming) can be accepted through a modem, the Internet, an LPT port, or a COM port. Direct connections, also listed as an incoming connection, are made through an LPT, COM, or infrared port.

A Windows 2000 dial-up client can use the Serial Line Internet Protocol (SLIP) to connect to legacy dial-up servers, the Microsoft RAS Protocol (AsyBEUI) to connect to legacy Windows NT dial-up servers, or the Point-to-Point Protocol (PPP). You should *always* use connections based on PPP if the dial-up server supports PPP because it is the only protocol that allows for advanced security features and performance features. The Windows 2000 *dial-up* facility supports both AsyBEUI and PPP dial-up clients.

PPP connections in Windows 2000 include a number of important security features such as secure user authentication, mutual authentication, data encryption, and callback. You control the configuration of these features either through the properties of a connection or using Local Group Policy settings. You can secure an inbound connection by setting remote access permissions. Additional features available in Windows 2000 Server Routing and Remote Access service (RRAS) include caller-ID verification, Network Group Policy settings, and Remote Access Policy settings.

The **Internet Connection Sharing (ICS)** feature makes a dial-up client connection available to other computers on the network. This feature works similarly to APIPA by assigning an IP address and default mask to clients on the same network. Unlike APIPA, ICS sets a default gateway on client computers so that packets destined for another network are sent to the computer configured for ICS. The computer with the ICS dial-up or VPN connection acts as a router for incoming and outgoing packets.

Demand dialing automatically dials a connection when required. Combining demand dialing with ICS makes the connection configured for ICS available when users send packets to their default gateway. The default gateway in this case is the network adapter of the computer configured for ICS.

A feature designed to improve dial-up performance is dynamic multiple device dialing (Multilink). When a connection is configured for Multilink, additional bandwidth is available to the connection by establishing additional physical connections to the dial-up server. All connections are combined and load balanced to improve performance. When bandwidth requirements decrease, you can configure Multilink to drop the number of operational links to save on connection costs. This feature relies on the Bandwidth Allocation Protocol (BAP), and both the dial-up server and the client must be configured to support Multilink.

A remote access client supports two types of VPN connections: Point-to-Point Tunneling Protocol (PPTP) and Layer Two Tunneling Protocol (L2TP) with **IP Security (IPSec)**. A VPN connection allows you to securely tunnel packets of data through a public network such as the Internet. The packet tunnel uses TCP/IP, but the protocol inside the tunnel can be TCP/IP, IPX/SPX, or NetBEUI.

Note AppleTalk remote access for incoming connections to a computer running Windows 2000 Professional is supported by the AppleTalk Control Protocol (ATCP). The Windows 2000 Server operating system running RRAS includes the added benefit of acting as an AppleTalk router for incoming connections.

Dial-up and VPN connections support a variety of advanced user authentication methods, such as Extensible Authentication Protocol-Transport Level Security (EAP-TLS), which provides certificate-based encrypted authentication. Other authentication protocols from unencrypted Password Authentication Protocol (PAP) to Microsoft CHAP version 2 (MS-CHAP v2) are supported. EAP and MS-CHAP v2 are the only two authentication protocols that support mutual authentication. Mutual authentication verifies the identity of both the client and the server involved in the remote connection. You must choose an authentication protocol that meets or exceeds your security requirements and that is supported by the client and the remote access server.

Data encryption is supported between the remote access client and the remote access server using either Microsoft Point-to-Point Encryption (MPPE) or IPSec. MPPE requires either EAP-TLS or any of the MS-CHAP authentication protocols. You can use MPPE for either dial-up PPP or PPTP-based VPN connections. IPSec can apply to any connection, including the local area network (LAN) connection. IPSec provides L2TP with encryption services so that data is transmitted securely from the remote access client to its final destination on the remote network. Because IPSec is providing encryption services to L2TP, any authentication protocol including PAP and Shiva Password Authentication Protocol (SPAP) is allowed. L2TP is only a tunneling protocol; with IPSec, L2TP operates as a VPN.

Several important troubleshooting tools aid in solving configuration problems with the dial-up facility. For example, you can use PPP logging for troubleshooting PPP connections. You will establish most dial-up connections you make using PPP. PPP logging is available on a Windows 2000 dial-up server and on the client. To enable PPP logging on a client, use the Netsh dial-up scripting utility. Type **netsh ?** at the command line for information on using this utility. If you suspect that the problem is related to modem communications, review the Modem log contained in *%systemroot%*\Modemlog_*model*.txt. The log is automatically overwritten unless you adjust the logging settings using the Phone and Modem Options program in Control Panel.

If you are able to establish a connection with the remote network but you are unable to communicate with remote resources, run Netdiag to review a summary report of network communications. If a dial-up device is unavailable for configuration in the Network And Dial-Up Connections window, check the dial-up hardware in Device Manager and use the Add/Remove Hardware Wizard to install the device.

Objective 6.2 Questions

70-210.06.02.001

You want to use your Windows 2000 Professional computer with two external modems to dial in to your ISP. You configure a dial-up connection using the two modems, but when the connection is completed, only one of the modems is being used. What should you do in Windows 2000 Professional to dial both modems?

A. Use the Modems tab of the Phone And Modem Options dialog box.

B. Use the Advanced tab of the Phone And Modem Options dialog box.

C. Use the Options tab of the *connection_name* Properties dialog box to enable Multilink connections.

D. Use the Networking tab of the *connection_name* Connection Properties dialog box to enable Multi-link connections.

70-210.06.02.002

You are the administrator of your company's network supporting computers running Windows 2000 Professional. Management wants you to enable every computer on the network to browse Internet resources. Your only available Internet connection is a dial-up connection to an ISP using a 56 Kbps analog modem. You install the modem in one of the computers running Windows 2000 Professional, and make a new connection for it in the Network And Dial-Up Connections window. What else must you do? (Choose two.)

A. Enable ICS on the computer where the modem resides.

B. Enable ICS on all computers running Windows 2000 Professional.

C. Manually assign IP addresses to all computers without modems that are running Windows 2000 Professional.

D. Configure all Windows 2000 Professional computers without a modem to obtain an IP address automatically.

70-210.06.02.003

You want to connect to a remote Windows 2000 computer using a VPN connection from your computer running Windows 2000 Professional. The dial-up server to be used for the VPN connection does not support encrypted authentication. In this case, which two protocols can you use together to provide tunneling and encryption services for a secure VPN connection? (Choose two.)

A. IPSec

B. L2TP

C. MPPE

D. PPTP

70-210.06.02.004

You attempt to dial in to a remote access server, and you monitor the progress of the connection. The status indicates connecting, authorizing, and disconnecting. You specify the option to bring up a terminal window after dialing, but this causes an unintelligible combination of characters to be displayed before disconnecting.

Review the diagram below to view the Security tab in the Dial-Up Connection To Internet Properties dialog box.

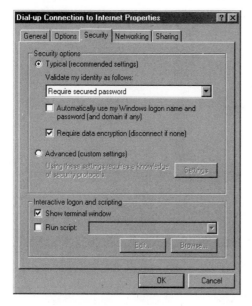

What should you do to allow the connection to be completed?

A. Specify the option to allow an unsecured password, and clear the Show Terminal Window check box.

B. Specify the option to require a secured password, select the Run Script check box, and then select %systemroot%\System32\Ras\Pppmenu.scp from the drop-down list box to establish a connection with the PPP host.

C. Select the Automatically Use My Windows Logon Name And Password check box, and clear the Show Terminal Window check box.

D. Select the Advanced (Custom Settings) radio button, and then click the Settings button. In the Advanced Security Settings dialog box, select the Use Extensible Authentication Protocol (EAP) radio button and click OK.

Objective 6.2 Answers

70-210.06.02.001

▶ **Correct Answers: C**

A. **Incorrect:** In the Modems tab of the Phone And Modem Options dialog box, you install any modems that were not automatically detected through Plug and Play enumeration. Clicking the Add button in the Phone And Modem Options dialog box starts the Add/Remove Hardware Wizard and shows the Install New Modem screen. The Modems tab is also an important place to begin troubleshooting modem problems. To troubleshoot an installed modem, select the modem and then click Properties. In the *modem* Properties dialog box, you can adjust the modem's configuration, perform modem diagnostics, and adjust the modem logging function so that the Modem log contained in *%systemroot%\Modemlog_model*.txt is appended to rather than overwritten.

B. **Incorrect:** In the Advanced tab of the Phone And Modem Options dialog box, you install and configure telephony providers. Telephony Service Providers (TSPs) resolve the protocol-independent call model of the Telephony API (TAPI) into protocol-specific call-control mechanisms.

C. **Correct:** All dial-up hardware devices installed in Windows 2000, including infrared ports, appear in the Connect Using box in the General tab of the *connection_name* Properties dialog box. After you select the devices that should be used to establish a Multilink connection, click the Options tab to enable Multilink. If you select multiple devices for the connection, then the Multiple Devices drop-down list box will be available near the bottom of the Options tab. This drop-down list box contains three settings: Dial Only First Available Device, Dial All Devices, and Dial Devices Only As Needed. The second and third options enable Multilink dialing. The third option, Dial Devices Only As Needed, allows you to set additional configuration options to control the bandwidth thresholds that cause additional devices to be connected or disconnected.

D. **Incorrect:** You use the Networking tab of the *connection_name* Properties dialog box to specify the type of dial-up server to use—either PPP or SLIP—to configure advanced PPP settings, and to configure the installed networking components. The advanced setting Negotiate Multi-Link For Single Link Connections allows PPP to throttle bandwidth over a single line if the server supports this feature. This might slightly improve download performance from the dial-up server.

70-210.06.02.002

▶ **Correct Answers: A and D**

A. **Correct:** After the modem is installed and a connection is created for it, you must access the properties of the connection, click the Sharing tab, and then select the Enable Internet Connection Sharing For This Connection check box. When you enable this check box, the On-Demand Dialing check box is enabled. This setting instructs ICS to automatically dial the connection when users on the network attempt to send data whose destination is the external network.

   After ICS is configured, the computer containing the connection will be assigned the IP address of 192.168.0.1 and a class C subnet mask of 255.255.255.0. On-demand dialing, the DHCP allocator, and the DNS proxy are enabled, and the ICS service is started. The DNS proxy allows the ICS computer to resolve host names to IP addresses on behalf of the clients using the connection.

   Advanced settings for the ICS connection are available by clicking the Settings button. These settings allow you to configure network applications that should be available to computers sharing the connection and services to provide to users on remote networks. If your goal is to simply provide Web site access (port 80) through the ICS connection, it is not necessary to configure advanced settings.

B. **Incorrect:** Only one computer on the network should be configured for ICS. All computers on the network will then use the computer configured for ICS to reach external resources available from the connection.

C. **Incorrect:** When the ICS service is started, the DHCP allocator is enabled. Like a DHCP server, the DHCP allocator automatically assigns an IP address, subnet mask, and default gateway to client computers. The allocator is configured with a default scope of 192.168.0.1 to 192.168.0.254 and a subnet mask of 255.255.255.0. 192.168.0.1 is assigned to the ICS computer's LAN connection, and all other computers receive an address from the scope. All computers that will use the ICS computer to reach external resources are assigned the default gateway address of 192.168.0.1.

D. **Correct:** The DHCP allocator in the ICS computer assigns each computer on the network IP addressing information so that packets destined for a remote network will be sent to the ICS computer. The DHCP allocator can assign the IP address, subnet mask, and default gateway only if the computers that will use the ICS computer are configured to obtain an IP address automatically.

   If the DHCP Server service is running on the network, you should not use ICS. In this case, the DHCP Server service will allocate addressing information to the client computers and the ICS service will not be available to the clients. ICS is designed for small office or home networks.

70-210.06.02.003

▶ **Correct Answers: A and B**

A. **Correct:** Forming a tunnel does not guarantee the creation of a VPN. A VPN requires that the tunneled data travels securely. IPSec provides encryption to make an L2TP tunnel a VPN. IPSec provides end-to-end encryption services without regard to the authentication protocol. Therefore, even if a dial-up server supports only PAP, the data can travel securely over the transit internetwork using IPSec. A transit internetwork is the shared or public network used by encapsulated data. A typical transit internetwork is the Internet or a private intranet.

B. **Correct:** L2TP encapsulates PPP frames and sends the frames over the transit internetwork. Unlike PPTP, L2TP does not encrypt the data; instead, IPSec provides this service to L2TP. L2TP can be used as a tunneling protocol over the Internet or over private intranets.

C. **Incorrect:** PPTP uses MPPE. MPPE is available only when either EAP-TLS (smart card or other certificate-based services) or one of the MS-CHAP security protocols is used between the dial-up client and the dial-up server. This is required because MPPE uses EAP or MS-CHAP to generate the encryption key pairs.

D. **Incorrect:** PPTP uses MPPE for data encryption services. Because MPPE requires either EAP-TLS (smart card or other certificate-based services) or MS-CHAP to generate the encryption key, the dial-up server cannot use PAP for encrypted PPTP traffic.

70-210.06.02.004

▶ **Correct Answers: A**

A. **Correct:** Based on the Required Secure Password setting appearing in the diagram, this dial-up connection requires that the dial-up server use either CHAP, MS-CHAP, or MS-CHAP v2 to authenticate the dial-up client's identity. The client begins the connection process, and then when the client enters the authentication phase, the connection attempts to send identity information securely, but the dial-up server isn't accommodating that request. Therefore, the client disconnects the call. To verify that this is what is happening, at the command prompt, type **netsh ras set tracing ppp enabled** and then attempt the connection again. After the call is disconnected, type **netsh ras set tracing ppp disabled** to stop the PPP logging process. Then review the contents of the PPP.LOG file created in the *%systemroot%*\Tracing folder. To resolve this problem, select the Allow Unsecured Password option.

The terminal window appears because the Show Terminal Window check box is selected. The terminal window contains unintelligible characters probably because the dial-up server or security host does not require manual or scripted input or because nothing was entered into the window within a specified time. A security host is an authentication device located between the client and the server that verifies whether a connection is authorized to connect to a dial-up server. If you are connecting directly to a Windows 2000 Server RRAS server, then the terminal window is not necessary. To stop the terminal window from appearing, clear the Show Terminal Window check box.

B. **Incorrect:** The Require A Secured Password option means that the client's identity must be transmitted securely using CHAP, MS-CHAP, or MS-CHAP v2 authentication protocols. If the server is unable to accommodate this request, the connection is dropped.

A terminal window is appearing with unreadable text probably because it doesn't need to be displayed to gain access. Assigning the PPPMENU.SCP script file to the connection's attributes will cause the client to send scripted data back to the dial-up server or intermediate host. The question does not indicate that this data is required to establish a connection with the server.

C. **Incorrect:** Nothing in the question indicates that the dial-up server expects user identity information that matches your Windows 2000 logon name, password, and optionally, domain name.

A connection configured to automatically use the Windows logon name, password, and optionally, domain name is useful for mobile client computers that are operated by different corporate users. The connection's user ID will match the identity of the user logging on to the computer. The option to automatically use the Windows logon name, password, and optionally, domain name is available only if you select the Require A Secured Password option.

As described in the previous answer explanations for this question, the terminal window is not necessary, so clearing the Show Terminal Window check box is correct.

D. **Incorrect:** If the connection is failing, setting the EAP option isn't likely to solve the problem. To use this option, the client and server must be configured to use one of two EAP types: either EAP-TLS or EAP-MD5. EAP-TLS requires a user certificate on the client and a machine certificate on the server. A client certificate is typically stored locally on a device such as the fixed disk or smart card. The client and server exchange and verify each other's certificates. If the client is configured for MD5-Challenge (EAP-MD5), authentication is performed during the connection authentication phase rather than during the link negotiation phase, but a certificate is not used for authentication.

OBJECTIVE 6.3

Connect to shared resources on a Microsoft network.

In the first two objectives of this chapter, you explored the physical connections and most common protocols used to transport packets, authenticate users, and encrypt both user identity and data being transmitted across a network. This objective investigates accessing file system resources in a Microsoft network after you establish a connection to the network.

File system resources (folders and files) are made available to network users by creating shares. A share points to either a disk or a folder. The Server service and the Computer Browser service make shares available to the network. The Computer Browser service publishes computer name and share information; the Server service allows users to connect to these resources. These services are part of the File and Printer Sharing for Microsoft Networks component.

You can create a share in a number of ways. For example, at the command line, you can type **net share home=e:\homefolders /unlimited /remark:"shared home folder"** to share a folder named Homefolders with a share name of home. The /unlimited switch grants an unlimited number of users access to it, and the /remark switch adds a comment to describe the share's purpose. You can create a folder share in the user interface in the Sharing tab in the *foldername* Properties dialog box. You can open this dialog box in Windows Explorer by selecting a folder and on the context menu, clicking Sharing. You can follow this same procedure to share a drive by first selecting a drive.

You can connect to a share or a folder below a share in a number of ways. For example, at the command line, you can type **net use * \\server01.domain01.local\home\user1** to connect the first available drive letter to a Windows 2000 Server named server01.domain01.local with a share named home and a folder named User1. If drive J were the next available drive on the computer, then opening the J drive would show the contents of the User1 folder. You can connect to a share in the user interface in the Map Network Drive dialog box. This dialog box is available by opening Windows Explorer and clicking the Map Network Drive command on the Tools menu.

File system resources are protected by the Server service using **share permissions**, and they are protected on an NTFS partition by using **local permissions**. All file systems can be protected over the network using share permissions, but only partitions formatted with NTFS can be protected locally and over the network using local permissions.

The three share permissions are Read, Change, and Full Control. The Read share permission allows a user to view and open all folders and files in the share and access the properties of these file system objects. The Read share permission provides adequate privileges for running most applications. The Change share permission grants the user the privilege to modify the attributes, edit the contents, and delete folders and files below the share. You should grant the Read share permission along with the Change share permission, or users will not be able to access the share. The Change share permission provides adequate privileges for data that users need to modify. The Full Control permission grants the user all Read and Change permissions plus the privilege to edit the discretionary access control list (DACL) and take ownership. These privileges apply to the share and the folders and files below the share if the share is located on a partition formatted for NTFS. Shares, folders, and files located on a FAT partition do not contain DACLs or ownership information.

Note DACL and ownership features are NTFS local permissions.

A user's effective rights for all shares are the combination of the share permissions assigned to the user and any groups in which the user is a member. The Deny assignment overrides any other permissions granted to the share. For example, if a group in which a user is a member is granted the Read share permission but the user is explicitly denied the Read share permission, the user's effective right is Deny on Read. For shares located on NTFS partitions, local permissions and share permissions can conflict. The rule in this case is that the most restrictive permissions apply. For example, if a user is granted the Full Control share permission to a folder named User1 but the local permission granted to the user for this folder is Read, then the user's effective right is Read.

All permissions (share and local) are inherited unless inheritance is specifically blocked. By default, the Everyone group is granted the Full Control share permission when a share is created. If a folder or file is created on an NTFS partition, the object inherits the local permission of its parent folder. If local permissions are not modified on an NTFS partition or parent folder, the default local permission is Full Control granted to the Everyone group.

Objective 6.3 Questions

70-210.06.03.001

You are the administrator of a workgroup supporting computers running Windows 2000 Professional. The Reports shared folder resides on an NTFS partition in a computer running Windows 2000 Professional. Some users report that they can open files but not make changes. You want to enable users to edit files without granting more rights and permissions than necessary. Which additional permissions should you grant? (Choose two.)

A. The Read share permission

B. The Change share permission

C. The Write local permission

D. The Modify local permission

70-210.06.03.002

You are the network administrator of a workgroup supporting computers running Windows 2000 Professional. You hire LisaC to share folders, install and configure software, and install Plug and Play hardware. To which local group should you add her user account?

A. The Administrators group

B. The Backup Operators group

C. The Power Users group

D. The Users group

70-210.06.03.003

You are the administrator of a LAN supporting computers running Windows 2000 Professional. You want to connect to the Sales shared folder on a computer named Corp1. Which syntax should you use in the Run dialog box?

A. \Corp1\Sales\

B. \\Sales\Corp1

C. \\Corp1\Sales

D. \Sales\Corp1\\

Objective 6.3 Answers

70-210.06.03.001

▶ **Correct Answers: B and C**

A. **Incorrect:** The users are able to open files, but they are not able to make changes. The Read share permission provides this privilege level. With the Read permission alone, users are not able to modify the attributes of folders and files or edit their contents.

B. **Correct:** The Change share permission grants the users the ability to modify the attributes of folders and files below the share. Share permissions apply only when users access the contents of a share over the network. The Read share permission already assigned to the share must remain for users to access the share.

C. **Correct:** A local permission is a combination of a specific set of privileges called special permissions. The Write local permission provides the Create Files/Write Data, Create Folders/Append Data, Write Attributes, and Write Extended Attributes special permissions. The Write local permission *does not* grant the Change Permissions special permission. This special permission is different than the Change share permission—it grants the right to change the DACL on files and folders.

Because the users are able to open files contained in the Reports folder, the Read local permission must already be assigned to the folders and files below this share. The Read local permission provides the List Folder/Read Data, Read Attributes, Read Extended Attributes, and the Read Permissions special permissions.

In summary, the users are granted the Read and Change share permissions and the Read and Write local permissions. This combination of rights meets the requirements of this question: Users are able to edit the contents of files below the share. Users are also able to modify the attributes on files. However, this combination of permissions *does not* allow the users to move, rename, or delete folders or files below the share.

To ease administration and avoid share permission and local permission conflicts on NTFS partitions, consider modifying local permissions and leaving the share permission on a folder set to Full Control for the Everyone group.

D. **Incorrect:** The Modify local permission grants the users a different set of privileges than they require. This permission grants the user *some* of the privileges provided by the Write permission plus the Traverse Folder/Execute File, List Folder/Read Data, Read Extended Attributes, and Delete special permissions.

70-210.06.03.002

▶ **Correct Answers: C**

A. **Incorrect:** The Administrators group will allow LisaC to complete the tasks listed in the question, but it also gives her additional privileges that are unnecessary to meet the requirements. Members of the Administrators group are unlimited in their power to perform system administration tasks.

B. **Incorrect:** The Backup Operators group will allow LisaC to restore files on the computer, regardless of any permissions that protect those files. Members of the Backup Operators group can log on to the computer and shut it down, but they cannot share folders, install and configure software, or install hardware, Plug and Play or otherwise.

C. **Correct:** The Power Users group will allow LisaC to share folders and configure applications. She will also be able to install applications that do not modify operating system files or install system services. She will not be able to add or remove any Windows components. The question doesn't specifically outline which applications need to be installed, but limiting it to applications that are not Windows components and that do not modify operating system files or install system services is prudent. She will also be able to install Plug and Play hardware as long as the operating system detects the hardware. The operating system must detect the hardware because members of the Power Users group are not allowed to run the Add/Remove Hardware Wizard.

D. **Incorrect:** The Users group is too limited in its privileges for LisaC to complete any of the tasks outlined in the question. Users group membership provides a secure environment in which to run programs. Members of the Users group cannot modify systemwide registry settings, operating system files, or program files. They can shut down computers running Windows 2000 Professional, install Plug and Play hardware, run certified Windows 2000 programs that have been installed by administrators, create local groups, and manage the local groups that they create.

If a legacy application will not run, you may have to adjust the user's privileges or make the user a member of the Power Users group. Members of the Users group have full control of data files they create, their local profile, and the part of the registry represented by the HKEY_CURRENT_USER key.

70-210.06.03.003

▶ **Correct Answers: C**

A. **Incorrect:** Connecting to a share on another computer by typing a command in the Run dialog box opens a window to the share. The computer name always precedes the share name. However, the syntax shown in this answer is incorrect because a Universal Naming Convention (UNC) name always begins with two backslashes.

B. **Incorrect:** The computer name always precedes the share name when specifying UNC syntax. This answer shows the share name preceding the computer name.

C. **Correct:** The correct syntax using the UNC is *computername**sharename*. The syntax shown in the question is correct to connect to a computer with a NetBIOS name of Corp1 hosting a share named sales.

If Corp1 had a fully qualified domain name (FQDN) of corp1.microsoft.com, you could access the share by typing **\\corp1.microsoft.com\sales**. A UNC name can also use an IP address instead of a NetBIOS computer name or a FQDN. For example, if the IP address of corp1.microsoft.com is 10.1.1.100, you can connect to the share by typing **\\10.1.1.100\sales**.

If Corp1 is running Microsoft Internet Information Services (IIS), specifically the World Wide Web Publishing Service of IIS, then you can share the folder using the Web Sharing tab in the *foldername* Properties dialog box. If the folder is Web shared with Read and Directory Browsing access permissions enabled, then the same folder can be opened through a Web browser using any of the following addresses: *http://corp1/sales*, *http://corp1.microsoft.com/sales*, or *http://10.1.1.100/sales*.

D. **Incorrect:** The computer name always precedes the share name when specifying UNC syntax. The answer shows the share name preceding the computer name. Also, the UNC name always begins with two backslashes.

Implementing, Monitoring, and Troubleshooting Security

Configuring and managing security is a critical and often overlooked task when installing standalone or networked computers. Physical security is an important first step in securing computing resources and data from unauthorized access. Because mobility and network data access are critical to today's network operations, physical isolation of all computing resources is unrealistic. Computers that are networked or mobile make data more accessible and are at an even greater risk than computers that are physically secure and not connected to a network. Therefore, the next important security measure is protecting the computer's data through **user authentication**.

On most networks, user authentication is achieved by entering a username/password combination. Microsoft Windows 2000 enhances the user authentication process through a number of important technologies, including **Group Policy** and **smart cards**. The authentication process is further protected through sophisticated **authentication algorithms** and **encryption services**. The data that traverses the network is protected using virtual private networks (VPNs), which were explored in Objective Domain 6, and **IP Security (IPSec)**. You can use New Technology File System (NTFS) permissions and the **Encrypting File System (EFS)** to protect file system data from unauthorized access. You can also use shares to provide some additional protection for over-the-network resource access. However, NTFS and EFS provide a significantly more robust security infrastructure than shares do. If you suspect unauthorized data or computing resource access, Windows 2000 **auditing** allows you to track access to objects such as printers, folders, and files.

Configuring security is a complex task. To ease the configuration and deployment of a consistent security policy, Windows 2000 allows you to import security policy from one computer to another or to import predefined **security templates**. The **Security Configuration and Analysis snap-in** allows you to simplify the process of configuring and deploying security. This tool provides for the configuration and deployment of consistent security settings, including Group Policy application, event-log access, restricted group membership, system-service configuration, registry access, and file system access.

Tested Skills and Suggested Practices

The skills you need to successfully master the Implementing, Monitoring, and Troubleshooting Security Objective Domain on Exam 70-210: Installing, Configuring, and Administering Microsoft Windows 2000 Professional include the following:

- **Use EFS and recover encrypted data.**

    - Practice 1: Encrypt and decrypt folders and files.

    - Practice 2: Recover encrypted files from a computer running Windows 2000 in a workgroup and in a domain.

    - Practice 3: At the command prompt, type **cipher /?** to view the Cipher command-line switches. Run the switch used to encrypt a folder and its contents, run the switch that displays hidden and system files that are not encrypted by default, and run the switch that creates a new encryption key.

    - Practice 4: At the command prompt, type **efsinfo /?** to view the Efsinfo command-line switches.

    - Practice 5: Create a recovery agent using Microsoft Windows 2000 Server Certificate Services, and then add it to a standalone or workgroup computer using the Local Security Settings console.

- **Configure and troubleshoot local Group Policy security settings.**

    - Practice 1: Open the Local Security Settings console on a workgroup or standalone computer, and configure the two types of account policies: password policy and account lockout policy.

    - Practice 2: In the Local Security Settings console, open each of the IP Security policies appearing in the details pane. Review the various settings, and verify that default Kerberos authentication applies to all preconfigured rules. Review the General tab appearing in the Properties dialog box of each IP Security policy.

- Practice 3: Create a custom console containing the IP Security Policy Management snap-in. Set the focus of the snap-in to the local computer. Then create a new IPSec policy using the IP Security Policy Wizard. Configure the policy with a default response setting and Kerberos authentication. Notice that if the computer is not a member of a Windows 2000 domain, Kerberos authentication is not used. Do not assign this policy to the computer.

- Practice 4: Review the contents of and features available in the Manage IP Filter Lists And Filter Actions dialog box.

- **Configure, administer, and troubleshoot user accounts in a workgroup.**

  - Practice 1: Create users and groups using the Local Users and Groups snap-in in the Computer Management console.

  - Practice 2: Open the Local Security Settings console, and select the User Rights Assignment folder below the Local Policies node. Click the Action menu, and then click Export List. Save the exported list as a comma-delimited file (.csv). Open the .csv file in Microsoft Excel, and review the local groups appearing in the Local Setting column to determine each group's user rights assignments.

  - Practice 3: Experiment with the policies appearing in the User Rights Assignment and Audit Policy folders.

- **Configure and troubleshoot Windows 2000 workgroup and domain authentication.**

  - Practice 1: Create a local user account, log on interactively with this account, and then attempt to access network resources.

  - Practice 2: Create two identically named local user accounts on two computers running Windows 2000 Professional. Assign both user accounts the same password. Attempt to access resources on one computer from the other computer.

  - Practice 3: Create a user account in a Windows 2000 domain. Join the domain, and log on with this user account. Be sure you log on to the domain at least twice: the first time with the user account name and the second time with the UPN.

- **Configure and apply a consistent security configuration to multiple computers.**

  - Practice 1: Configure the policy settings appearing in the Security Options node in a local GPO.

  - Practice 2: Import a security template to multiple computers using the Local Security Settings console.

- Practice 3: Use the Security Configuration and Analysis snap-in to analyze a computer's security configuration. Configure the computer's security using the snap-in. Save the database as a new template, and import the template to other computers in a workgroup.

- Practice 4: View the log file created by the Security Configuration and Analysis snap-in after you run the Configure Computer Now command.

- Practice 5: Import a security template to a domain-based GPO.

Further Reading

This "Further Reading" section provides lists of important readings to supplement your current understanding of the skills tested within this Objective Domain. The lists are delineated into pertinent readings for each objective within this Objective Domain. If you feel that you need additional preparation prior to taking the exam, study these sources thoroughly.

Objective 7.1

Microsoft Corporation. "Encrypting File System for Windows 2000." You can download this article by searching on its title at *http://www.microsoft.com/windows2000*.

Microsoft Corporation. *MCSE Training Kit—Microsoft Windows 2000 Professional*. Redmond, Washington: Microsoft Press, 2000. Read and complete the practices in Lesson 3, Chapter 18, "Managing Data Storage."

Microsoft Corporation. *Microsoft Windows 2000 Professional Resource Kit*. Redmond, Washington: Microsoft Press, 2000. Read about EFS and PKI on pp. 587–620, Chapter 13, "Security"; read pp. 735–737, Chapter 17, "File Systems."

Microsoft Corporation. *MCSE Training Kit—Microsoft Windows 2000 Server*. Redmond, Washington: Microsoft Press, 2000. Read Lesson 2, Chapter 11, "Public Key Technologies."

Objective 7.2

Microsoft Corporation. *Microsoft Windows 2000 Professional Resource Kit*. Redmond, Washington: Microsoft Press, 2000. Read pp. 560–572, Chapter 13, "Security," and pp. 289–302, Chapter 7, "Introduction to Configuration and Management."

Microsoft Corporation. "Step-by-Step Guide to Configuring Enterprise Security Policies." You can download this article by searching on its title at *http://www.microsoft.com/windows2000*.

Microsoft Corporation. "Step-by-Step Guide to Understanding the Group Policy Feature Set." You can download this article by searching on its title at *http://www.microsoft.com/windows2000*.

Microsoft Corporation. *MCSE Training Kit—Microsoft Windows 2000 Professional*. Redmond, Washington: Microsoft Press, 2000. Read and complete the practices in Chapter 17, "Configuring Group Policy and Local Security Policy."

Objective 7.3

Microsoft Corporation. "Default Access Control Settings." You can download this article by searching on its title at *http://www.microsoft.com/windows2000*.

Microsoft Corporation. *Microsoft Windows 2000 Professional Resource Kit Group Policy Reference* online help file. Redmond, Washington: Microsoft Press, 2000. Read explanations of the Group Policy settings for audit policy and user rights assignments.

Microsoft Corporation. *Microsoft Windows 2000 Professional Resource Kit*. Redmond, Washington: Microsoft Press, 2000. Read pp. 545–559, Chapter 13, "Security."

Microsoft Corporation. *MCSE Training Kit—Microsoft Windows 2000 Professional*. Redmond, Washington: Microsoft Press, 2000. Read and complete the practices in Lesson 3, Chapter 16, "Auditing Resources and Events."

Objective 7.4

Microsoft Corporation. *Microsoft Windows 2000 Professional Resource Kit*. Redmond, Washington: Microsoft Press, 2000. Read pp. 540–545, Chapter 13, "Security."

Microsoft Corporation. *MCSE Training Kit—Microsoft Windows 2000 Professional*. Redmond, Washington: Microsoft Press, 2000. Read and complete the practices in Chapter 10, "Setting Up and Managing User Accounts"; and read Lesson 1, Chapter 21, "Configuring Remote Access."

Microsoft Corporation. "Smart Card Logon." You can download this article by searching on its title at *http://www.microsoft.com/windows2000*.

Microsoft Corporation. "Windows 2000 Kerberos Interoperability." You can download this article by searching on its title at *http://www.microsoft.com/windows2000*.

Objective 7.5

Microsoft Corporation. "Step-by-Step Guide to Using the Security Configuration Tool Set." You can download this article by searching on its title at *http://www.microsoft.com/windows2000*.

Microsoft Corporation. *Microsoft Windows 2000 Professional Resource Kit*. Redmond, Washington: Microsoft Press, 2000. Read pp. 572–575 and pp. 583–587, Chapter 13, "Security."

OBJECTIVE 7.1

Encrypt data on a hard disk by using Encrypting File System (EFS).

All versions of New Technology File System (NTFS) use local permissions to restrict access to files. However, local permissions won't protect data if the partition is accessed locally using an operating system other than Microsoft Windows NT or Windows 2000. When NTFS was released with Windows NT 3.1, Windows NT was the only operating system able to locally access files on NTFS partitions protected with local permissions. Since then, third-party utilities have been released that bypass local permissions to allow partial or full access to NTFS partitions even when running other operating systems, such as MS-DOS or Microsoft Windows 98.

Microsoft includes **Encrypting File System (EFS)** support with Windows 2000 to counter the vulnerability of protected data located on an NTFS partition. EFS provides file encryption services by using a **symmetric encryption algorithm** and a **file encryption key**. A partition *must* be running NTFS version 5 to support encryption. Encryption is applied as a folder or file attribute. You can use one of two common methods to set the encryption attribute: either from Windows Explorer or from the command line using CIPHER.EXE.

To enable encryption from Windows Explorer, access the properties of a folder or file and, in the General tab, click the Advanced button to open the Advanced Properties dialog box. The last option in this dialog box is the Encrypt Contents To Secure Data check box. This check box is mutually exclusive of the Compress Contents To Save Disk Space check box. This is because an encrypted file cannot be compressed, and a compressed file cannot be encrypted. The Cipher command-line utility allows you to view encryption settings on folders and files as well as encrypt and decrypt them. Additional management functions provided with Cipher include the ability to force encryption and create a new file encryption key.

A command-line utility for displaying details of file encryption settings is EFS-INFO.EXE. This utility displays the following file encryption information: the user allowed to decrypt a file, the recovery agent or agents, and the certificate thumbnail (identifier). Running Efsinfo is an easy way to find out the recovery agents for an encrypted folder or file. Efsinfo is included with the Windows 2000 Professional and Server Resource Kits.

When you set the encryption attribute on a folder, you have the option of encrypting just the folder or all of its contents (including subfolders). Any new files created in an encrypted folder are automatically encrypted, including files copied to the folder. An encrypted file remains encrypted if it is copied or moved to one of the following:

- The same partition
- A different NTFS partition on the same computer
- An NTFS partition on another computer running Windows 2000

Note If an encrypted file is copied to another computer running Windows 2000, the other computer must support an equal or greater level of encryption to preserve the encryption attribute.

An encrypted file is decrypted if it is moved to a **file allocation table (FAT)** partition or another computer running a version of NTFS earlier than version 5. You must be allowed to decrypt the file; otherwise, a copy or move operation to a partition that does not support encryption will fail. If you open an encrypted file in a program and that program creates temporary files in an encrypted folder, the temporary files are encrypted. If the program creates temporary files in an unencrypted folder, the temporary files are not encrypted. Therefore, encrypt the temporary folder to maximize file security.

Because EFS is tightly integrated with NTFS, encryption and **decryption** are completed in the background with little user intervention. The process of generating a **public-key pair** and getting the public key certified is completed silently and in the background. Even though encryption and decryption are background processes, the EFS infrastructure provides a high level of security. To decrypt a file, a user must have access to a valid **certificate** and associated **private key**. You can store the certificate and private key locally or on a device such as a **smart card** or floppy disk.

To tighten security further, use the Microsoft Windows 2000 System Key (SysKey) utility to configure security for the private startup key. After encryption is enabled, either by using this tool or by encrypting a folder or file, encryption cannot be disabled. Using SysKey, you can specify the password key that must be entered on startup to unlock the system, or you can use the system-generated password key. If you use the system-generated password key, you can store the key on a floppy disk that must be inserted to start the system or store the key locally. Local storage of a system-generated password key is the default setting.

The danger of such a high level of security is that the loss of a private key used to encrypt the file could mean that the file cannot be decrypted. Windows 2000 protects against this by requiring that at least one user account be configured with a recovery agent certificate and a private key. On a standalone or workgroup computer, the user account created at the first logon following operating system installation is designated as the recovery agent. This is typically the local Administrator account, but it will be a different account if one is created during operating system installation.

You can add alternate recovery agents to a standalone or workgroup computer from the Add Recovery Agent Wizard. To start this wizard, open the Local Security Settings console, select the Encrypted Data Recovery Agents folder located below the Public Key Policies folder, click the Action menu, and then click Add. The Add Recovery Agent Wizard will request a certificate (.cer) file created for recovery. You must use Certificate Services running on Windows 2000 Server to create alternate recovery agent certificates.

If a computer running Windows 2000 Professional is made a member of a Windows 2000 domain, the domain Administrator account becomes the recovery agent. The domain Administrator account is designated as the data recovery agent in the Default Domain Policy Group Policy object (GPO). Additional recovery agents are added to any domain-based GPO, such as an organizational unit (OU) GPO.

Objective 7.1 Questions

70-210.07.01.001

You administer a Pentium III computer running Windows 2000 Professional. You want to encrypt a folder using a command prompt. Which command-line utility should you use?

A. Cipher

B. Efsinfo

C. Drivers

D. Nfsadmin

70-210.07.01.002

You are the administrator of a workgroup supporting computers running Windows 2000 Professional. Sandra stores her files on an encrypted NTFS partition. She is out of town on a business trip, and you need to access some of her encrypted files for an important meeting. You do not know Sandra's password, but you know that the default recovery agent is the Administrator account. Which procedure is recommended for accessing Sandra's encrypted files?

A. Log on to Sandra's computer as Administrator, and decrypt the files.

B. Log on to Sandra's computer as a member of the Backup Operators group, and decrypt the files.

C. Log on to Sandra's computer as a member of the Backup Operators group, and take ownership of the files.

D. Log on to another computer as Administrator, restore a backup version of the files, and decrypt the files.

70-210.07.01.003

You are the administrator of a domain supporting 80 computers running Windows 2000 and 4 computers running Windows 2000 Server. Users save work to home folders on a server. The NTFS partition containing the home folders uses EFS. Ingo leaves the company, and you move his files from the home folder to his manager's folder. The manager attempts to open the files, but an Access Denied error message appears. The default recovery agent is in use. How can you access the encrypted files?

A. Grant the manager NTFS Full Control permission.

B. Grant the manager NTFS Take Ownership permission.

C. Log on as the local Administrator, and recover the files.

D. Log on as the domain Administrator, and recover the files.

70-210.07.01.004

You are the administrator of a workgroup supporting computers running Windows 2000 Professional. A remote computer running Windows 2000 Professional named Win2000rem is used for remote encryption. You want to achieve these results:

- Use EFS to encrypt files on Win2000rem.

- Use EFS to encrypt data transferred over the network.

- Use EFS to encrypt the \Docs folder on your computer running Windows 2000 Professional.

- Set an OU Group Policy for recovery of EFS-encrypted data.

Your proposed solution is to log on to your computer as Administrator, use Windows Explorer to encrypt the \Docs folder, and use the Cipher command-line utility to encrypt the appropriate folders and files on Win2000rem.

Which results does the proposed solution provide? (Choose two.)

A. Files in the \Docs folder on Win2000rem are encrypted using EFS.

B. Data transferred over the network is encrypted using EFS.

C. The \Docs folder on your computer is encrypted using EFS.

D. An OU Group Policy is defined for recovery of EFS-encrypted data.

Objective 7.1 Answers

70-210.07.01.001

▶ **Correct Answers: A**

A. **Correct:** The Cipher command-line utility (CIPHER.EXE) allows you to create new file encryption keys and view, encrypt, and decrypt folders and files. To encrypt a folder using this utility, type **cipher /e** *path_name\ folder_name*, where *path_name* is the folder path and *folder_name* is the name of the folder you want to encrypt. To encrypt a folder and all of its subfolders, type **cipher /e /s: path_name\ folder_name**. To encrypt a folder, all of its subfolders, and all files in the folder hierarchy, type **cipher /e /s:** *path_name\ folder_name* **/a**.

B. **Incorrect:** The Efsinfo command-line utility (EFSINFO.EXE) provides detailed information on encrypted files and folders. Suppose you use the Cipher command-line utility to create a new encryption key for the current user by typing **cipher /k**. If you later wanted to view the encryption key thumbnail you created, you would type **efsinfo /y**. You can't use Efsinfo to encrypt or decrypt folders or files.

C. **Incorrect:** The Drivers command-line utility (DRIVERS.EXE) lists all of the drivers in the *%systemroot%*\System32\Drivers folder that are currently running. You can use this utility to identify a driver that might be causing problems because of corruption or because it is missing, not loaded, or outdated. This utility is part of both the Windows 2000 Professional and Windows 2000 Server Resource Kits; you can't use it to manage EFS.

D. **Incorrect:** The Nfsadmin command-line utility (NFSADMIN.EXE) allows you to configure and administer a Windows 2000 client running the NFS Client to access a Network File System (NFS) resource. You can't use this utility to manage EFS.

70-210.07.01.002

▶ **Correct Answers: A**

A. **Correct:** In a workgroup, the Administrator local user account is set as the default recovery agent when the operating system is installed, and a new user account is *not* created during setup. To decrypt the files, log on as Administrator and decrypt the files using either Windows Explorer or the Cipher command-line utility.

To verify that the local administrator is the default recovery agent, log on with the Administrator account and open the Local Security Settings console. To open this console, click the Start menu, point to Programs, point to Administrative Tools, and then click Local Security Policy. In the Local Security Settings console, expand the Public Key Policies container and then select the Encrypted Data Recovery Agent folder. Notice that the Administrator certificate appears in the details pane. From here, you can add recovery agents and export certificates and keys (if available) using the Certificate Export Wizard. Use Efsinfo to check the recovery agent or agents assigned to a folder or file. For example, to check the recovery agent for a file named DOCUMENT.DOC in the D:\Home\Sandra folder on a computer named Computer1, type **efsinfo /r d:\home\sandra\document.doc** on Computer1. Efsinfo will return something like this:

```
document.doc: Encrypted
Recovery Agents: COMPUTER1\Administrator (OU=EFS File Encryption Certificate, L=EFS,
CN=Administrator)
```

B. **Incorrect:** The members of the Backup Operators group are not assigned as recovery agents. A user is assigned as an alternate recovery agent on a standalone or workgroup computer by adding the user's .cer certificate file. You add the .cer file by using the Add Recovery Agent Wizard available from the Local Security Settings console on a computer containing the user's certificate. You must create certificate files for recovery in Certificate Services and then import them using the Add Recovery Agent Wizard. Certificate Services is available in Windows 2000 Server. To manage certificates stored locally, you can use the Certificates snap-in. This snap-in is not part of a console installed by default, so you must create a custom console containing this snap-in.

C. **Incorrect:** Members of the Backup Operators group are not granted the right to take ownership. Even if they were granted the Take Ownership right, taking ownership does not grant the right to decrypt files.

D. **Incorrect:** The Windows 2000 version of Microsoft Windows Backup (NTBACKUP.EXE) retains the encryption attributes of folders and files. If a recovery procedure cannot be completed on Sandra's computer and a backup file contains the encrypted folders and files, the backup can be sent to a computer containing a valid recovery agent. Before you can restore the backup file and decrypt the data, import a recovery agent certificate and private key that is valid on Sandra's computer to the computer used for data recovery.

This procedure is unnecessary because you can log on to Sandra's computer using the local Administrator account and decrypt the encrypted files.

70-210.07.01.003

▶ **Correct Answers: D**

A. **Incorrect:** The encryption attribute is separate from NTFS local permissions. You will be able to change the discretionary access control list (DACL) on Ingo's files if you have the appropriate permissions to do so. However, the manager will not be able to decrypt Ingo's files because he is not designated as the recovery agent.

B. **Incorrect:** The encryption attribute is separate from the NTFS Take Ownership permission. You will be able to assign the Take Ownership permission to Ingo's former manager if you have the appropriate permissions to do so. However, the manager will not be able to decrypt Ingo's files because he is not designated as the recovery agent.

C. **Incorrect:** After a computer is joined to a Windows 2000 domain, the default recovery agent becomes *domain_name*\Administrator, where *domain_name* is the name of the domain to which the computer is joined. You can verify the recovery agent for a folder or file by running Efsinfo with the /r switch. .

D. **Correct:** When a Windows 2000 Professional computer becomes a member of a Windows 2000 domain, the domain Administrator account becomes the recovery agent. The domain Administrator account is designated as the encryption recovery agent in the Default Domain Policy GPO.

70-210.07.01.004

▶ **Correct Answers: A and C**

A. **Correct:** Encryption is available by default and is activated by setting the encryption attribute on a file or folder. By encrypting the \Docs folder on the remote computer, any files created in this folder are encrypted. You should apply this encryption when the folder is empty. If files are in the folder and you choose to apply encryption to the folders, subfolders, and files, other users who are not recovery agents on the computer will not be able to decrypt the files.

B. **Incorrect:** Data encryption is integrated with NTFS version 5 and functions locally. Data is *not* encrypted by EFS as it traverses the network. You can use IP Security (IPSec) to encrypt data as it travels over the network. Data can be encrypted over a dial-up line by implementing a virtual private network (VPN), such as Point-to-Point Tunneling Protocol (PPTP) or Layer Two Tunneling Protocol (L2TP) over IPSec.

C. **Correct:** As with the remote computer (Win2000rem), encryption is available by default. On both the remote computer and the local computer, the first user created during the Windows 2000 setup routine or the local Administrator account is designated as the recovery agent.

D. **Incorrect:** An OU is a construct of a Windows 2000 domain. If the computers are members of a Windows 2000 domain, you can assign a GPO to the OU containing the computers and then configure a recovery agent Group Policy setting in this GPO. By default, the domain Administrator account is designated as the recovery agent in the Default Domain Policy GPO.

OBJECTIVE 7.2

Implement, configure, manage, and troubleshoot local security policy.

You apply workgroup and standalone computer security to a computer running Windows 2000 Professional through **local security policy**. You configure and view local security policy from the **Local Security Settings console**, which you open from the Local Security Policy icon in Administrative Tools.

Four categories of local security policies exist: **account policies**, **local policies**, **public key policies**, and **IP Security policies**. In Objective 7.1, you examined the **Encrypting File System (EFS)** recovery policy, which is a public key policy setting. This policy setting appears in the Public Key Policies\Encrypted Data Recovery folder of the Local Security Settings console. This objective explores the other three policy categories. Account policies are categorized by password policy and account lockout policy. Local policies are categorized by audit policy, user rights assignment, and security options. IP Security policies are categorized by three types of IP Security (IPSec) rules, from Unsecured to Require Secured Communication Between Two Endpoints.

To configure most policy settings, select a node or folder object in the console tree appearing in the Local Security Settings console. Then double-click the security setting appearing in the details pane to set the properties of the setting. For example, to deny the local Guest account from logging on locally, expand the Local Policies node and then select the User Rights Assignment folder. In the details pane, double-click the Log On Locally setting to open the Local Security Policy Setting dialog box. To the right of *computer_name*\Guest, clear the Local Policy Setting check box.

When a computer becomes a member of a Windows 2000 domain, domain-based security policy overrides local security policy. The Default Domain Policy Group Policy object (GPO) is applied to the computer unless Group Policy settings are changed. The security applied to a computer in the domain appears in the Domain Security Policy console and is part of the Default Domain Policy GPO.

The greater the number of GPOs and settings within each GPO configured for a computer, the longer it takes for the computer to start up and complete the logon process. Therefore, minimize the number of GPOs applied to a computer in a domain and minimize the settings applied to a computer in a domain, in a workgroup, or on a standalone computer.

Objective 7.2 Questions

70-210.07.02.001

You are the administrator of a workgroup supporting computers running Windows 2000 Professional. You want to use Group Policy to configure a user account password policy that enforces a minimum password length on all workgroup computers. How can you accomplish this task?

A. Open the Users and Passwords program in Control Panel, select the Password Policy check box, and click the Advanced Password Settings button. In the Advanced Password Settings dialog box, configure minimum password length.

B. Open the Local Security Policy icon in the Administrative Tools folder. In the Local Security Settings console, use the Account Policies node to configure password settings.

C. Open the Computer Management icon from the Administrative Tools folder. In the Computer Management console, click the Security Settings node, and in the details pane, configure password settings.

D. Create a custom Microsoft Management Console (MMC), add the Group Policy snap-in, save it with the name GPO, and select the check box called Allow The Focus Of The Group Policy Snap-In To Be Changed When Launching From The Command Line. This Only Applies If You Save The Console. Using the custom Group Policy console, connect to each computer in the workgroup and configure minimum password length.

70-210.07.02.002

You want to prevent users from using passwords that contain user account names. Which GPO should you configure?

A. Enforce Password History

B. Minimum Password Age

C. Minimum Password Length

D. Passwords Must Meet Complexity Requirements

70-210.07.02.003

You are the administrator of a workgroup supporting Windows 2000 Professional computers. You want to configure an Account Lockout Policy that locks users out after four invalid logon attempts. You have configured the Account Lockout Threshold policy setting value to 4. You also want users to be locked out indefinitely until the Administrator unlocks the user account. What should you do?

A. Set Account Lockout Duration to 0.

B. Set Account Lockout Threshold to 0.

C. Set Account Lockout Duration to 99,999.

D. Take no action because this is the default setting.

Objective 7.2 Answers

70-210.07.02.001

▶ **Correct Answers: B**

A. **Incorrect:** The Users and Passwords program contains many of the features available through the Local Users and Groups snap-in. In the Users tab in this program, you can add, remove, and modify the properties of local user accounts and set passwords. In the Advanced tab, you can manage certificates, start the Local Users and Groups snap-in, and configure whether users are required to press Ctrl+Alt+Delete before logon. You can't use this program to configure Group Policy settings.

B. **Correct:** The Local Security Settings console contains the Security Settings extension of the Group Policy snap-in. You configure security settings for a standalone or workgroup computer from this extension. Configuring policy in this way applies to the computer where the Local Security Settings console is run. Therefore, you must run this console on each computer in the workgroup to set minimum password length.

To configure minimum password length on a computer, open the Local Security Settings console from the Local Security Policy icon. In the Local Security Settings console, expand the Account Policies node and then click the Password Policy folder. In the details pane, double-click the Minimum Password Length policy setting. In the Local Security Policy Setting dialog box, set the password length. The default is 0, which means no password is required.

C. **Incorrect:** The Security Settings node is not part of the Computer Management console.

D. **Incorrect:** Security Settings is an extension of the Group Policy snap-in. The extension containing security settings for a workgroup computer appears in the Windows Settings folder located below the Computer Configuration node. After you have navigated to this location, you can follow the procedure previously to configure minimum password length. This procedure works *only* on the local computer.

As outlined in the question, you can view Group Policy settings on other computers in the workgroup using a saved console. You can also use the default Group Policy console (GPEDIT.MSC) to complete this task. Before configuring Group Policy settings on another computer, you must be able to connect to it with local administrator privileges. To open Group Policy on another computer in the workgroup named Computer0 with a saved Group Policy named GPO, first open a command prompt and locate the folder containing the custom console. From the folder, type **gpo.msc /gpcomputer:"computer01"**. Using the default Group Policy console, you can type **gpedit.msc /gpcomputer:"computer01"** to open Group Policy on another computer.

This answer is incorrect because in the release version of Windows 2000 Professional, the only computer configuration security settings available remotely in a workgroup are IP Security Policies. The Account Policies, Local Policies, and Public Key Policies nodes do not appear. As outlined previously, you configure minimum password length from the Password Policy folder below the Account Policies node. You can run the Group Policy snap-in locally to configure this policy.

70-210.07.02.002

▶ **Correct Answers: D**

A. **Incorrect:** This policy setting does *not* enforce the content of a password. The Enforce Password History policy setting dictates the number of unique new passwords that a user logging on to a computer must use before an old password can be reused. The password history value ranges between 0 and 24 passwords. This setting enhances security by ensuring that the password change policy isn't negated by a user changing a password to an old password.

By default, this policy setting is defined in the Default Domain Policy GPO with a value of 1. On standalone or workgroup computers running Windows 2000 Professional, the local security policy for this value is set to 0.

B. **Incorrect:** This policy setting does *not* enforce the content of a password. The Minimum Password Age policy setting dictates the period of time (in days) that a password must be used before the user can change it. You can allow immediate password change with a policy setting value of 0, or you can configure values between 1 and 999 days.

By default, this policy setting is defined in the Default Domain Policy GPO. It is also defined in the local security policy of standalone and workgroup computers running Windows 2000 Professional with a value of 0. This means that the user can change his or her password immediately.

For the Enforce Password History policy setting to be effective, configure the Minimum Password Age policy setting to a value other than 0. Even if this policy setting is configured with a value of 1 or more, an administrator can change the user's password at any time.

C. **Incorrect:** The Minimum Password Length policy setting does enforce the content of a password by requiring a minimum number of characters in the password. In most cases, this policy setting does allow the password to contain the user account name. The only exception to this rule is if the user account name does not meet the Minimum Password Length policy setting value. For example, if the Minimum Password Length policy setting is set to 5, the MaxN user account cannot be the password because it doesn't contain enough characters.

By default, this policy setting is defined in the Default Domain Policy GPO and in the local security policy of standalone and workgroup computers running Windows 2000 Professional with a value of 0.

D. **Correct:** The Passwords Must Meet Complexity Requirements policy setting does enforce the content of a password by verifying that the password meets a specific set of complexity requirements. The requirements are that the password cannot contain all or part of the user's account name, is at least six characters long, and contains characters from three of the following items: English uppercase characters (A...Z), English lowercase characters (a...z), base 10 digits (0...9), and nonalphanumeric characters (for example, !,$#,%). This policy is enforced only when a user account is created or a password is changed.

By default, this policy setting is disabled in the Default Domain Policy GPO and in the local security policy of standalone and workgroup computers running Windows 2000 Professional.

70-210.07.02.003

▶ **Correct Answers: A**

A. **Correct:** The Account Lockout Duration policy setting dictates the number of minutes a locked-out account remains locked out before automatically becoming unlocked. The range is 1 to 99,999 minutes. By setting the lockout duration to 0, the account will be locked out until an administrator explicitly unlocks it.

By default, this policy setting is not defined because it has meaning only when you specify an account lockout threshold.

B. **Incorrect:** The question states that this policy setting value was configured to four invalid logon attempts. Setting this value to 0 means that the account will *never* be locked out. The Account Lockout Threshold policy setting dictates the number of failed logon attempts that will cause a user account to be locked out. A locked-out account cannot be used until an administrator resets it or the Account Lockout Duration expires. You can set values between 1 and 999 failed logon attempts, or you can specify that the account will never be locked out by setting the value to 0.

When you assign the Account Lockout Threshold policy setting a value other than 0, a Suggested Value Changes dialog box appears recommending that the Account Lockout Duration and Reset Account Lockout Counter After policy setting values be changed from Not Defined to 30 Minutes. Therefore, if you set the Account Lockout Threshold policy setting value to four invalid logon attempts and a user attempts four logons with incorrect passwords, the account will be locked for 30 minutes. If a user attempts fewer than four invalid logons in a 30-minute period, the invalid logon attempts counter will be reset to 0. Because you are configuring the Account Lockout Duration policy setting value to 0, the Reset Account Lockout Counter After policy setting has no effect.

Failed password attempts against standalone or workgroup computers that have been locked using either Ctrl+Alt+Delete or password-protected screen savers do not count as failed logon attempts.

C. **Incorrect:** An Account Lockout Duration of 99,999 means that an account will be disabled for 99,999 minutes, or approximately 69 days. After 69 days, the account will be automatically enabled. This is the maximum lockout duration that the computer automatically resets. This does not satisfy the requirement described in the question that the users be locked out indefinitely until the Administrator unlocks the user account.

D. **Incorrect:** The Account Lockout Threshold policy setting value is 0, and the Account Lockout Duration and Reset Account Lockout Counter After policy settings are not defined. These are the default setting values in the Default Domain Policy GPO and in the local security policy of standalone and workgroup computers running Windows 2000 Professional.

OBJECTIVE 7.3

Implement, configure, manage, and troubleshoot local user accounts.

A critical security measure in all networks is controlling initial access through user account configuration. In Windows 2000 Professional and Windows 2000 Server running as a standalone or member server, user accounts and groups are stored locally in a security accounts database. Windows 2000 domain user accounts and other domain objects, such as security groups and **Group Policy**, exist in the Microsoft Active Directory store. The Active Directory store is shared and managed by computers running Windows 2000 Server as domain controllers.

This objective covers **local user account** administration, including creating and modifying user accounts, account settings, group membership, and local policy configuration. Specific emphasis is placed on configuring local policies for auditing user account activity and assigning user rights.

Note Account policies (Password Policy and Account Lockout Policy) were explored in the previous objective.

You complete most local user account administration from the **Local Users and Groups snap-in** appearing in the Computer Management console. This snap-in contains the Users and Groups folders. You can also use the **User and Passwords program** in Control Panel to complete user administration tasks using wizards.

From the Users folder, you create, modify, and delete local user accounts. By default, the Users folder contains two built-in accounts: Administrator and Guest. You can rename these accounts, but you cannot delete them. The Guest account is disabled by default. In the GUI-Mode phase of a Windows 2000 Professional setup procedure, you can create an account that is initially named by extracting the value specified in the User Name text box. This account is automatically granted administrator privileges. Except for the built-in Administrator account, you can disable all accounts.

From the Groups folder, you create, modify, and delete group accounts. By default, the Groups folder contains the Administrators, Backup Operators, Guests, Power Users, Replicator, and Users built-in **local groups**. The following privileges are assigned to user accounts that are members of these groups:

- Administrators have complete and unrestricted access to the computer. The default member of this group is Administrator. If a user is created during the installation of Windows 2000 Professional, it is also made a member of this group.

- Backup Operators override security restrictions for the sole purpose of backing up or restoring files. This group contains no members by default.

- Guests are granted the same access as any member of the Everyone special group. The default member of this group is the Guest user account, which is more restricted than user accounts manually added to the Guests group.

- Power Users possess most administrative powers with some restrictions. Power Users can run legacy applications in addition to certified applications. This group contains no members by default.

- Replicator supports file replication in a domain. This group contains no members by default.

- Users are prevented from making accidental or intentional systemwide changes. Users can run certified applications but not most legacy applications. The Authenticated Users and Interactive special groups are members of the Users group. When a user account is created, it is automatically made a member of the Users group.

User rights assignments dictate what a user or group is able to do on the computer. By default, the Everyone group and the local groups (except for the Guests group) are assigned various user rights. No user account is directly assigned user rights by default, but you can assign user rights to user accounts or other groups. For example, the Users group is granted the rights to shut down the computer, remove the computer from a docking station, log on locally, access the computer from the network, and bypass traverse checking. The Bypass Traverse Checking user right determines whether you can move through a folder hierarchy on the computer even though you might not have the permissions to view a folder or folders in the hierarchy. You configure user rights from the **User Rights Assignment folder** under the Local Policies node in the Security Settings console.

Note Any policies configured in a domain-based Group Policy object (GPO) override local policy settings, including user rights assignment.

Audit policy settings dictate which security-related activity the Event Log service should log in the Security log. By default, nothing is audited. Audit policy tracks success and failure attempts. You configure whether one or both types of attempts should be tracked. For example, when you enable the Audit Logon Events audit policy, you configure whether to log successful attempts, failed attempts, or both types of attempts in the Security log. You configure audit policy from the **Audit Policy folder** under the Local Policies node in the Security Settings console.

Note Objective 7.5 explores the Security Options folder under the Local Policies node.

Objective 7.3 Questions

70-210.07.03.001

You are the administrator of a computer running Windows 2000 Professional that multiple users share. An unauthorized user is suspected of deleting your documents. You want to audit the activity of the user to detect unauthorized actions. What should you do? (Choose two.)

A. Enable success auditing of the Audit Object Access policy setting.

B. Add the suspected user account to the SACL of the folder containing your documents.

C. Enable failure auditing of the Process Tracking policy setting.

D. Enable success auditing of the Process Tracking policy setting.

70-210.07.03.002

You are the administrator of a computer running Windows 2000 Professional that multiple users share. A user is suspected of changing the system time. You want to establish an audit policy to detect whether a user changes the system time. What should you do?

A. Enable auditing of the Audit Logon Events policy setting.

B. Enable auditing of the Audit Object Access policy setting.

C. Enable auditing of the Audit Privilege Use policy setting.

D. Enable auditing of the Audit System Events policy setting.

70-210.07.03.003

You are the administrator of a network supporting computers running Windows 2000 Professional. Geof, a user, is leaving the company and is being replaced by Alix. You want to deny access to the Geof user account and assign the Alix user account the same level of access that the Geof user account had. How can you accomplish these goals with minimum administration?

A. Copy the Geof user profile to the Alix user account.

B. Rename Geof's user account to Alix, and change the password.

C. Delete the Geof user account, create a new user account for Alix, and assign it the same permissions that Geof's account was assigned.

D. Disable the Geof user account, create a new user account for Alix, and assign it the same permissions that the Geof user account was assigned.

70-210.07.03.004

Jolie is a member of the local Administrators group on your computer running Windows 2000 Professional, which is shared among multiple users. A few users report that Jolie has accidentally deleted some of their Microsoft Word documents. Their documents are stored in individual folders assigned to each user who logs on to the computer, and each user is granted full control of his or her documents folder. You restore the missing documents from backup. You want to limit Jolie's access by allowing her only to back up data and reinstall applications. What should you do?

A. Remove the Jolie user account from the local Administrators group, and add the account to the Users group.

B. Remove the Jolie user account from the local Administrators group, and add it to the Power Users group. Add the Administrator local group to the parent folder containing all user documents and remove the Everyone group from the same folder.

C. Remove the Jolie user account from the local Administrators group, and add it to the Backup Operators and Power Users groups. Add the Administrators local group to the parent folder containing all user documents, and remove the Everyone group from the same folder.

D. Allow Jolie's user account to remain in the local Administrators group, and configure NTFS permissions to restrict her access to Read permissions on user documents.

70-210.07.03.005

You are the administrator of a workgroup supporting computers running Windows 2000 Professional. Which user rights assignment policies should you restrict to prevent unauthorized access to network resources and denial-of-service attacks? (Choose two.)

A. Bypass Traverse Checking

B. Enable Computer And User Accounts To Be Trusted For Delegation

C. Increase Quotas

D. Deny Access To This Computer From The Network

Objective 7.3 Answers

70-210.07.03.001

► **Correct Answers: A and B**

A. **Correct:** Configuring the Audit Object Access policy setting to monitor access attempts allows you to enable object auditing of objects such as folders and files on a New Technology File System (NTFS) partition, registry keys, and printers. Each of these objects contains an empty system access control list (SACL). Success audits generate an audit entry in the Security log when a user successfully accesses an object that has a configured SACL. Failure audits generate an audit entry in the Security log when a user unsuccessfully attempts to access an object. Defining the Audit Object Access policy setting to monitor failure audits isn't necessary because your goal is to track a user's success in deleting your documents.

B. **Correct:** Configuring the Audit Object Access policy setting is necessary to enable object auditing, but it does *not* begin object access security logging. After you define this policy setting, you must configure an object's SACL. An object containing an SACL is configured for auditing in the Security tab in the object's Properties dialog box. In the Security tab, click the Advanced button to open the Access Control Settings dialog box for the object. Click the Auditing tab in the Access Control Settings dialog box, add users or groups who should be audited, and then select the types of events you want to audit.

To track a specific user who you suspect is deleting your files, add the user to the audit list for the SACL on the folder containing your documents. Apply the audit entry to the folder, subfolders, and files, and configure the Delete and Delete Subfolders And Files access events. You might want to configure auditing for other successful access events such as List Folder/Read Data and Create Files/Write Data. After the suspected user has used the computer, check the Security log in Event Viewer.

C. **Incorrect:** Configuring the Audit Process Tracking policy setting to monitor access attempts allows you to audit detailed tracking information for events such as program activation, process exit, handle duplication, and indirect object access. Failure audits generate an audit entry when the process being tracked fails.

D. **Incorrect:** Success audits generate an audit entry when the process being tracked completes the audited event successfully.

70-210.07.03.002

▶ **Correct Answers: C**

A. **Incorrect:** Configuring the Audit Logon Events policy setting to monitor access attempts allows you to audit each instance of a user logging on or logging off a computer where the computer was used to validate the account. Success audits generate an audit entry when account logon occurs successfully. Failure audits generate an audit entry when an attempted occurrence of the account logon fails.

B. **Incorrect:** Configuring the Audit Object Access policy setting to monitor access attempts allows you to enable object auditing of objects such as folders and files on an NTFS partition, registry keys, and printers. Success audits generate an audit entry in the Security log when a user successfully accesses an object that has a configured SACL. Failure audits generate an audit entry in the Security log when a user unsuccessfully attempts to access an object.

C. **Correct:** Configuring the Audit Privilege Use policy setting to monitor access attempts allows you to audit each time a user exercises a user right. Success audits generate an audit entry when a user right is successfully exercised. Failure audits generate an audit entry when the exercise of a user right fails.

The Change The System Time user rights assignment is granted to the Power Users and Administrators groups by default. If you haven't changed this user rights assignment, the user changing the time must be a Power Users or Administrators group member. After you configure the Audit Privilege Use policy setting for successful attempts and the system time is changed, review the Security log for this event. The event ID for this event is 577, and the privilege is SeSystemtimePrivilege. You can look up event IDs using the *Windows 2000 Professional Resource Kit* Error and Event Messages Help file.

D. **Incorrect:** Configuring the Audit System Events policy setting to monitor access attempts allows you to audit when a user restarts or shuts down the computer or when an event has occurred that affects either the system security or the Security log. Success audits generate an audit entry when a system event is successfully executed. Failure audits generate an audit entry when a system event is unsuccessfully attempted.

70-210.07.03.003

▶ **Correct Answers: B**

A. **Incorrect:** Assuming that the Geof user profile is accessible by the Alix user account, the Alix user profile settings will match Geof's. However, depending on how security is configured, the Alix user account will probably not have access to Geof's files on an NTFS partition or in shares accessed over the network. Also, the Geof user account remains active, so if Geof is able to connect to the internal network, he will be able to gain access to his file resources.

B. **Correct:** Each user account contains a unique security ID (SID). The SID is granted access to resources and is symbolically represented by a user account name. Therefore, renaming the Geof user account to Alix will maintain the Geof user account security settings with a new name of Alix. Changing the password helps ensure that Geof will not be able to access resources previously available to him. This implicitly denies Geof access because the Geof user account no longer exists with the same username and password combination.

C. **Incorrect:** This will achieve the final objective of granting the Alix user account access to resources previously available to Geof, and it removes the Geof user account so that Geof can no longer access the network. However, this might require a significant amount of administrative effort, depending on the number of resources accessible by the Geof user account and the complexity of the security configuration.

D. **Incorrect:** Disabling the Geof user account achieves the objective of denying Geof access to resources. However, creating a new Alix user account and assigning the same permissions that the Geof user account had requires the same amount of administrative effort outlined previously.

70-210.07.03.004

▶ **Correct Answers: C**

A. **Incorrect:** Members of the Users local group are not able to back up data and install applications. Therefore, making the Jolie user account a member of only the Users local group will not allow Jolie to complete the administrative tasks that are her responsibility.

B. **Incorrect:** Members of the Power Users local group are able to install applications but are unable to back up and restore data. You can verify this by viewing the user right assignments Backup Files And Directories and Restore Files And Directories. The Administrators and Backup Operators local groups are assigned these privileges by default. No other group is assigned these user rights.

C. **Correct:** Members of the Power Users local group are able to install applications, so this membership satisfies one of Jolie's administrative responsibilities. Members of the Backup Operators local group are able to back up and restore files on the computer regardless of any permissions protecting the files. This permission satisfies her other administrative responsibility.

Removing Full Control from the Everyone group to the parent folder restricts access to the folder. By default, all folders and files in the parent folder inherit this permission. Adding the Administrators local group to the parent folder ensures easy access to members of the Administrators local group. Because the Jolie user account is no longer a member of the Administrators local group, Jolie will not be able to accidentally delete other users' documents.

D. **Incorrect:** NTFS permissions are cumulative unless a specific access denial is configured. Therefore, as a member of the Everyone group, Jolie's effective rights are Full Control. Even if her effective permissions were Read, as a member of the Administrators local group, she can take ownership of files and reassign rights to herself and then delete files.

70-210.07.03.005

▶ **Correct Answers: B and C**

A. **Incorrect:** The Bypass Traverse Checking user rights assignment grants the privilege to navigate through a folder structure even if a user does not have rights to the folders in the hierarchy. Users are not able to view the contents of folders with this user right. The Everyone, Users, Power Users, Backup Operators, and Administrators groups are granted this user rights assignment by default.

B. **Correct:** The Enable Computer And User Accounts To Be Trusted For Delegation user rights assignment grants the privilege to access resources on another computer using a client's delegated credentials. This user rights assignment is typically granted to a service account. The service account is assigned to a process that accesses other computer resources on the network. This privilege is not granted to any users or groups by default because it makes the computer vulnerable to attack by Trojan horse programs—programs that masquerade as another program in an attempt to obtain information such as username and password.

C. **Correct:** The Increase Quotas user rights assignment grants the privilege to use a process with write property access to another process to increase the processor quota assigned to the other process. This privilege is useful for system tuning, and it is required by the Cluster service account in Windows 2000 clusters. You can use this privilege to launch a denial-of-service attack, an explicit attempt to prevent legitimate users of a service from using that service. Using the Increase Quotas privilege, the attacker attempts to disrupt service to a specific system by excessively increasing the processor quota assigned to a process. The Administrators local group is granted this assignment by default.

D. **Incorrect:** The Deny Access To This Computer From The Network user rights assignment restricts users from connecting to a computer over the network. This user right is applied to users or groups. When users with this user rights assignment attempt to access the computer over the network, a message box appears stating that the user has not been granted the requested logon type. This policy is highly restrictive and is not assigned to any users or groups by default.

Implement, configure, manage, and troubleshoot local user authentication.

A user's credentials are authenticated against a database of identity information. In a workgroup or standalone computer, the database of identity information is the local security accounts store. In a Windows 2000 domain, the database of identity information is the Active Directory store. Certificate stores are important identity information stores for high security. Certificate stores are associated with users, services, and computers.

This objective covers supporting **user authentication** using the local security accounts store and the Active Directory store. Specifically, you must know how to configure and troubleshoot authentication to either store.

User authentication is the process of verifying a user's identity. You log on interactively to gain initial access to their computer or to the network. After the interactive logon process is complete, you access network resources using a network authentication method, such as Kerberos version 5. If you log on locally, you must provide network authentication credentials to access network resources. If you log on to a Windows 2000 domain (the Active Directory store), the interactive logon credentials are used to transparently authenticate you to network resources. You can obtain **logon credentials** by entering a username/password combination or by inserting a **smart card** and entering a personal identification number (PIN).

If you intend to log on interactively to a standalone or workgroup computer with a username/password combination, the Log On To text box contains the name of the computer. After a computer joins a Windows 2000 domain, the Log On To text box is populated with the logon domain and other domains in the hierarchy. A computer must be joined to the domain before a domain user can log on interactively. When you log on to a Windows 2000 domain, the Log On To text box contains the domain name. To avoid having to select the appropriate domain from the Log On To text box, you can log on with a **user principal name (UPN)**. A UPN is identical in syntax to an e-mail name: *username@ domain_name*, where *username* is the user account name and *domain_name* is the fully qualified domain name (FQDN) or custom suffix defined in the Active Directory store.

If you intend to log on interactively to a Windows 2000 domain from a Windows 2000 client using a smart card, the process begins by inserting a smart card into a smart card reader. This event causes a prompt for a PIN to appear. The PIN you enter is used to authenticate to the smart card, not to the domain. A public key certificate stored on the smart card is used to authenticate to the domain using the Kerberos version 5 protocol. Extensible Authentication Protocol-Transport Level Security (EAP-TLS) is used for Point-to-Point Protocol (PPP)-based logon with a smart card.

You use a variety of authentication protocols in a number of communication scenarios. For example, you use **Kerberos authentication** when a Windows 2000 Professional workstation logs on to a Windows 2000 domain. **IP Security (IPSec)** also uses Kerberos authentication by default. You can configure both network logon and IPSec for other authentication methods, such as certificates and shared secret keys. Remote access using PPP, which was explored in Objective 6.2, provides additional authentication protocols to secure remote access connections.

Objective 7.4 Questions

70-210.07.04.001

You are the administrator of your company's network. You add two new user accounts, FlorianV and ClausR, to a computer running Windows 2000 Professional that several users share. When FlorianV attempts to log on, an error message appears stating, "The system is unable to copy \Documents and Settings\All Users to \Documents and Settings\FlorianV. DETAIL – Access is denied." What should you do to allow FlorianV to log on?

A. Copy the All Users profile to the Default User profile.

B. Copy the Default User profile to the All Users profile.

C. Reset the permissions on the \Documents and Settings\All Users folder.

D. Reset the permissions on the \Documents and Settings\Default User folder.

70-210.07.04.002

You are the administrator of a domain supporting Windows 2000 computers. You create a local user account named AlanC on a computer running Windows 2000 Professional. You are unable to assign access permissions for domain resources to AlanC. How can you assign permissions for domain resources to this user?

A. Create a local user account on a member server.

B. Create a local user account on a domain controller.

C. Create a domain user account on a member server.

D. Create a domain user account on a domain controller.

70-210.07.04.003

You are the administrator of a domain supporting computers running Windows 2000 Professional. You want to implement a smart card logon process for your mobile clients. Which protocol should you use?

A. PAP

B. SPAP

C. CHAP

D. EAP-TLS

E. MS-CHAP

F. MS-CHAP v2

Objective 7.4 Answers

70-210.07.04.001

▶ **Correct Answers: D**

A. **Incorrect:** You generate local user profiles in one of two ways: when Windows 2000 Professional is installed and when a user logs on for the first time. The two user profiles automatically created when Windows 2000 Professional is installed are the All Users profile and the Default User profile. These two profiles serve distinct roles, so you should not copy the All Users profile to the Default User profile.

B. **Incorrect:** These two profiles serve distinct roles, so you should not copy the Default User profile to the All Users profile.

C. **Incorrect:** If the FlorianV user account is denied access to the All Users folder, when she attempts to log on, an error message appears stating that "D:\Documents and Settings\All Users\Desktop is not accessible. Access is denied." However, Florian can click OK and continue the logon process. The FlorianV user account will not have access to the contents of the All Users profile.

D. **Correct:** When a user with no user profile under the Documents and Settings folder logs on, a profile folder is automatically generated for that user by copying the contents of the Default User folder to a folder uniquely named for the user. By default, the Default User folder inherits the local permissions of Full Control assigned to the Everyone group. If this permission is removed and no alternate permission is assigned to allow the new user to access the Default User folder, a profile cannot be created for the user. If a profile cannot be created, the user is not allowed to log on. A solution to this problem is to reset the permissions on the Default User folder and then have the new user log on interactively.

70-210.07.04.002

▶ **Correct Answers: D**

A. **Incorrect:** You can create a local user account on the member server named AlanC with an identical password as the other AlanC user account. Then assign access permissions for local resources on the member server to the local user account. This will provide transparent access to resources on the member server. However, this does not provide access to other domain resources. Also, this method requires significant administrative overhead.

B. **Incorrect:** Domain controllers contain domain user accounts, not local user accounts. Therefore, it is not possible to create local user accounts on a domain controller.

C. **Incorrect:** Member servers contain local user accounts and are joined to a Windows NT or Windows 2000 domain. You cannot create domain user accounts *on* a member server. You can, however, create domain user accounts *from* a member server, but the account is located in the Active Directory store on domain controllers.

D. **Correct:** The AlanC local user account is designed to provide access to local resources on the computer. The full name of the AlanC local user account is *computername*\AlanC, where *computername* is the name of the computer where the local user account was created. This type of account is not granted access to domain resources. Instead, create a domain user account named AlanC. The full name of the AlanC user account name is AlanC@*domain_name* or AlanC@*unique_suffix*. Domain user accounts are designed to provide access to domainwide resources. After creating the account, make AlanC a member of a group or groups that are granted access permissions for domain resources. You can also directly assign permissions to the AlanC user account for domain resources.

70-210.07.04.003

▶ **Correct Answers: D**

A. **Incorrect:** Password Authentication Protocol (PAP) sends identity data unencrypted from a PPP client to the server. PAP is not used in the smart card logon process.

B. **Incorrect:** Shiva Password Authentication Protocol (SPAP) authenticates PPP clients to Shiva remote access servers and Windows 2000 remote access servers. SPAP follows a similar authentication process as PAP except that the password is encrypted before it is sent to the remote access server. SPAP is not used in the smart card logon process.

C. **Incorrect:** Challenge Handshake Authentication Protocol (CHAP) is an improvement over PAP and SPAP because the user's password is never sent over the PPP connection. Instead, the client runs the Message Digest 5 (MD5) hashing algorithm against the password entered locally, the session ID, and a challenge string sent by the dial-in server. The user name in clear text and the return string (hash) is sent to the dial-in server. The dial-in server duplicates the operation against the locally stored client password and compares the result with the response sent by the client. If there is a match, the dial-in server grants the client access. You can't use CHAP in the smart card logon process.

D. **Correct:** EAP-TLS uses transport layer security when a PPP connection is established. Mutual authentication and encryption services are provided between client and server using certificates. The client exchanges a user certificate that can be stored on a smart card or on the local disk, and the server sends a machine certificate.

E. **Incorrect:** Microsoft-CHAP (MS-CHAP) carries out a similar challenge response process as outlined for CHAP except that the password is already encrypted using the MD4 hashing algorithm. The dial-in server compares the encrypted password sent by the client with the locally stored encrypted version of the password. MS-CHAP is not used in the smart card logon process.

F. **Incorrect:** Microsoft-CHAP version 2 (MS-CHAP v2) is more secure then MS-CHAP and is also used for PPP communications. The dial-in server sends the client a session ID and a challenge string. The PPP client responds with its username, a client challenge string, and a response to the server's challenge string that is encrypted using the Secure Hash Algorithm (SHA). SHA hashes the server and client challenge string, the session ID, and the user's encrypted password. When the dial-in server receives the response from the client, it returns a success or failure response and an authenticated response using all of the data sent to it from the client. After the client verifies the return data, the connection is established. MS-CHAP v2 is not used in the smart card logon process.

O B J E C T I V E   7 . 5

Implement, configure, manage, and troubleshoot a security configuration.

The previous objectives in this chapter examined all of the security policies except those contained in the **Security Options** folder. On a standalone or workgroup computer, the Security Options folder is located below the Local Policies node. The policies contained in the Security Options folder are applied to the computer and affect all users who use the computer. Some of the policies are extensions of other policies, such as the Audit Use Of Backup And Restore Privilege policy setting. This policy adds to the events that can be audited on a computer running Windows 2000. Other policy settings change the default behavior of Windows 2000, such as the Disable Ctrl+Alt+Delete requirement for logon.

As you might have surmised by now, the sheer number of policy settings, file system permissions, and security groups and the way these security features interact with each other make configuring security on a single computer a complex task. Even more difficult is implementing a consistent security configuration from one computer to the next. Centralized permissions, domain-based Group Policy objects (GPOs), security groups, and user accounts ease the administrative burden of applying a consistent security configuration across the network, but they don't decrease the complexity of security configuration. **Security templates** are used for this purpose.

A security template is an .inf file containing security configuration settings. You apply the policy settings to a standalone or workgroup computer by importing them into the Security Settings node of the local GPO. To import a security template, select the Security Settings node in the Local Security Settings console and, on the Action menu, click Import Policy. You can import a security template into all of the computers in a workgroup to apply consistent security policy. You can also import a security template into a domain-based GPO. Through normal GPO client processing, the policy settings in the domain-based GPO are disseminated to all computers affected by the GPO. Microsoft includes a number of security templates in the *%systemroot%*\Security\Templates folder. Each template is a profile of security settings for a variety of computing environments requiring differing levels of security.

You can also use the **Security Configuration and Analysis snap-in** to import one or more security templates. This snap-in goes beyond applying security policy settings contained in a single template. The Security Configuration and Analysis snap-in allows you to merge multiple security templates to create a composite template and apply event log, restricted group, system services, registry, and file system configurations. You also use this snap-in to analyze a computer's security configuration against an existing security template or a composite template.

Objective 7.5 Questions

70-210.07.05.001

You are the administrator of a workgroup supporting computers running Windows 2000 Professional. Users need to run legacy applications on Windows 2000 Professional, but you do not want the users to be members of the Power Users group. Which security template type should you use?

A. Basic

B. Optional Component File Security

C. Compatible

D. Secure

E. High Secure

70-210.07.05.002

You are the administrator of a domain supporting computers running Windows 2000 Professional, Windows 98, and Windows NT 4. Windows 98 and Windows NT 4 computers access resources on computers running Windows 2000. Which types of security templates might you consider applying to the computers running Windows 2000? (Choose four.)

A. Basic

B. Optional Component File security

C. Compatible

D. Secure

E. High Secure

70-210.07.05.003

You are the administrator of a workgroup supporting computers running Windows 2000 Professional in North America. You want to configure a remote IP Security (IPSec) communication policy that will help protect against known key attacks. What should you do? (Choose four.)

A. Use the Data Encryption Standard (DES) algorithm.

B. Use the 3DES algorithm.

C. Use session key lifetimes less than 50 MB.

D. Use session key lifetimes greater than 50 MB.

E. Enable Perfect Forward Secrecy (PFS) for the master key.

F. Enable PFS for the session key.

Objective 7.5 Answers

70-210.07.05.001

▶ **Correct Answers: C**

A. **Incorrect:** There are three Basic security templates: BASICDC.INF for Windows 2000 domain controllers, BASICSV.INF for Windows 2000 standalone servers, and BASICWK.INF for Windows 2000 Professional workstations. The Basic security templates apply Windows 2000 default access control settings. Apply this template type if you are trying to troubleshoot a computer running Windows 2000 and you suspect that the problem is related to the security configuration. Also, to update a security configuration, apply this template type to a computer upgraded from Windows NT 4 to Windows 2000.

B. **Incorrect:** There are two Optional Component File security templates: OCFILESS.INF for Windows 2000 Server domain controller and standalone servers, and OCSFILESW.INF for Windows 2000 Professional workstations. The Optional Component File security templates apply default access control settings to Windows 2000 optional components installed during or after the Windows 2000 installation process. You should apply this type of template after applying a Basic security template.

C. **Correct:** Applying the Compatible security template, COMPATWS.INF, configures security settings that allow members of the Users group to run legacy applications. After this security configuration is applied, users do not need to be members of the Power Users group to run legacy applications.

D. **Incorrect:** There are two Secure security templates: SECUREDC.INF for Windows 2000 domain controllers and SECUREWS.INF for Windows 2000 Server standalone servers and Windows 2000 Professional workstations. This template type focuses on configuring more restrictive group membership, enabling policy settings that are part of audit policy and account policy, configuring restricted event log access, and modifying registry settings for security.

E. **Incorrect:** There are two High Secure security templates: HISECDC.INF for Windows 2000 domain controllers and HISECWS.INF for Windows 2000 Server standalone servers and Windows 2000 Professional workstations. Many of the settings in the Secure security template are even more restrictive in the High Secure security template. After applying a Secure or High Secure security template type, test the configuration thoroughly before moving the computer into a production environment.

70-210.07.05.002

▶ **Correct Answers: A, B, C, and D**

A. **Correct:** The Basic security templates apply Windows 2000 default access control settings to computers running Windows 2000. These settings are more secure than the default settings found on a computer running Windows NT 4 or Windows 98. However, down-level clients should still be able to access resources running on Windows 2000 computers configured with default access control settings.

B. **Correct:** The Optional Component File security templates apply default access control settings to Windows 2000 optional components installed during or after the Windows 2000 installation process. As described in answer explanation A, the default settings found on a computer running Windows 2000 are appropriate for down-level client access.

C. **Correct:** Applying the Compatible security template configures security settings that allow members of the Users group to run legacy applications. This is less secure than the default security settings. Therefore, down-level clients will not have trouble accessing resources secured with this template.

D. **Correct:** This template type applies a security configuration that is more secure than the default settings. However, the Secure template type does not modify file system permissions. Therefore, users configured with the appropriate permissions should still be able to access resources on this computer, even when access is achieved from a down-level client.

E. **Incorrect:** This template type applies the most secure configuration of any defined template type. Applying this template to the Windows 2000 computers accessed by Windows NT 4 or Windows 98 clients might cause access problems. Careful testing should follow the application of any template that applies a security configuration greater than the default settings.

70-210.07.05.003

▶ **Correct Answers: B, C, E, and F**

A. **Incorrect:** IPSec uses Internet Key Exchange (IKE) for security negotiation and for authentication between sender and receiver. During security negotiation, the sender and receiver agree on the encryption algorithm, the hash algorithm, the authentication method, and the length of keying material to be exchanged to create the shared master and session keys. Security negotiation might be initially encrypted, but this depends on the negotiated authentication method. IKE uses an encryption protocol to secure the authentication process, and IPSec uses an encryption algorithm to protect data following successful authentication. The encryption algorithm used in all IPSec communication is either DES or Data Encryption Standard 3 (3DES). DES is less secure than 3DES because DES uses a 56-bit key.

B. **Correct:** The 3DES encryption algorithm uses a longer key than DES for greater security. Computers running Windows 2000 require the High Encryption Pack to use the 3DES encryption algorithm. If a Windows 2000 computer not running the High Encryption Pack receives a request to negotiate 3DES encryption, it might not be able to negotiate a connection. IPSec policy determines this, which might or might not allow for the less secure DES encryption algorithm to be negotiated. Because of export restrictions, it is not legal to use the High Encryption Pack in all countries.

C. **Correct:** Session key lifetimes determine when new session keys are regenerated to continue communication between two endpoints. You can use default session key lifetimes defined in IPSec rules or specify the intervals between key regeneration. The intervals between session key regeneration are based on the *amount of data* transferred and the *number of seconds* the session key has been in use. Limiting session key lifetimes to 50 MB means that a new session key will be regenerated after 50 MB of data has been transferred.

D. **Incorrect:** Session key lifetimes longer than 50 MB of data transfer give an attacker more time to initiate a key attack.

E. **Correct:** The intervals between master key regeneration are based on the *number of minutes* the key has been in use and the *number of session keys* that have been regenerated with a single master key. Configuring intervals determines *when* a key is regenerated, not how. PFS determines *how* a new key is generated to guarantee that compromising a single key permits access only to data protected by that single key. Therefore, enabling PFS for the master key ensures that no previously used master keying material or master keys will be reused for key regeneration.

F. **Correct:** Enabling session key PFS ensures that no previously used session keys or keying material will be reused for key regeneration.

Index

Numbers and Symbols

3DES (3 Data Encryption Standard), 288, 290

A

Accelerated Graphics Port (AGP), 83
access control entries (ACEs), 46
accessibility services, 170, 173, 213–17
access rights. *See* permissions
account lockout policy, 250, 266, 269
account policies, 263
accounts, group. *See* group accounts
accounts, user. *See* user accounts
ACEs (access control entries), 46
ACPI (Advanced Configuration and Power Interface), 35, 89–91, 93, 111
Active Desktop, 172, 197–98
  enabling, 198
  wallpaper, 200, 202
Active Directory
  desktop settings, 198
  Group Policy, 170, 198
  identity information database, 279
Add Printer Wizard, 59, 61, 64
Add Recovery Agent Wizard, 257
Add/Remove Hardware Wizard
  I/O devices, 96
  modems, 102
Add Standard TCP/IP Printer Port Wizard, 61–62
Administrators local group, 56–57, 271, 274, 277
  driver installation, 107, 109
  privileges assigned, 271–72
  recovery agents, 257–58, 260–62
Advanced Configuration and Power Interface (ACPI), 35, 89–91, 93, 111
Advanced Options menu, 124, 162
Advanced Power Management (APM), 89–93
Advanced Programmable Interrupt Controller (APIC), 73, 111
advertising applications, 193, 196
AGP (Accelerated Graphics Port), 83
Alerts feature, 126, 150
aliases. *See* Web sharing
All Users profile, 177, 281–82
APIC (Advanced Programmable Interrupt Controller), 73, 111

APIPA (Automatic Private IP Addressing), 117, 119, 220, 225
APM (Advanced Power Management), 89–93
APM BIOS, 73, 91–93
AppleTalk, 117, 234
AppleTalk Control Protocol (ATCP), 234
application permissions, 54
applications
  advertising, 193, 196
  assigning to users, 192–96
  availability, 169
  compatibility, 24, 26–27
  components, 191
  features, 191
  forcing termination of, 149
  Group Policy, 192, 194
  permissions, 192, 194
  publishing, 193–94, 196
  reinstalling at logon, 192–95
  Windows Installer Service, 191–96
ASMP (Asymmetric multiprocessing), 113, 115
AsyBEUI, 233
Asymmetric multiprocessing (ASMP), 113, 115
ATCP (AppleTalk Control Protocol), 234
AT utility, 125, 135, 139
audio. *See* sound
Audit policy, 249–50, 272–73, 275–77
authentication, 279–90
  dial-up networking, 235
  domains, 279
  enhancements, 249
  Kerberos, 250–51, 280
  logons, 279
  mutual, 235
  PPP, 280
  skills, list of required, 251
  user, 249
automated installation, 15–21
Automatic Caching For Documents, 142, 146
Automatic Private IP Addressing (APIPA), 117, 119, 220, 225

B

Backup Operators local group, 56–57, 271–72, 274, 277
backups
  certificates, 162
  Copy, 166
  Differential, 164, 166
  encrypted file attribute, 162
  Incremental, 166

W

There's no
substitute
for
experience.

In-depth. Focused. *And* ready for work.

Get the technical drilldown you need to deploy and support Microsoft products more effectively with the MICROSOFT TECHNICAL REFERENCE series. Each guide focuses on a specific aspect of the technology—weaving in-depth detail with on-the-job scenarios and practical how-to information for the IT professional. Get focused—and take technology to its limits—with MICROSOFT TECHNICAL REFERENCES.

Data Warehousing with Microsoft® SQL Server™ 7.0 Technical Reference
U.S.A. $49.99
U.K. £32.99 [V.A.T. included]
Canada $76.99
ISBN 0-7356-0859-8

Microsoft SQL Server 7.0 Performance Tuning Technical Reference
U.S.A. $49.99
U.K. £32.99
Canada $76.99
ISBN 0-7356-0909-8

Building Applications with Microsoft Outlook® 2000 Technical Reference
U.S.A. $49.99
U.K. £32.99 [V.A.T. included]
Canada $74.99
ISBN 0-7356-0581-5

Microsoft Windows NT® Server 4.0 Terminal Server Edition Technical Reference
U.S.A. $49.99
U.K. £32.99 [V.A.T. included]
Canada $74.99
ISBN 0-7356-0645-5

Microsoft Windows® 2000 TCP/IP Protocols and Services Technical Reference
U.S.A. $49.99
U.K. £32.99 [V.A.T. included]
Canada $76.99
ISBN 0-7356-0556-4

Active Directory™ Services for Microsoft Windows 2000 Technical Reference
U.S.A. $49.99
U.K. £32.99
Canada $76.99
ISBN 0-7356-0624-2

Microsoft Windows 2000 Security Technical Reference
U.S.A. $49.99
U.K. £32.99
Canada $72.99
ISBN 0-7356-0858-X

Microsoft Windows 2000 Performance Tuning Technical Reference
U.S.A. $49.99
U.K. £32.99
Canada $72.99
ISBN 0-7356-0633-1

Microsoft Press® products are available worldwide wherever quality computer books are sold. For more information, contact your book or computer retailer, software reseller, or local Microsoft Sales Office, or visit our Web site at mspress.microsoft.com. To locate your nearest source for Microsoft Press products, or to order directly, call 1-800-MSPRESS in the U.S. (in Canada, call 1-800-268-2222).

Prices and availability dates are subject to change.

Microsoft®
mspress.microsoft.com

Microsoft® Resource Kits— powerhouse resources to minimize costs while maximizing performance

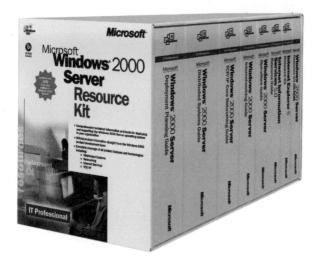

Deploy and support your enterprise business systems using the expertise and tools of those who know the technology best—the Microsoft product groups. Each RESOURCE KIT packs precise technical reference, installation and rollout tactics, planning guides, upgrade strategies, and essential utilities on CD-ROM. They're everything you need to help maximize system performance as you reduce ownership and support costs!

Microsoft® Windows® 2000 Server Resource Kit
ISBN   1-57231-805-8
U.S.A. $299.99
U.K.   £189.99 [V.A.T. included]
Canada $460.99

Microsoft Windows 2000 Professional Resource Kit
ISBN   1-57231-808-2
U.S.A. $69.99
U.K.   £45.99 [V.A.T. included]
Canada $107.99

Microsoft BackOffice® 4.5 Resource Kit
ISBN   0-7356-0583-1
U.S.A. $249.99
U.K.   £161.99 [V.A.T. included]
Canada $374.99

Microsoft Internet Explorer 5 Resource Kit
ISBN   0-7356-0587-4
U.S.A. $59.99
U.K.   £38.99 [V.A.T. included]
Canada $89.99

Microsoft Office 2000 Resource Kit
ISBN   0-7356-0555-6
U.S.A. $59.99
U.K.   £38.99 [V.A.T. included]
Canada $89.99

Microsoft Windows NT® Server 4.0 Resource Kit
ISBN   1-57231-344-7
U.S.A. $149.95
U.K.   £96.99 [V.A.T. included]
Canada $199.95

Microsoft Windows NT Workstation 4.0 Resource Kit
ISBN   1-57231-343-9
U.S.A. $69.95
U.K.   £45.99 [V.A.T. included]
Canada $94.95

Microsoft®

mspress.microsoft.com

MICROSOFT LICENSE AGREEMENT
Book Companion CD

IMPORTANT—READ CAREFULLY: This Microsoft End-User License Agreement ("EULA") is a legal agreement between you (either an individual or an entity) and Microsoft Corporation for the Microsoft product identified above, which includes computer software and may include associated media, printed materials, and "online" or electronic documentation ("SOFTWARE PRODUCT"). Any component included within the SOFTWARE PRODUCT that is accompanied by a separate End-User License Agreement shall be governed by such agreement and not the terms set forth below. By installing, copying, or otherwise using the SOFTWARE PRODUCT, you agree to be bound by the terms of this EULA. If you do not agree to the terms of this EULA, you are not authorized to install, copy, or otherwise use the SOFTWARE PRODUCT; you may, however, return the SOFTWARE PRODUCT, along with all printed materials and other items that form a part of the Microsoft product that includes the SOFTWARE PRODUCT, to the place you obtained them for a full refund.

SOFTWARE PRODUCT LICENSE

The SOFTWARE PRODUCT is protected by United States copyright laws and international copyright treaties, as well as other intellectual property laws and treaties. The SOFTWARE PRODUCT is licensed, not sold.

1. **GRANT OF LICENSE.** This EULA grants you the following rights:

    a. **Software Product.** You may install and use one copy of the SOFTWARE PRODUCT on a single computer. The primary user of the computer on which the SOFTWARE PRODUCT is installed may make a second copy for his or her exclusive use on a portable computer.

    b. **Storage/Network Use.** You may also store or install a copy of the SOFTWARE PRODUCT on a storage device, such as a network server, used only to install or run the SOFTWARE PRODUCT on your other computers over an internal network; however, you must acquire and dedicate a license for each separate computer on which the SOFTWARE PRODUCT is installed or run from the storage device. A license for the SOFTWARE PRODUCT may not be shared or used concurrently on different computers.

    c. **License Pak.** If you have acquired this EULA in a Microsoft License Pak, you may make the number of additional copies of the computer software portion of the SOFTWARE PRODUCT authorized on the printed copy of this EULA, and you may use each copy in the manner specified above. You are also entitled to make a corresponding number of secondary copies for portable computer use as specified above.

    d. **Sample Code.** Solely with respect to portions, if any, of the SOFTWARE PRODUCT that are identified within the SOFTWARE PRODUCT as sample code (the "SAMPLE CODE"):

    i. **Use and Modification.** Microsoft grants you the right to use and modify the source code version of the SAMPLE CODE, *provided* you comply with subsection (d)(iii) below. You may not distribute the SAMPLE CODE, or any modified version of the SAMPLE CODE, in source code form.

    ii. **Redistributable Files.** Provided you comply with subsection (d)(iii) below, Microsoft grants you a nonexclusive, royalty-free right to reproduce and distribute the object code version of the SAMPLE CODE and of any modified SAMPLE CODE, other than SAMPLE CODE, or any modified version thereof, designated as not redistributable in the Readme file that forms a part of the SOFTWARE PRODUCT (the "Non-Redistributable Sample Code"). All SAMPLE CODE other than the Non-Redistributable Sample Code is collectively referred to as the "REDISTRIBUTABLES."

    iii. **Redistribution Requirements.** If you redistribute the REDISTRIBUTABLES, you agree to: (i) distribute the REDISTRIBUTABLES in object code form only in conjunction with and as a part of your software application product; (ii) not use Microsoft's name, logo, or trademarks to market your software application product; (iii) include a valid copyright notice on your software application product; (iv) indemnify, hold harmless, and defend Microsoft from and against any claims or lawsuits, including attorney's fees, that arise or result from the use or distribution of your software application product; and (v) not permit further distribution of the REDISTRIBUTABLES by your end user. Contact Microsoft for the applicable royalties due and other licensing terms for all other uses and/or distribution of the REDISTRIBUTABLES.

2. **DESCRIPTION OF OTHER RIGHTS AND LIMITATIONS.**

    - **Limitations on Reverse Engineering, Decompilation, and Disassembly.** You may not reverse engineer, decompile, or disassemble the SOFTWARE PRODUCT, except and only to the extent that such activity is expressly permitted by applicable law notwithstanding this limitation.

    - **Separation of Components.** The SOFTWARE PRODUCT is licensed as a single product. Its component parts may not be separated for use on more than one computer.

    - **Rental.** You may not rent, lease, or lend the SOFTWARE PRODUCT.

- **Support Services.** Microsoft may, but is not obligated to, provide you with support services related to the SOFTWARE PRODUCT ("Support Services"). Use of Support Services is governed by the Microsoft policies and programs described in the user manual, in "online" documentation, and/or in other Microsoft-provided materials. Any supplemental software code provided to you as part of the Support Services shall be considered part of the SOFTWARE PRODUCT and subject to the terms and conditions of this EULA. With respect to technical information you provide to Microsoft as part of the Support Services, Microsoft may use such information for its business purposes, including for product support and development. Microsoft will not utilize such technical information in a form that personally identifies you.

- **Software Transfer.** You may permanently transfer all of your rights under this EULA, provided you retain no copies, you transfer all of the SOFTWARE PRODUCT (including all component parts, the media and printed materials, any upgrades, this EULA, and, if applicable, the Certificate of Authenticity), **and** the recipient agrees to the terms of this EULA.

- **Termination.** Without prejudice to any other rights, Microsoft may terminate this EULA if you fail to comply with the terms and conditions of this EULA. In such event, you must destroy all copies of the SOFTWARE PRODUCT and all of its component parts.

3. **COPYRIGHT.** All title and copyrights in and to the SOFTWARE PRODUCT (including but not limited to any images, photographs, animations, video, audio, music, text, SAMPLE CODE, REDISTRIBUTABLES, and "applets" incorporated into the SOFTWARE PRODUCT) and any copies of the SOFTWARE PRODUCT are owned by Microsoft or its suppliers. The SOFT-WARE PRODUCT is protected by copyright laws and international treaty provisions. Therefore, you must treat the SOFTWARE PRODUCT like any other copyrighted material **except** that you may install the SOFTWARE PRODUCT on a single computer provided you keep the original solely for backup or archival purposes. You may not copy the printed materials accompanying the SOFTWARE PRODUCT.

4. **U.S. GOVERNMENT RESTRICTED RIGHTS.** The SOFTWARE PRODUCT and documentation are provided with RESTRICTED RIGHTS. Use, duplication, or disclosure by the Government is subject to restrictions as set forth in subparagraph (c)(1)(ii) of the Rights in Technical Data and Computer Software clause at DFARS 252.227-7013 or subparagraphs (c)(1) and (2) of the Commercial Computer Software—Restricted Rights at 48 CFR 52.227-19, as applicable. Manufacturer is Microsoft Corporation/One Microsoft Way/Redmond, WA 98052-6399.

5. **EXPORT RESTRICTIONS.** You agree that you will not export or re-export the SOFTWARE PRODUCT, any part thereof, or any process or service that is the direct product of the SOFTWARE PRODUCT (the foregoing collectively referred to as the "Restricted Components"), to any country, person, entity, or end user subject to U.S. export restrictions. You specifically agree not to export or re-export any of the Restricted Components (i) to any country to which the U.S. has embargoed or restricted the export of goods or services, which currently include, but are not necessarily limited to, Cuba, Iran, Iraq, Libya, North Korea, Sudan, and Syria, or to any national of any such country, wherever located, who intends to transmit or transport the Restricted Components back to such country; (ii) to any end user who you know or have reason to know will utilize the Restricted Components in the design, development, or production of nuclear, chemical, or biological weapons; or (iii) to any end user who has been prohibited from participating in U.S. export transactions by any federal agency of the U.S. government. You warrant and represent that neither the BXA nor any other U.S. federal agency has suspended, revoked, or denied your export privileges.

DISCLAIMER OF WARRANTY

NO WARRANTIES OR CONDITIONS. MICROSOFT EXPRESSLY DISCLAIMS ANY WARRANTY OR CONDITION FOR THE SOFTWARE PRODUCT. THE SOFTWARE PRODUCT AND ANY RELATED DOCUMENTATION ARE PROVIDED "AS IS" WITHOUT WARRANTY OR CONDITION OF ANY KIND, EITHER EXPRESS OR IMPLIED, INCLUDING, WITHOUT LIMITA-TION, THE IMPLIED WARRANTIES OF MERCHANTABILITY, FITNESS FOR A PARTICULAR PURPOSE, OR NONINFRINGEMENT. THE ENTIRE RISK ARISING OUT OF USE OR PERFORMANCE OF THE SOFTWARE PRODUCT REMAINS WITH YOU.

LIMITATION OF LIABILITY. TO THE MAXIMUM EXTENT PERMITTED BY APPLICABLE LAW, IN NO EVENT SHALL MICROSOFT OR ITS SUPPLIERS BE LIABLE FOR ANY SPECIAL, INCIDENTAL, INDIRECT, OR CONSEQUENTIAL DAM-AGES WHATSOEVER (INCLUDING, WITHOUT LIMITATION, DAMAGES FOR LOSS OF BUSINESS PROFITS, BUSINESS INTERRUPTION, LOSS OF BUSINESS INFORMATION, OR ANY OTHER PECUNIARY LOSS) ARISING OUT OF THE USE OF OR INABILITY TO USE THE SOFTWARE PRODUCT OR THE PROVISION OF OR FAILURE TO PROVIDE SUPPORT SERVICES, EVEN IF MICROSOFT HAS BEEN ADVISED OF THE POSSIBILITY OF SUCH DAMAGES. IN ANY CASE, MICROSOFT'S ENTIRE LIABILITY UNDER ANY PROVISION OF THIS EULA SHALL BE LIMITED TO THE GREATER OF THE AMOUNT ACTUALLY PAID BY YOU FOR THE SOFTWARE PRODUCT OR US$5.00; PROVIDED, HOWEVER, IF YOU HAVE ENTERED INTO A MICROSOFT SUPPORT SERVICES AGREEMENT, MICROSOFT'S ENTIRE LIABILITY REGARDING SUPPORT SERVICES SHALL BE GOVERNED BY THE TERMS OF THAT AGREEMENT. BECAUSE SOME STATES AND JURISDICTIONS DO NOT ALLOW THE EXCLUSION OR LIMITATION OF LIABILITY, THE ABOVE LIMITATION MAY NOT APPLY TO YOU.

MISCELLANEOUS

This EULA is governed by the laws of the State of Washington USA, except and only to the extent that applicable law mandates govern-ing law of a different jurisdiction.

Should you have any questions concerning this EULA, or if you desire to contact Microsoft for any reason, please contact the Microsoft subsidiary serving your country, or write: Microsoft Sales Information Center/One Microsoft Way/Redmond, WA 98052-6399.

System Requirements

To use this book's Readiness Review compact disc, you need a computer equipped with the following minimum configuration:

- Microsoft Windows 95, Microsoft Windows NT 4 with Service Pack 3 or higher, Microsoft Windows 98, or Microsoft Windows 2000 Professional

- Internet Explorer 5.01 or higher

- Multimedia PC with a 75-Mhz Pentium or higher processor

- 16 MB RAM for Windows 95 or Windows 98 (minimum)

- 32 MB RAM for Windows NT (minimum)

- 64 MB RAM for Windows 2000 (minimum)

- 17 MB available hard disk space for installation

- A double-speed CD-ROM drive or better

- Super VGA display with at least 256 colors

- Microsoft Mouse or compatible pointing device